Y0-CUL-408

HIGH TEA

JACKIE BROOKS

HIGH TEA

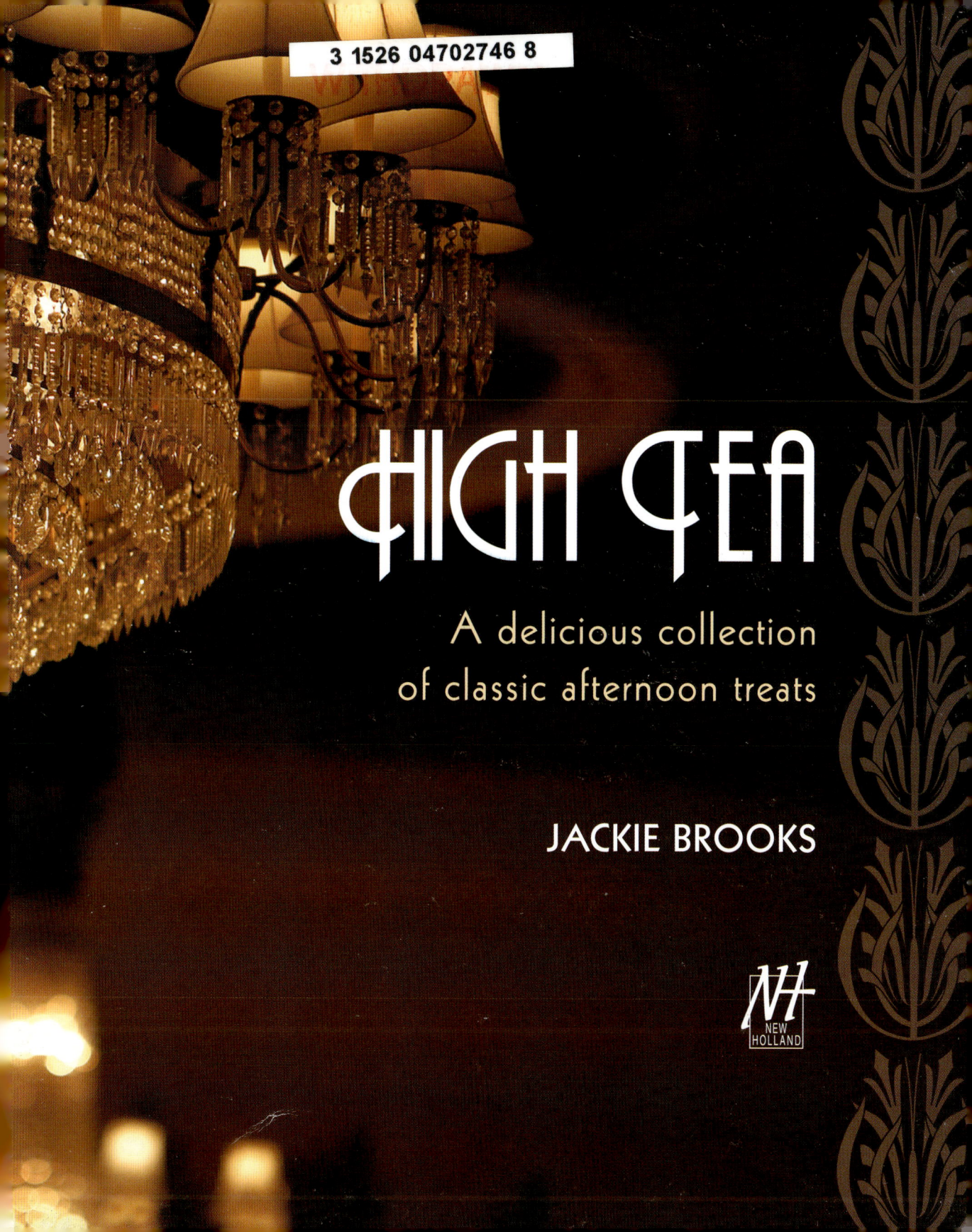

A delicious collection
of classic afternoon treats

JACKIE BROOKS

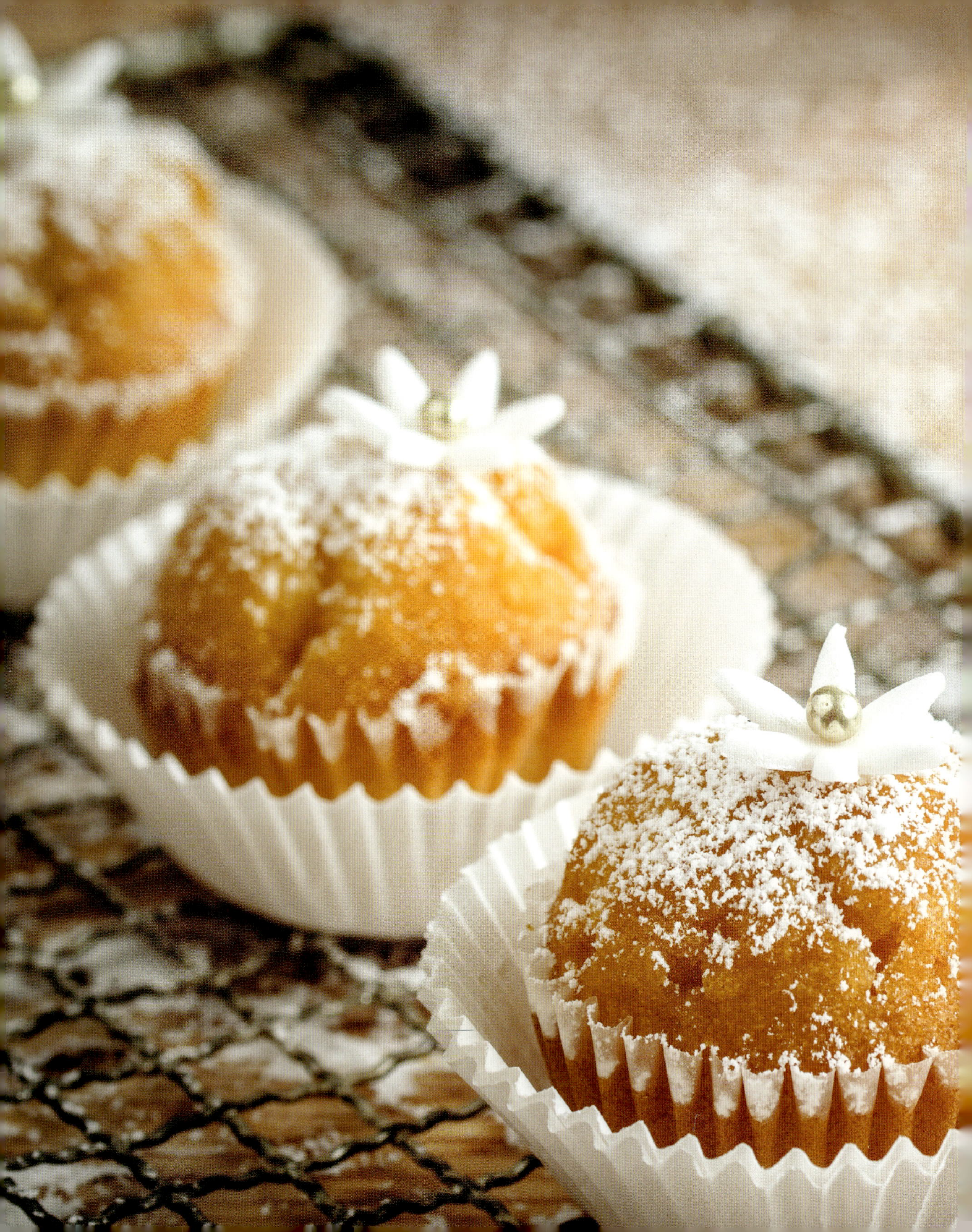

CONTENTS

Introduction	7
Tea	10
Coffee	24
Sandwiches	44
Scones & Muffins	58
Cupcakes	80
Slices	118
Cakes	148
Biscuits	182
Tarts	212
Cocktails	240
Index	254

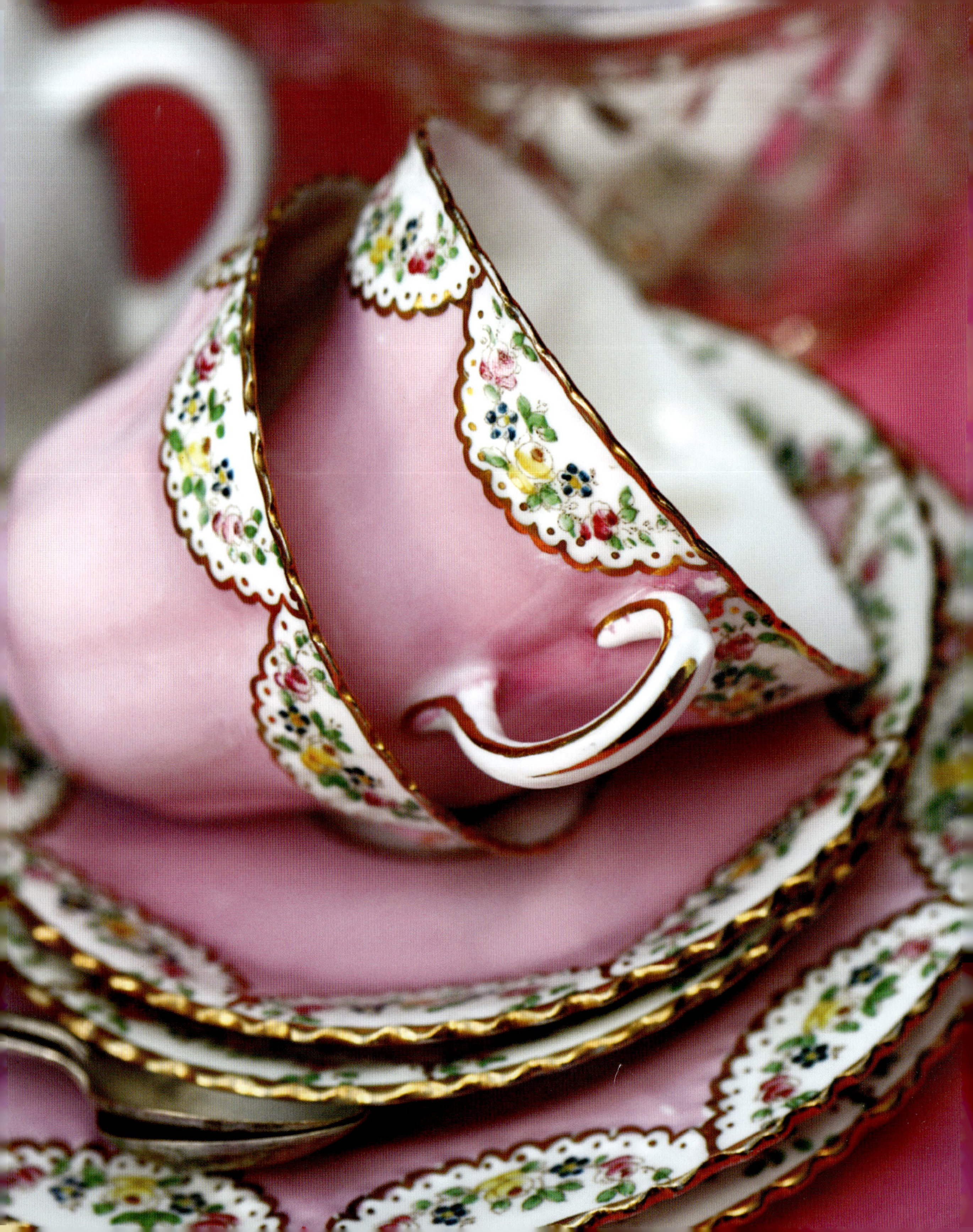

INTRODUCTION

There is nothing more quintessentially English than a traditional high tea. People have been enjoying sweet and savoury treats served in the afternoon with a fine pot of tea for centuries . . . and long may it continue.

The origin of High Tea is uncertain, but most High-tea historians place its beginnings at somewhere around the early 19th century. It is believed to have been started by Anna, the 7th Duchess of Bedford, who complained of 'having that sinking feeling' during the late afternoon when dinner wasn't served until eight. She began to order a pot of tea and a small bite to eat, alone in her boudoir, at about 4 o'clock. Soon she tired of eating alone and invited her friends to join her. The tradition of High Tea was born.

The trend caught on among the upper classes and soon respectable ladies everywhere were getting together every afternoon to drink tea and nibble sandwiches and cakes in parlours and hotels across Victorian England.

As with any tradition, High Tea came with its own set of rules and etiquette that any self-respecting guest would be expected to adhere to.

When attending a traditional High Tea, guests were expected to sit down, placing purses on their laps or behind them on their chair, and unfolding their napkin onto their laps. Sugar was placed into the teacup first, then lemon and finally the tea, poured from an ornate teapot. If guests preferred to drink their tea with milk, then that was added last, but never should tea be served with both milk and lemon.

The teaspoon was always placed behind the teacup on the saucer and was never left inside the teacup. Despite popular assumption, guests were not expected to hold their teacup 'pinky up', but to hold the cup by three fingers and to look into the teacup while they drank. It was not polite to look elsewhere.

Even the slicing of the scones was subject to etiquette. Guests were expected to split them with a knife and to place curd and cream on each bite individually. Of course, guests should then eat the scone neatly, using three fingers.

A traditional High Tea was eaten in stages: savouries like sandwiches first, scones second and finally sweets served on tiered cake stands.

Nowadays, of course, we have done away with much of the pomp and circumstance of the Victorian-era High Tea. And sadly, it is rare that most of us get to enjoy one at all. That is why on those special occasions that we do get to enjoy a High Tea, it is fun to give the occasion a little attention. In hotels and tearooms around the world, High Tea is still served the old-fashioned way, with sandwiches, scones with jam and cream and delicious finger-sized cakes served on delicate china plates and washed down with copious quantities of tea.

This book shows you how to make your own High Tea at home, perhaps for a special occasion like a baby shower, Christening or birthday, or perhaps just to make a regular afternoon a little bit special.

Although this book strives to include as many traditional High Tea treats as possible, it also contains many more recipes that also suit a 21st-century High Tea and a few modern-day naughties like cocktails and liquor coffees that the original takers of High Tea would certainly not have approved of.

Whether you want to recreate a traditional High Tea or take a modern-day twist on the occasion, put on your finest clothes, dust off your cake stand and your china teacups and embrace the decadence and spirit of High Tea.

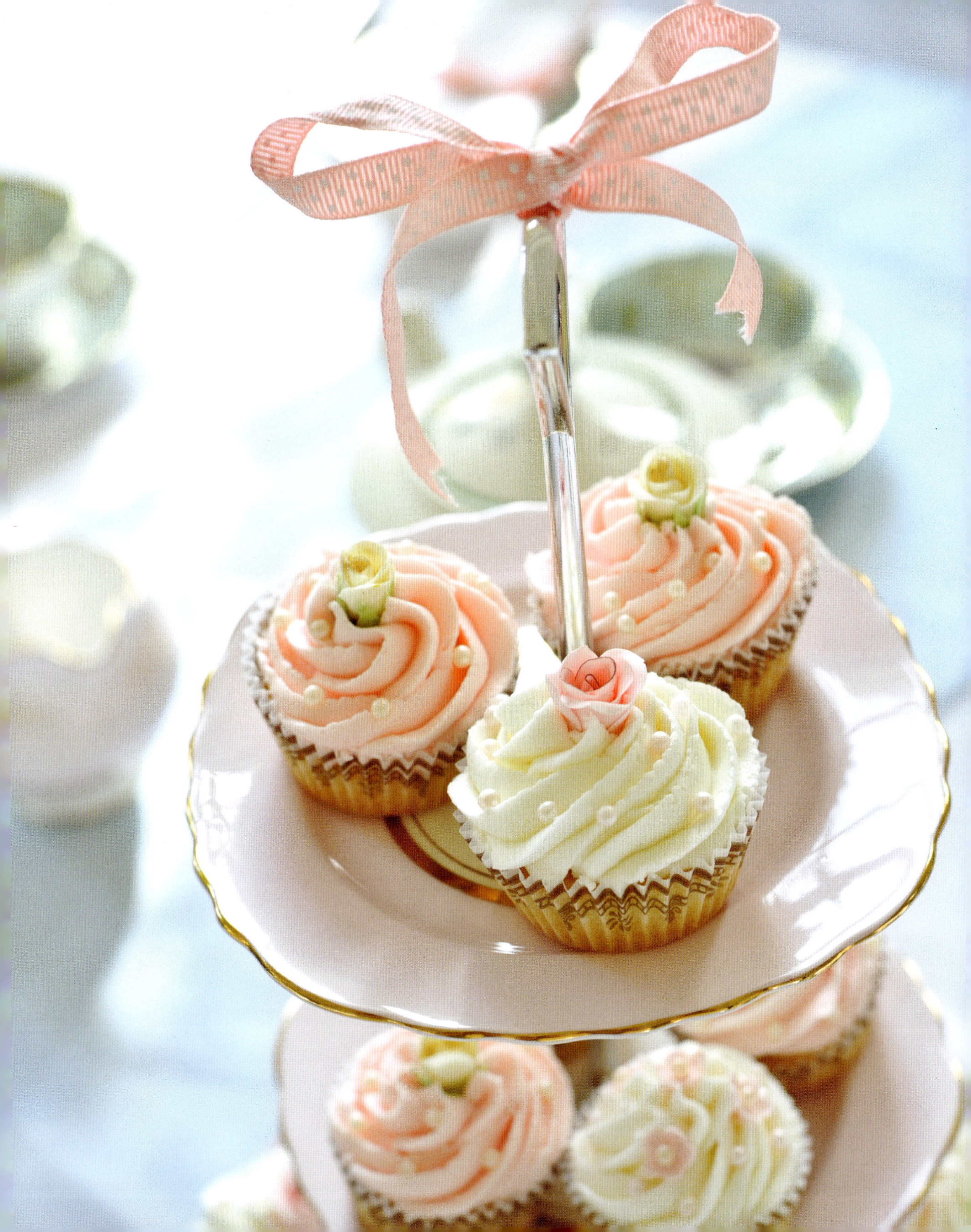

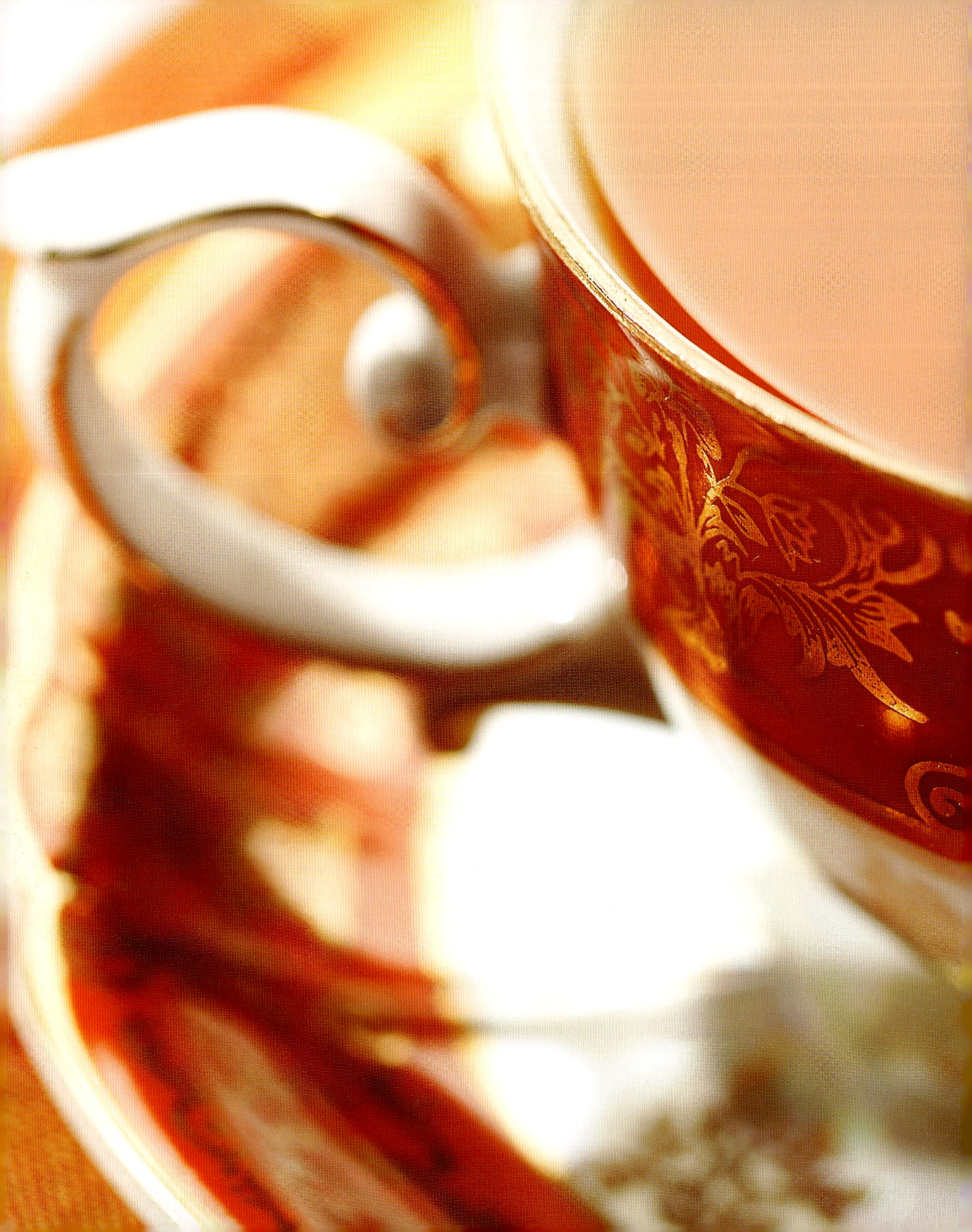

TEA

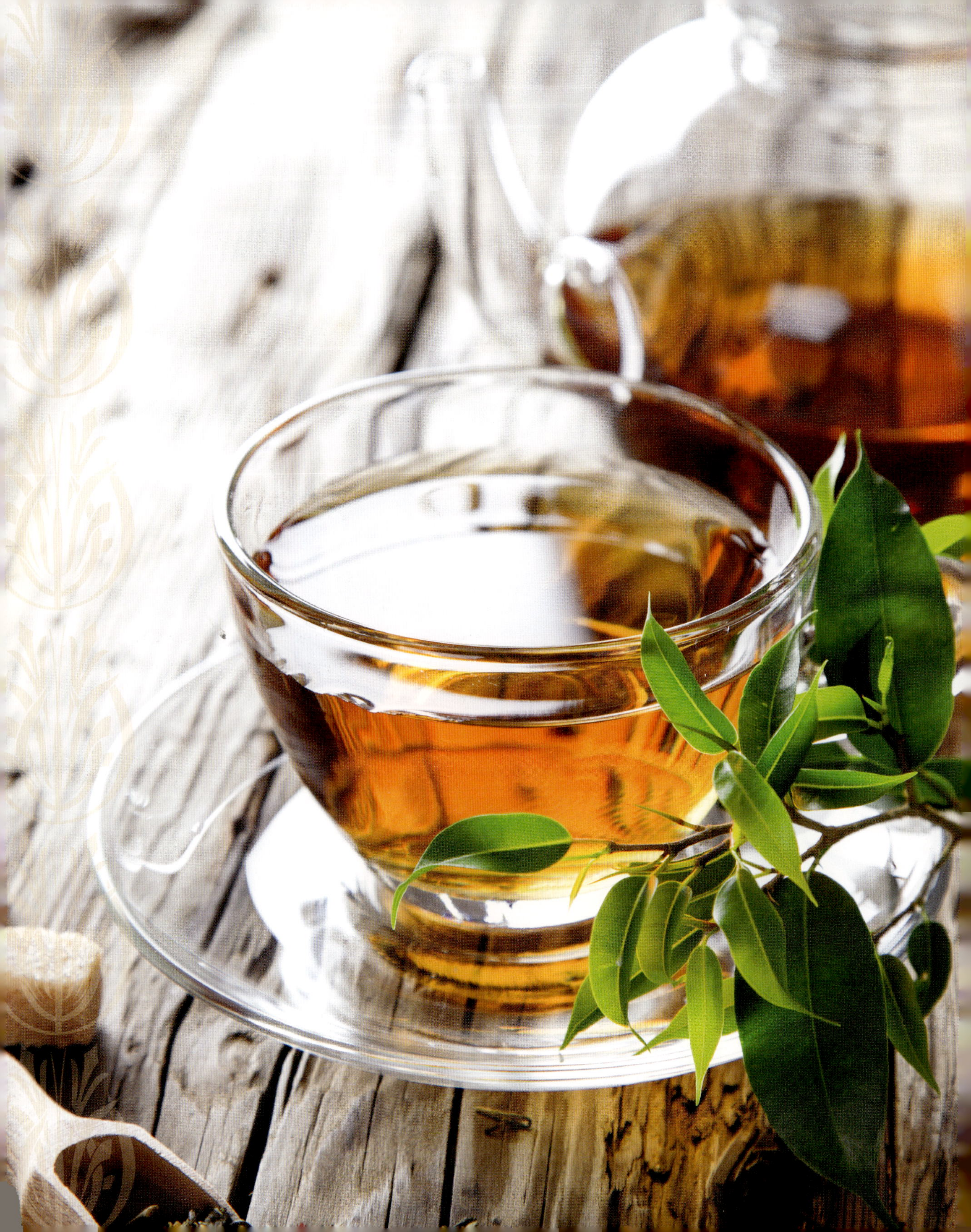

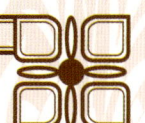

Bergamot Earl Grey Spicy Tea

Known as Oswego tea by the American Indians, this gloriously rich-flavoured tea has been around for centuries. The arresting flavour and fragrance of bergamot tea is similar to that of the Italian bergamot orange, Citrus bergamia, which gives Earl Grey tea its distinctive taste. By adding two fresh bergamot leaves to a pot of ordinary tea, you can immediately get that Earl Grey flavour.

INGREDIENTS:

1 Ceylon tea bag
2 bergamot leaves
1 cinnamon stick
cinnamon powder
1 fresh lemon slice
honey or sugar to taste

Serves 1

METHOD:

1. Pour 1 cup of boiling water over Ceylon tea bag and 2 bergamot leaves, 1 cinnamon stick and 1 lemon slice.
2. Remove the tea bag after 10–15 seconds.
3. Stand for 5 minutes and stir frequently with the cinnamon stick.
4. Strain, pour into a pretty mug and add a sprinkling of cinnamon powder, a fresh lemon slice and a touch of honey.

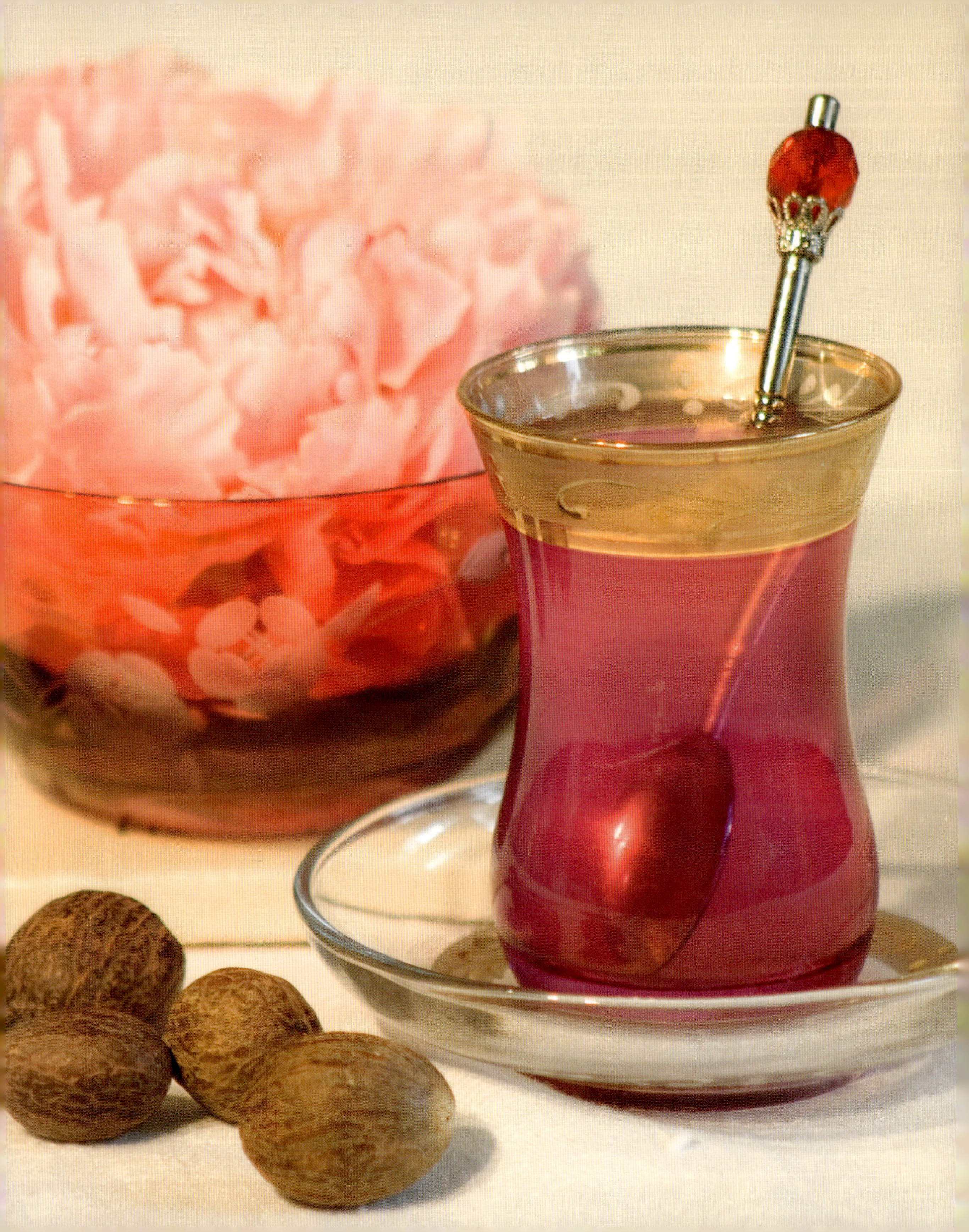

Ginger & Nutmeg Tea

There really is something quite compelling about freshly grated nutmeg. It's warming, comforting, delicious, charming, fragrant and, sprinkled onto hot milk or into a cup of hot water, it enfolds one in warmth and comfort and a nurtured feeling of wellbeing.

INGREDIENTS:

½ teaspoon freshly grated nutmeg

3 teaspoons freshly grated ginger

good squeeze of lemon juice

Serves 1

METHOD:

1 Pound grated nutmeg into grated ginger.

2 Stir into 1 cup of boiling water.

3 Add lemon juice to taste.

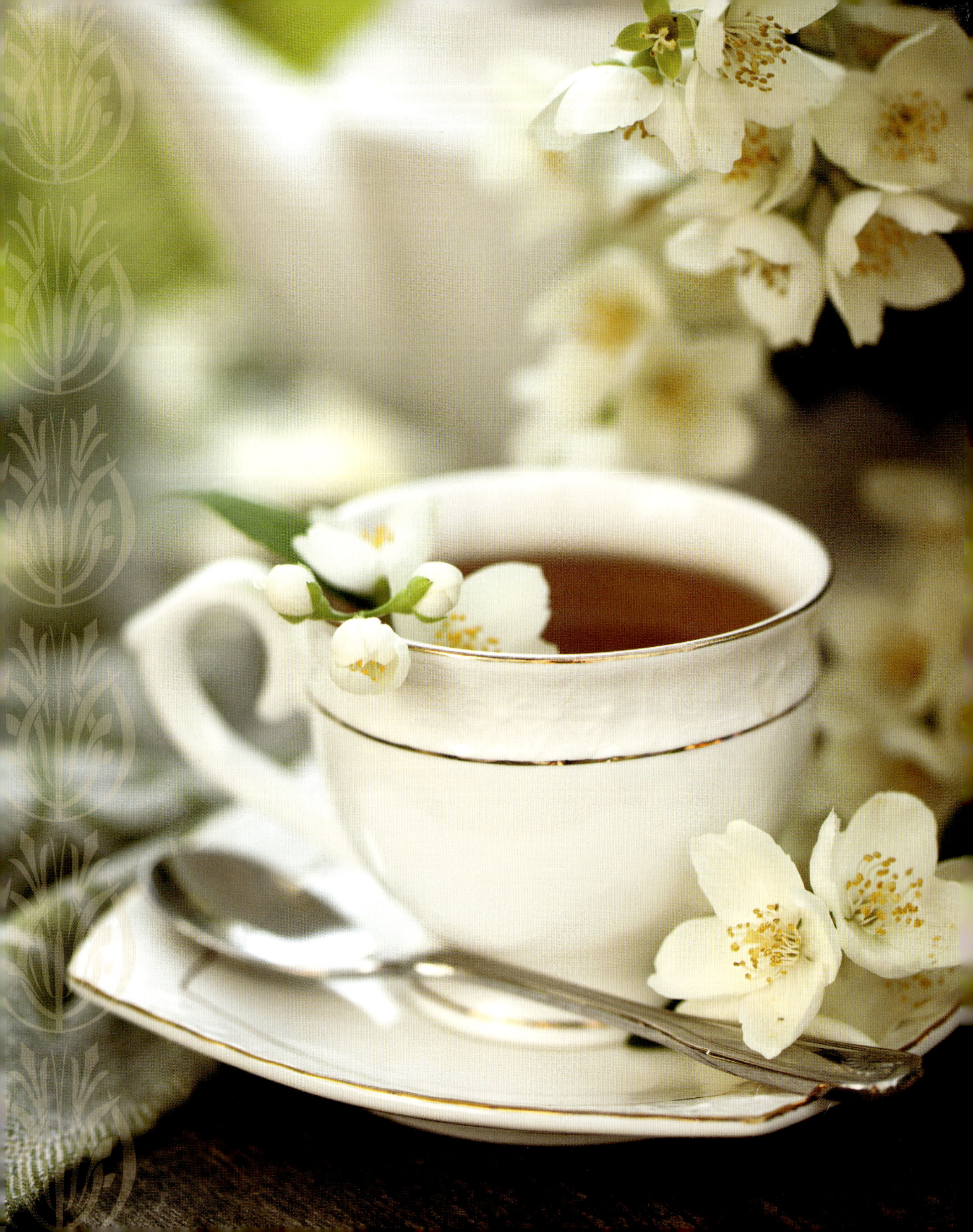

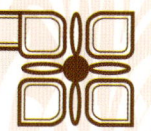

Jasmine Tea

Jasmine is exquisitely fragrant and one of the world's most treasured garden plants. The genus of about 200 species of jasmine is a glorious collection of this ancient plant that has been used through the centuries to make a calming, soothing and unwinding tea, often added to ordinary teas for its therapeutic effect.

It is the fresh flowers that are used (and not the leaves) in the scenting and flavouring of both China and Indian teas, and they make a rare and beautiful tea on their own.

Jasminum sambac or Arabian jasmine is a beautiful sprawling shrubby semi-climber or scrambler with clusters of flowers all through the year, and these flowers are particularly wonderful for scenting green tea.

INGREDIENTS:

several bunches of jasmine flowers
1 green tea tea bag
3 cloves
juice of ½ lemon
grated lemon zest
1 teaspoon honey

Serves 1

METHOD:

1 Dry the jasmine flowers on brown paper in the shade or on stainless-steel tables. When 95 per cent dry, add to green tea or ordinary Ceylon tea in the ratio of 1 cup of flowers to 4 cups of tea. Place in a large tin. Shake them up daily.
2 Now add ¼ cup of flowers and green tea to 1 cup of boiling water with cloves.
3 Stand for 3–5 minutes, stir often.
4 Strain and add lemon juice, a little grated lemon zest and honey.
5 Stir well.

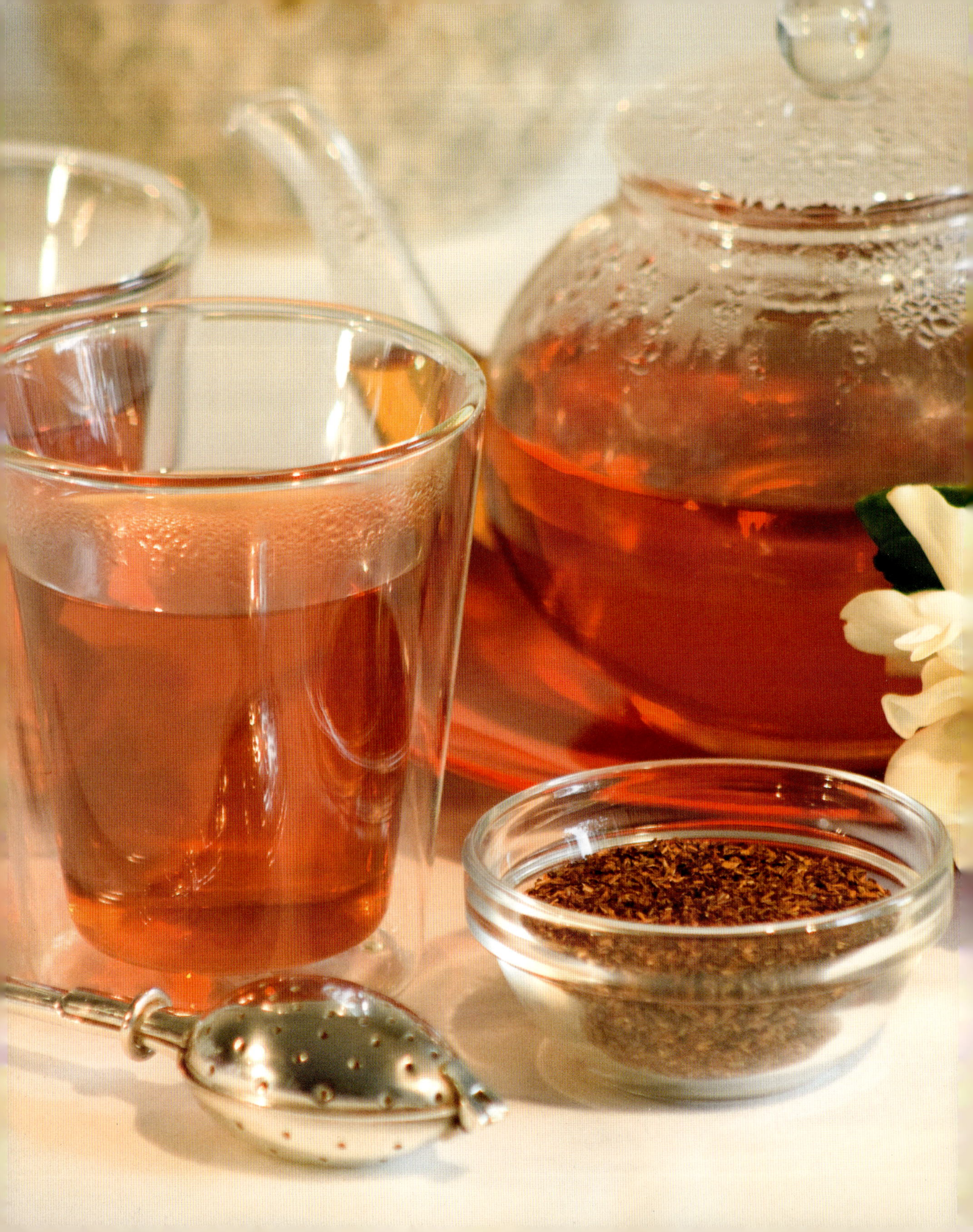

Rooibos Tea

Long ago, the Capoid people who inhabited the Cederberg area where rooibos grows naturally, were the first to discover the exceptional qualities of rooibos. They gathered it and prepared it by chopping it up, crushing it with a wooden mallet and drying it in the hot summer sun. Inexpensive and easily available, it has long been a favourite drink, and with its tonic, health-giving properties, rooibos is a household name, a favourite everywhere.

INGREDIENTS:

- 1 teaspoon or 1 teabag of rooibos
- 1 slice of fresh lemon and a good squeeze of lemon juice
- 3 thin slices of fresh ginger
- 3 cloves
- 2 sprigs of lemon balm leaves or a thumb-length sprig of spearmint

Serves 1

METHOD:

1. Take rooibos, fresh lemon and lemon juice, fresh ginger, cloves and lemon balm or spearmint. Pour over 2 cups of boiling water, stand for 5 minutes, strain.
2. Sweeten with a touch of honey.

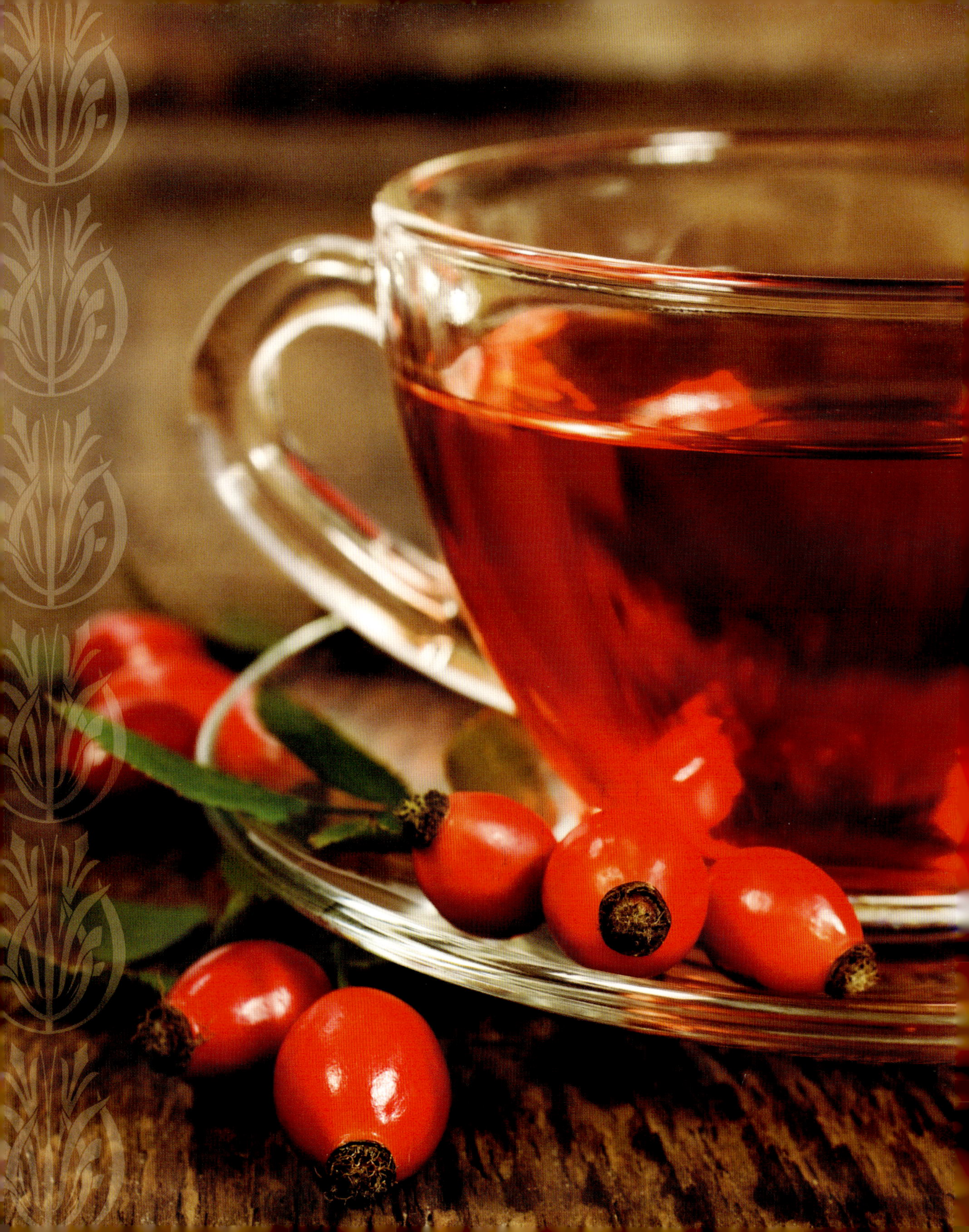

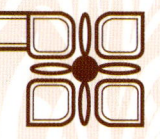

Rose Hip Tea

INGREDIENTS:

¼ cup crushed fresh rose hips
   or
⅓ cup dried rose hips
honey

Serves 1

METHOD:

1. Using fresh rosehips, pour 1 cup of boiling water over ¼ cup of crushed fresh rosehips and let it stand for five minutes.
2. Stir and crush well with the spoon.
3. Strain and add a little honey

If you are using dried rosehips:
1. Boil ½ cup of dried crushed hips in 3 cups of water for 15 minutes with the lid on.
2. Top up the water to the 3 cups if it boils away.
3. Strain and sweeten with honey (or cool and keep excess in the fridge and add fresh fruit juice for a refreshing cooldrink).

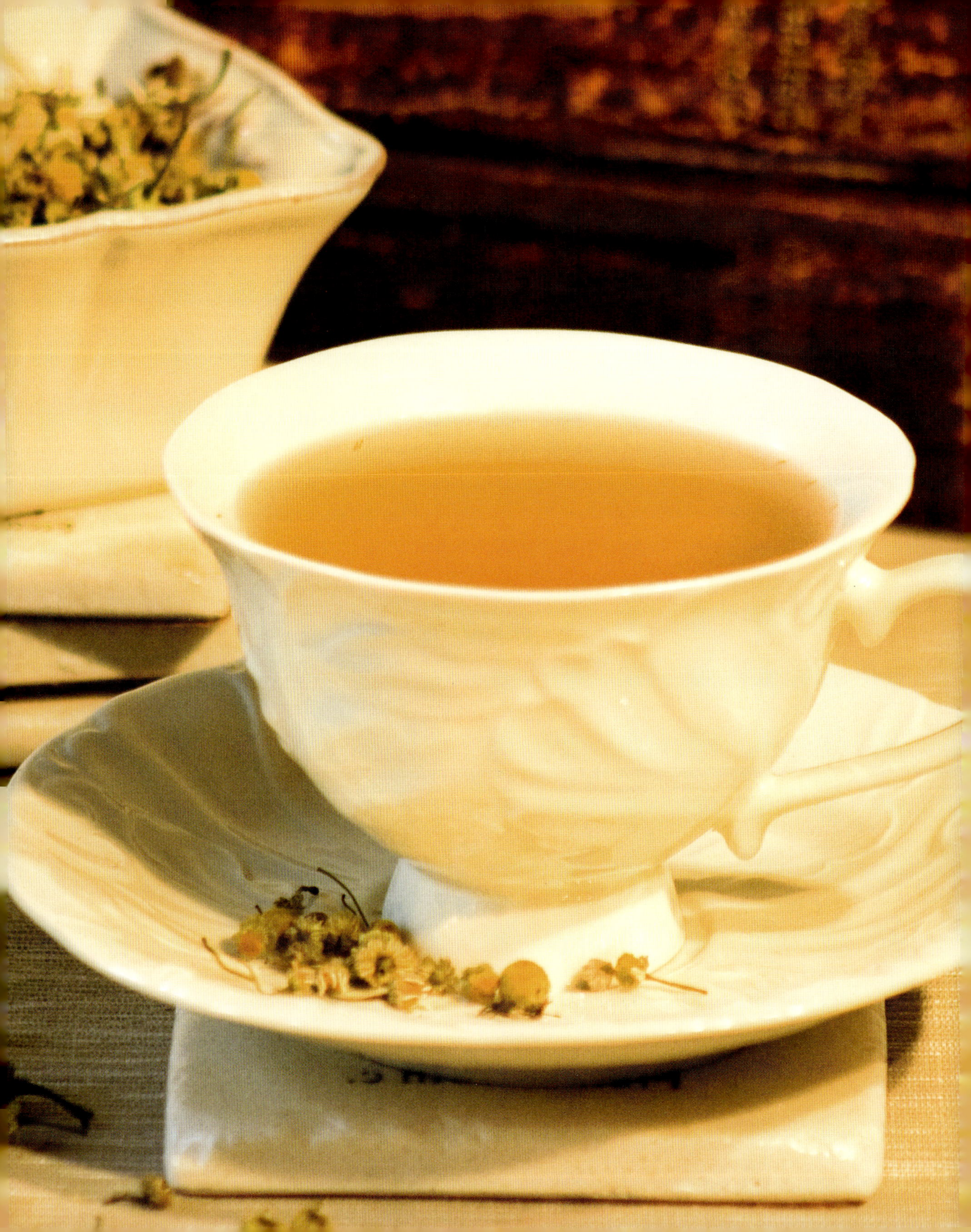

Classic Chamomile

Chamomile has to be one of the world's favourite herbal teas! They've been making chamomile tea since the 4th century and from the 14th century onwards chamomile was a registered medicine! It has the effect of soothing, calming and unwinding.

INGREDIENTS:

¼ cup fresh or less of dried chamomile flowers
thumb-length sprig of lemon balm
3 allspice berries, lightly cracked
a little honey

Serves 1

METHOD:

1. Cover chamomile flowers with 1 cup of boiling water.
2. Add lemon balm and allspice berries.
3. Stand for 5 minutes. Strain.
4. Add honey to sweeten and stir well.

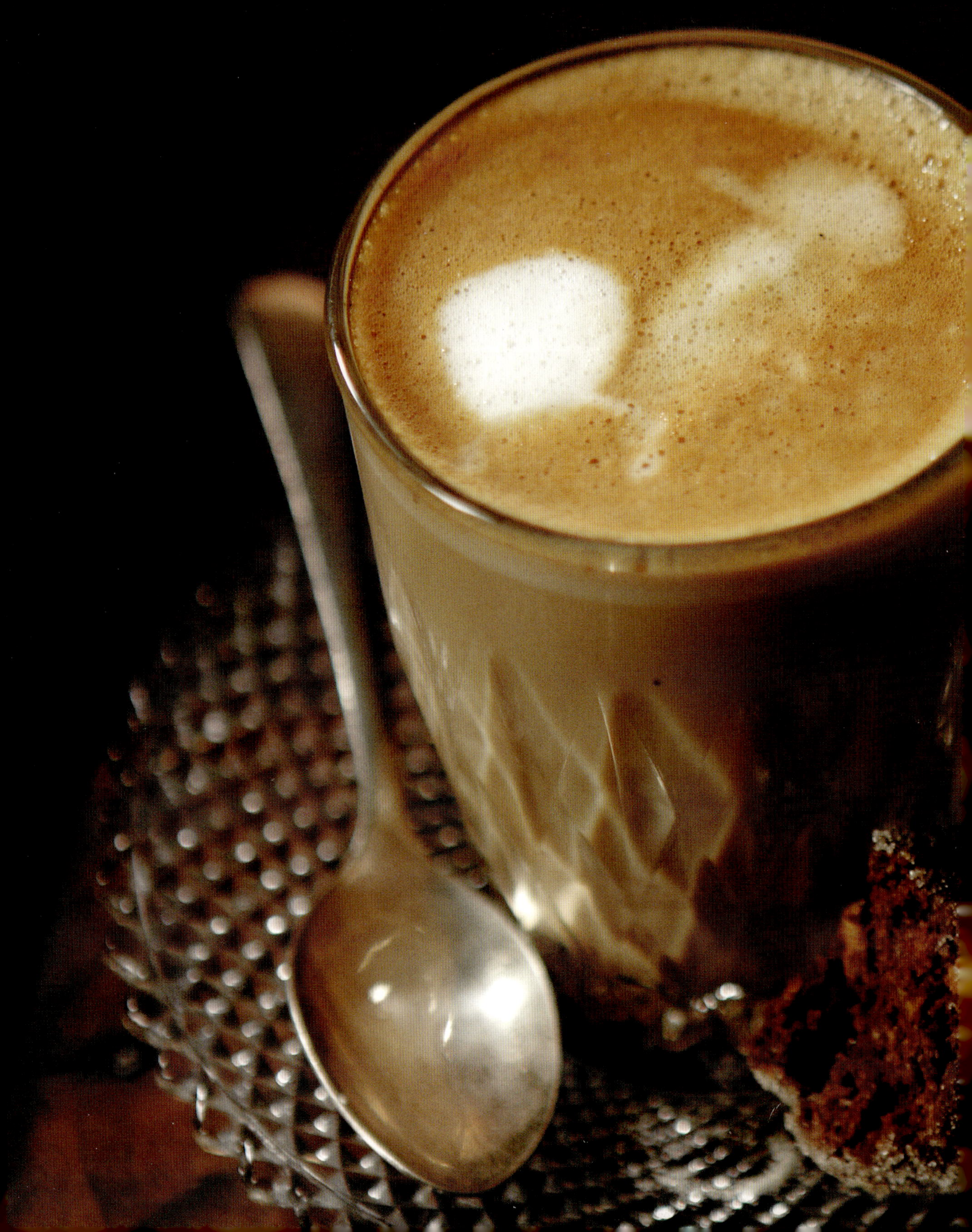

COFFEE

Vienna Coffee

Legend has it that soldiers of the Polish-Habsburg army, while liberating Vienna from the second Turkish siege in 1683, came accross a number of sacks of strange beans, which they first thought were camel feed and wanted to destroy. The Polish king granted the sacks to a Polish noble named Franz Georg Kolschitzky, who was instrumental in defeating the Turkish. He opened a coffee house called the Blue Bottle, and began serving coffee as it was prepared in Constantinople (as a concoction of pulp and water). The Viennese did not take to this and, after experimentation, Kolschitzky decided to filter the coffee and add cream and honey. Success was immediate.

INGREDIENTS:

2 shots espresso

whipped cream

Serves 1

METHOD:

1. Prepare strong shots of espresso into a standard cup or glass.
2. Top with cream (instead of milk or sugar).
3. Serve in a 90ml cup and drink through the cream top.

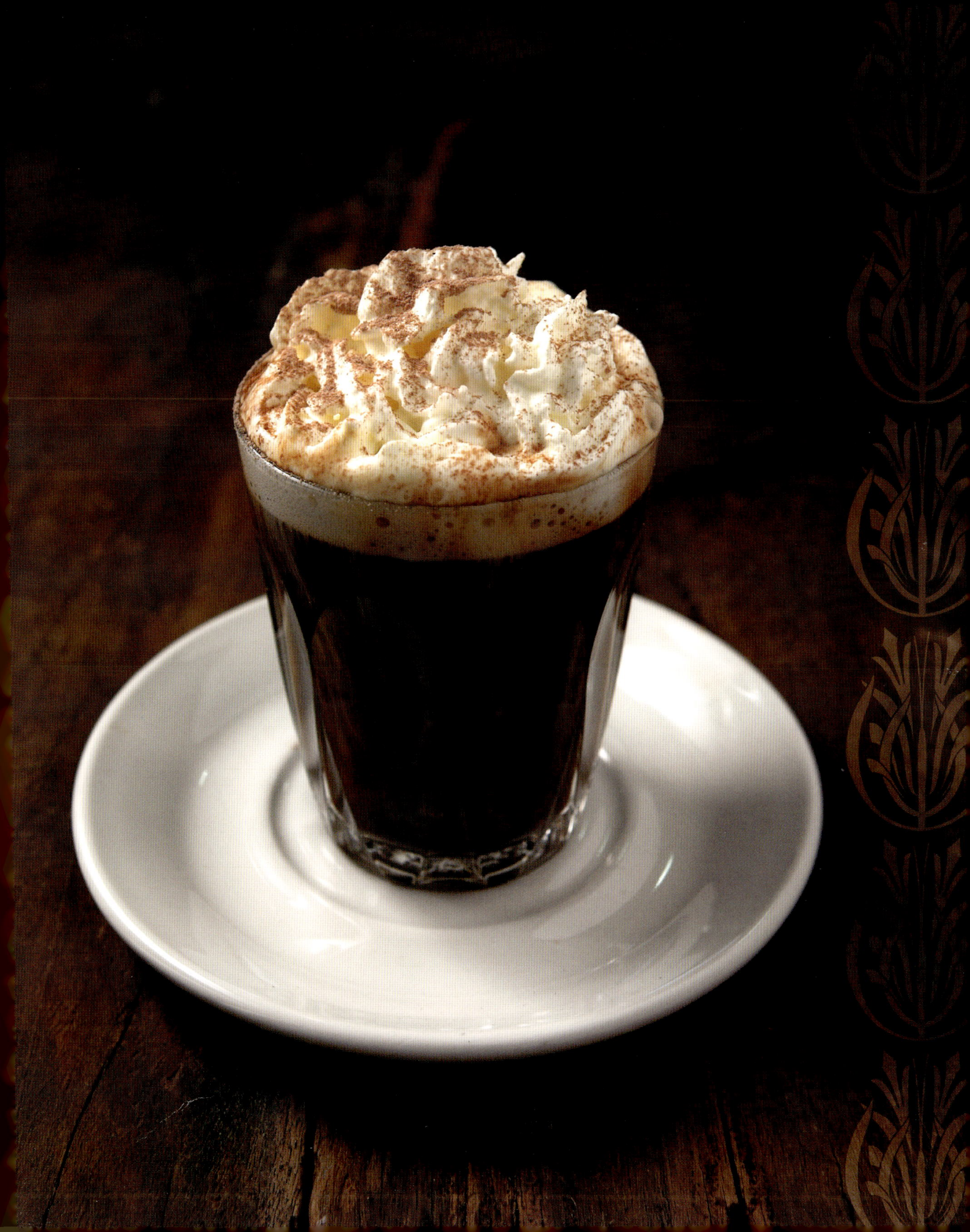

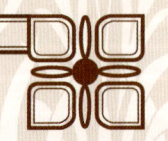

Affogato Agave

INGREDIENTS:

2 scoops vanilla bean ice cream

60 ml (2 fl oz) espresso coffee

2 tablespoons Patron XO Café Tequila, Frangelico or Kahlúa

1 teaspoon hazelnuts, chopped

Serves 1

METHOD:

1 Put the ice cream in the glass and drown it with the espresso coffee.

2 Pour over your choice of liqueur.

3 Garnish with chopped hazelnuts.

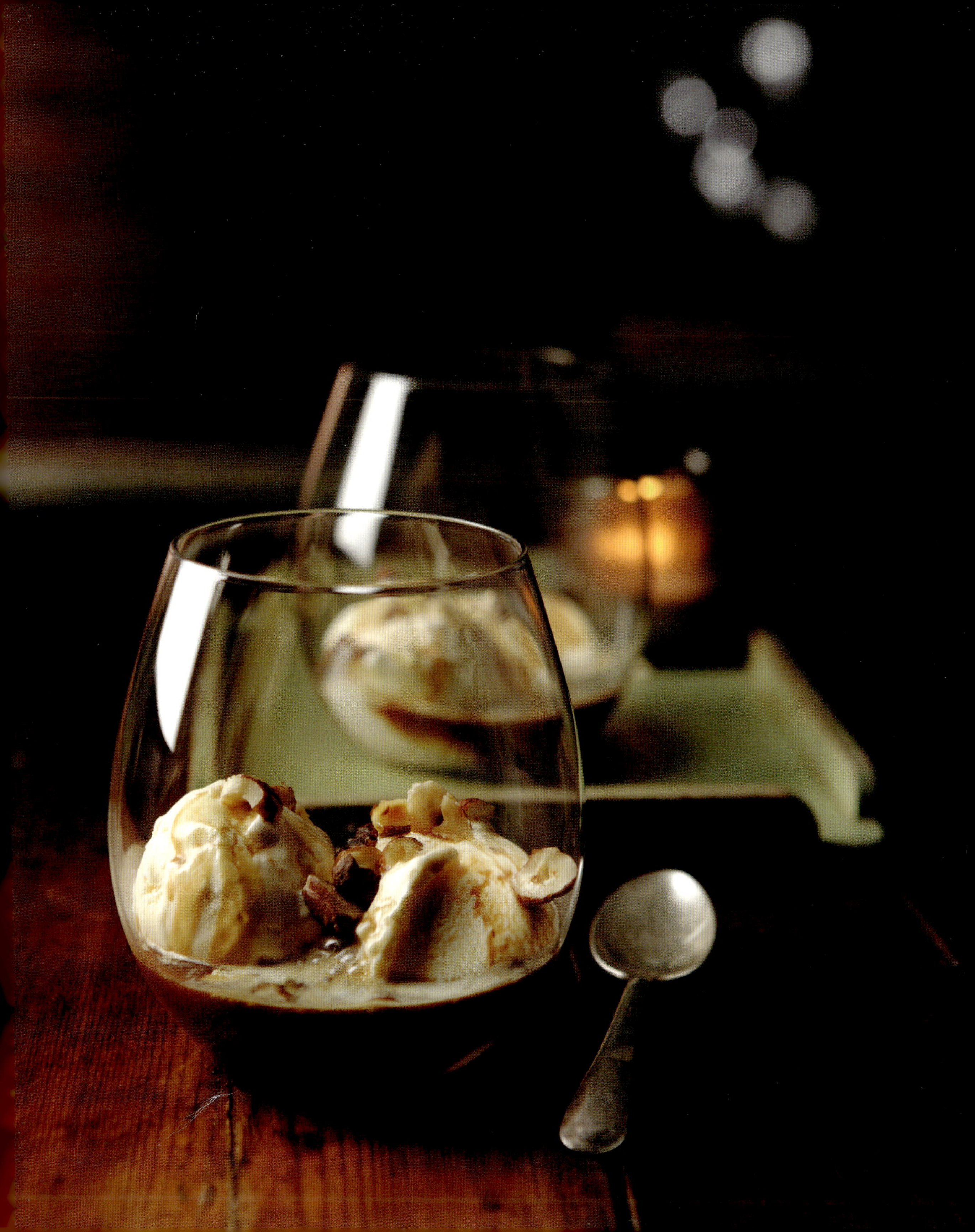

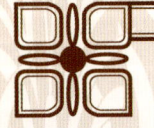

Iced Coffee

Iced coffee can be a refreshing afternoon treat. If it's really hot outside and you want to cool down but still get your caffeine and coffee flavour, iced coffee is the way to go.

There are many variations of iced coffee, depending on which country you are in.

In Australia, it is usually chilled coffee and milk with ice cream and/or whipped cream.

In Canada, it is known as an iced cappuccino or ice capps and it is a frozen coffee-flavoured slushie mixed with cream.

In Greece, there is a variation called a frappé. It is whipped in an electric mixer to create the foam on top. Milk is optional.

Many Italian cafes serve caffè freddo, which is straight espresso kept in the freezer and served as a slushie.

Thai iced coffee is strong black coffee sweetened with sugar, heavy cream and cardamon, quickly cooled and served over ice.

Vietnamese iced coffee is drip coffee with condensed milk over ice.

INGREDIENTS:

1 scoop ice cream
⅓ espresso
⅔ cold milk
whipped fresh cream

Serves 1

METHOD:

1. Make a strong coffee
2. Transfer the hot coffee to a carafe or pitcher.
3. Refrigerate until cold, about 2–3 hours.
4. Add 1 scoop of ice cream in a tall or milkshake glass.
5. Add cold coffee to glass until half-full—for a weaker serve add less coffee.
6. Pour cold milk to 1cm under the brim of the glass and stir a couple of times.
7. Finish with whipped or ice cream and garnish with chocolate powder and coffee beans.

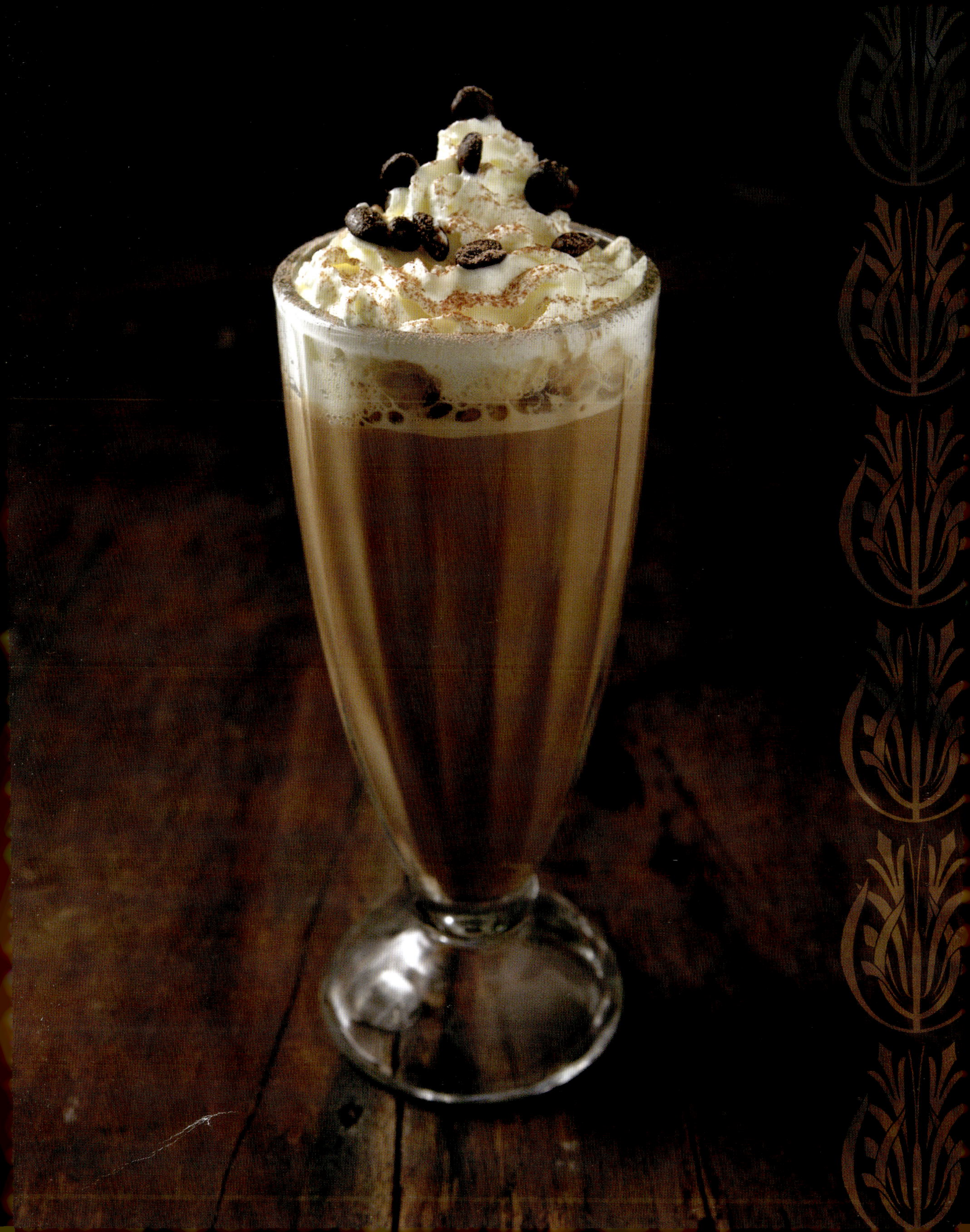

Irish Coffee

Variations: Alternatively, you can make Irish coffee with whisky by substituting a good Irish whisky such as Tullamore Dew or Jameson's for the Baileys. Other liqueur coffees are: French—brandy, English—gin, Russian—vodka, American—Bourbon, Calypso—dark rum, Jamaican—Tia Maria, Parisienne—Grand Marnier, Mexican—Kahlúa, Monks—Benedictine, Scottish—Scotch, Canadian—rye.

INGREDIENTS:

1 teaspoon brown sugar
2 tablespoons Baileys
hot black coffee
2 tablespoons fresh whipped cream
chocolate flakes or chocolate powder

Serves 1

METHOD:

1. Stir sugar into Baileys. Top up with coffee. Float fresh cream on top. Garnish with chocolate.

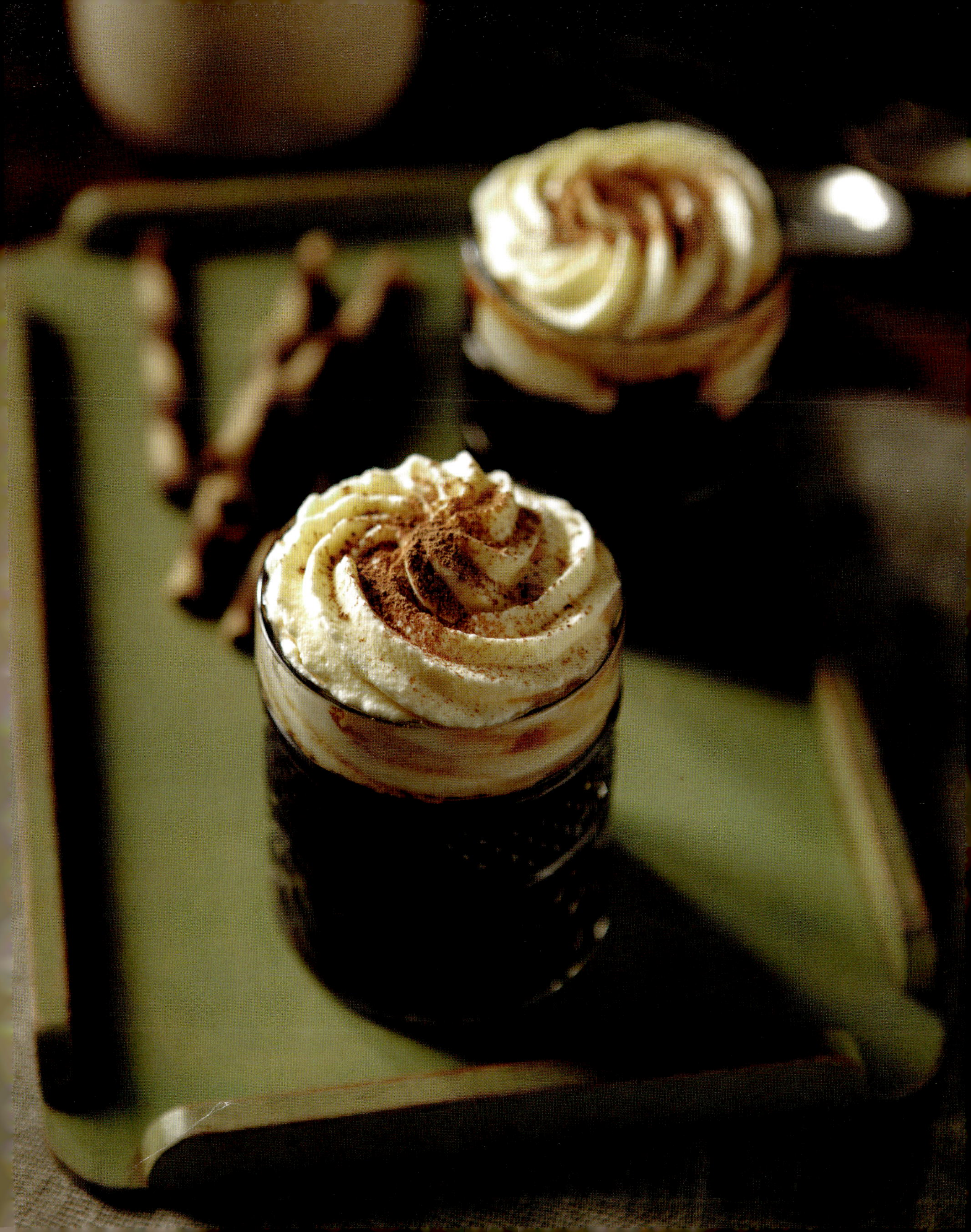

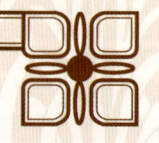

Café Agave

INGREDIENTS:

2 tablespoons Patron XO Café Tequila
2 tablespoons cocoa liqueur
60 ml (2 fl oz) espresso coffee
60 ml (2 fl oz) cream
1 chocolate flake

Serves 1

METHOD:

1. Shake all ingredients, except chocolate flakes, with ice and strain into the glass.
2. Serve in martini glass, garnished with chocolate flakes.

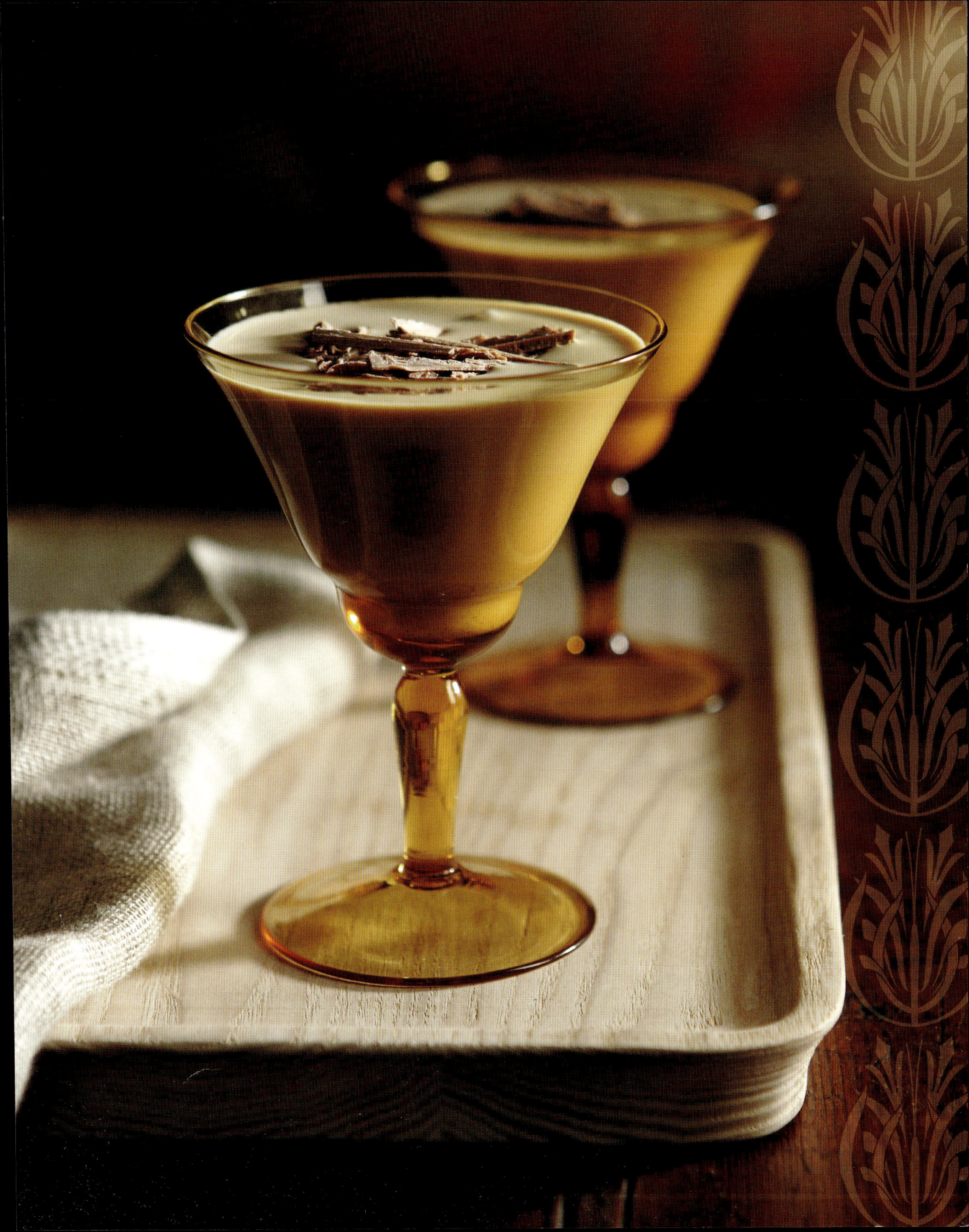

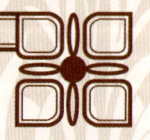

Coffee Break

Variations: Alternatively, you can make Peppermint Break by substituting crème de menthe for brandy.

INGREDIENTS:

½ cup hot black coffee

1 tablespoon brandy

1 tablespoon Kahlúa

3 tablespoons whipped cream

1 maraschino cherry

Serves 1

METHOD:

1. Pour coffee and liquors into an Irish coffee cup and sweeten to taste.
2. Float the cream on top, add a maraschino cherry and serve.

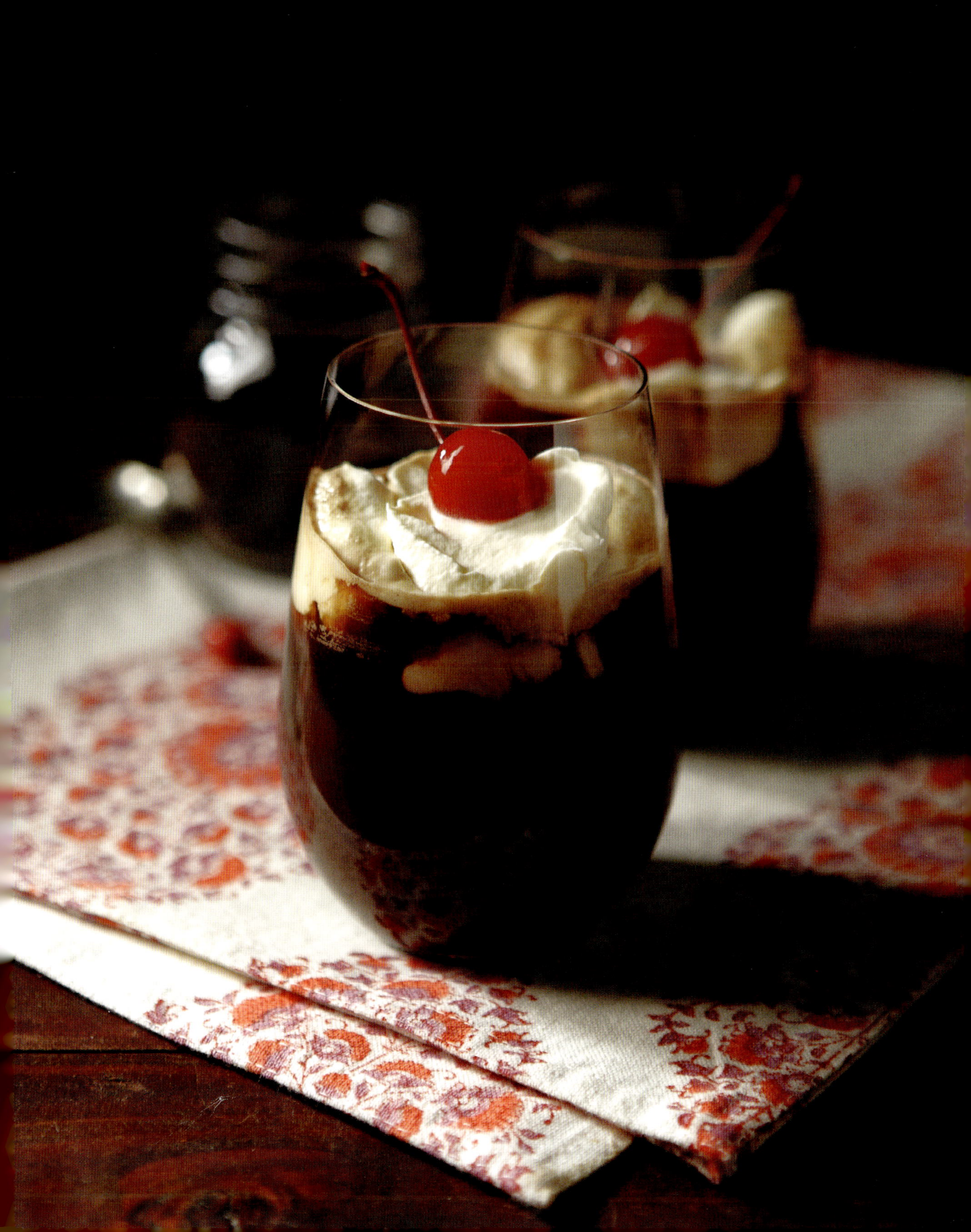

Caribbean Coffee

Variations: Alternatively, you can make this by substituting Kahlúa for the dark rum.

INGREDIENTS:

2 tablespoons dark rum

150 ml (4 fl oz) hot black coffee

3 tablespoons whipped cream

Serves 1

METHOD:

1 Pour rum and coffee into an Irish coffee cup and sweeten to taste.

2 Float the cream on top, sprinkle with grated chocolate.

3 Garnish with chocolate-coated coffee beans.

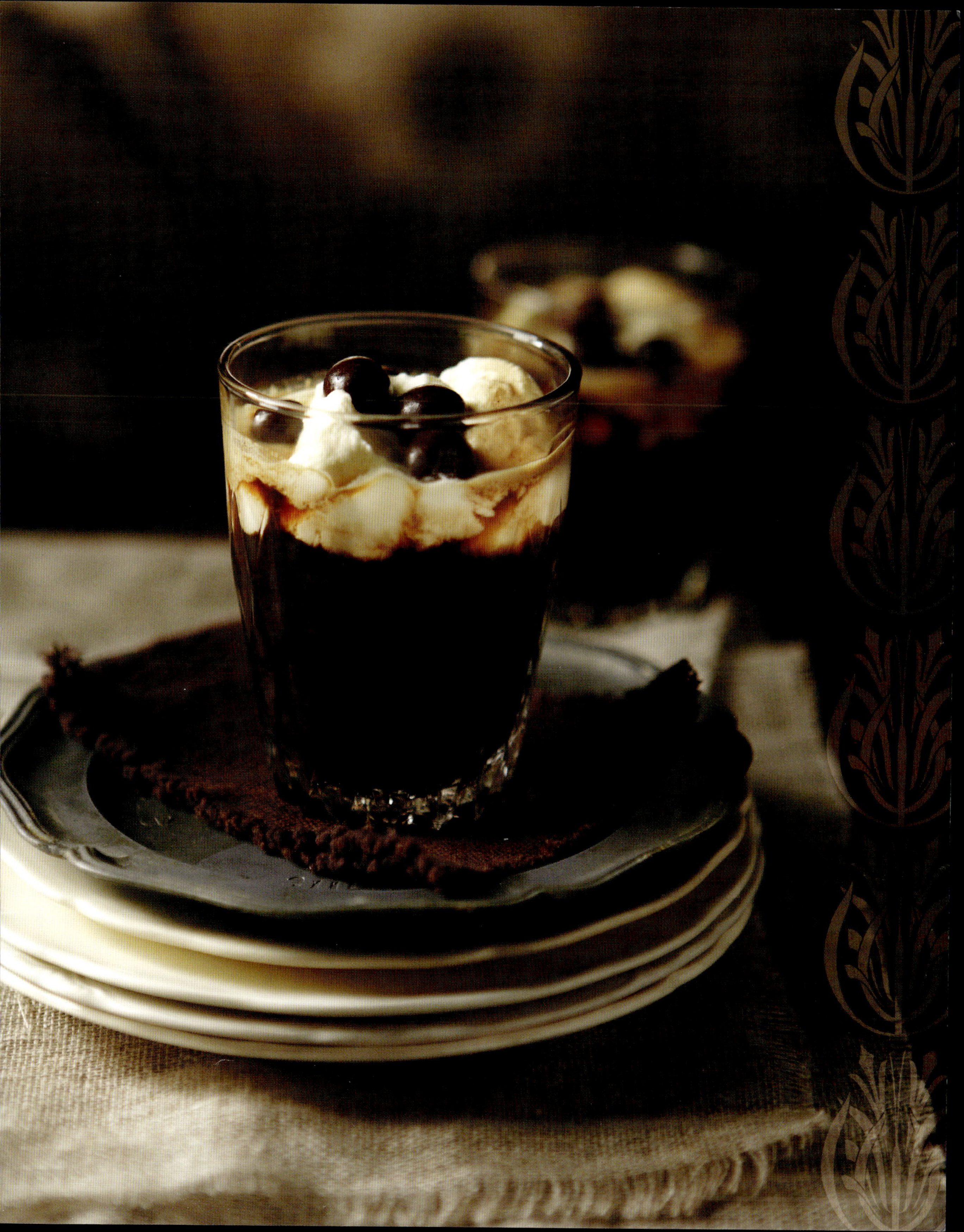

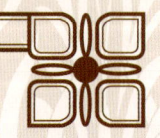

Café Oscar

INGREDIENTS:

1 tablespoon Kahlúa

1 tablespoon Amaretto di Galliano

hot coffee

double cream

1 scoop vanilla ice cream

Serves 1

METHOD:

1. Pour spirits into glass, then top up with coffee.
2. Float cream on top. Garnish with ice cream.

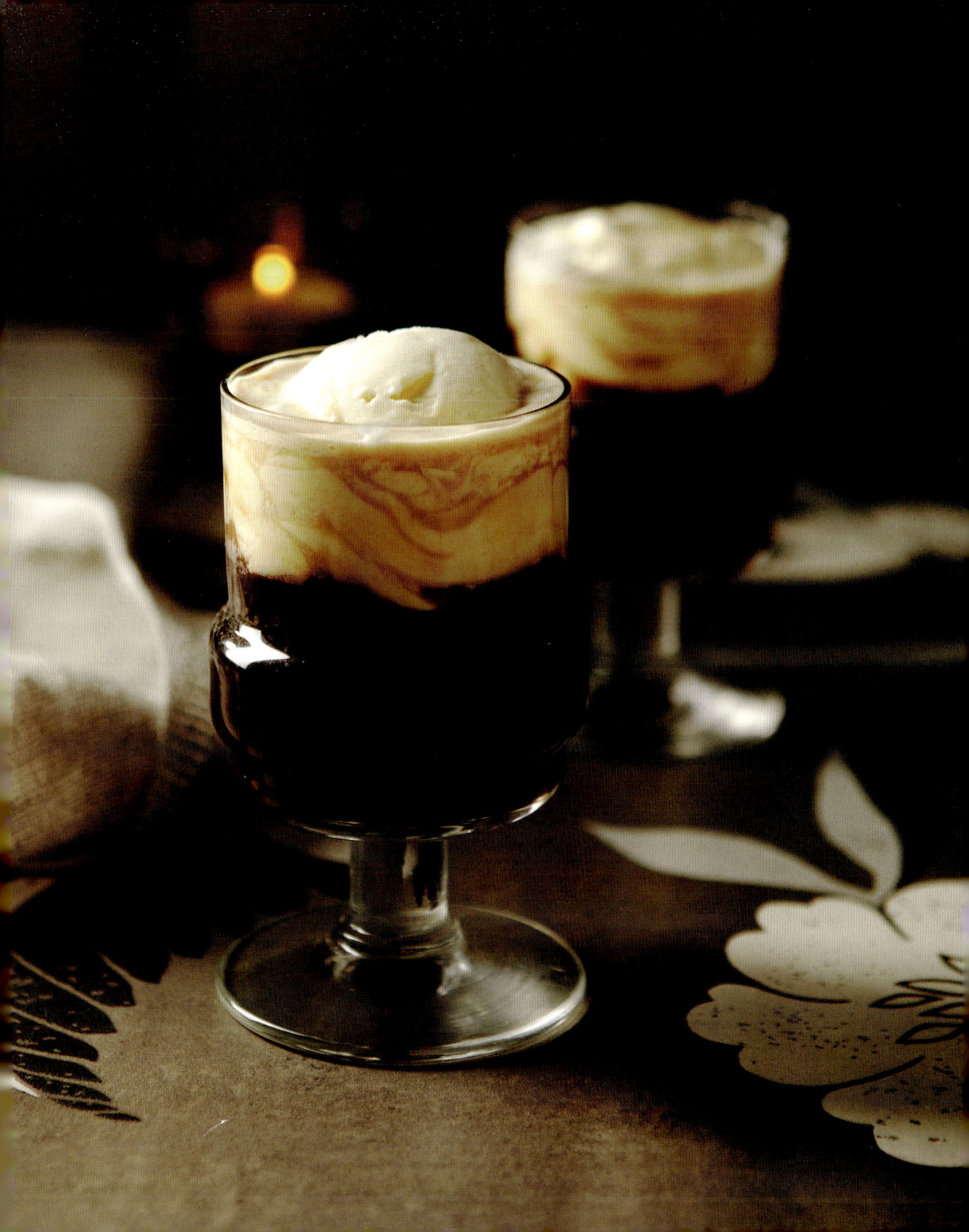

Royale Coffee

INGREDIENTS:

2 tablespoons Cognac

150 ml (5 fl oz) hot black coffee

3 tablespoons whipped cream

1 teaspoon grated chocolate

Serves 1

METHOD:

1. Add coffee and Cognac to an Irish coffee cup and sweeten to taste. Gently float whipped cream on top, sprinkle with grated chocolate and serve.

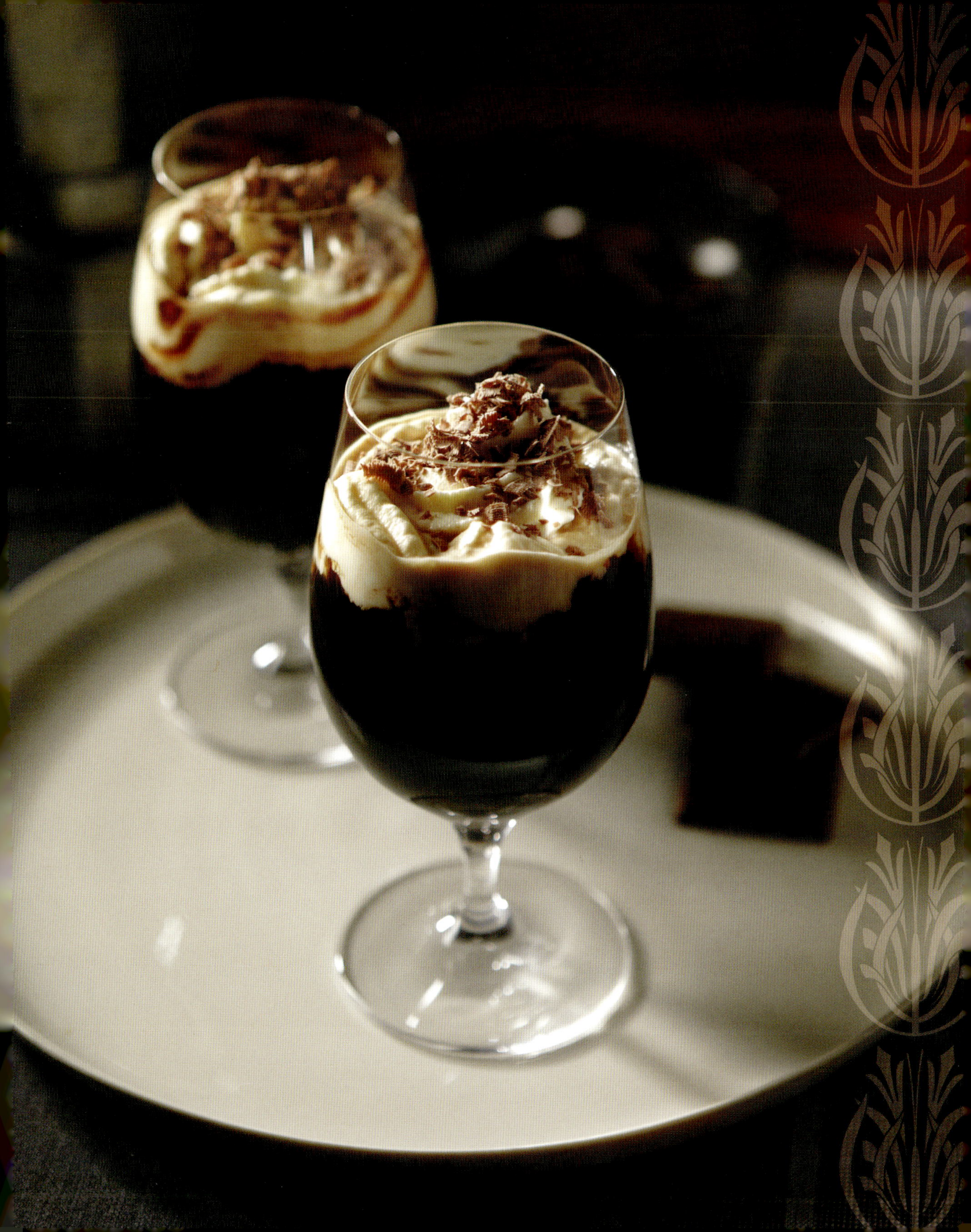

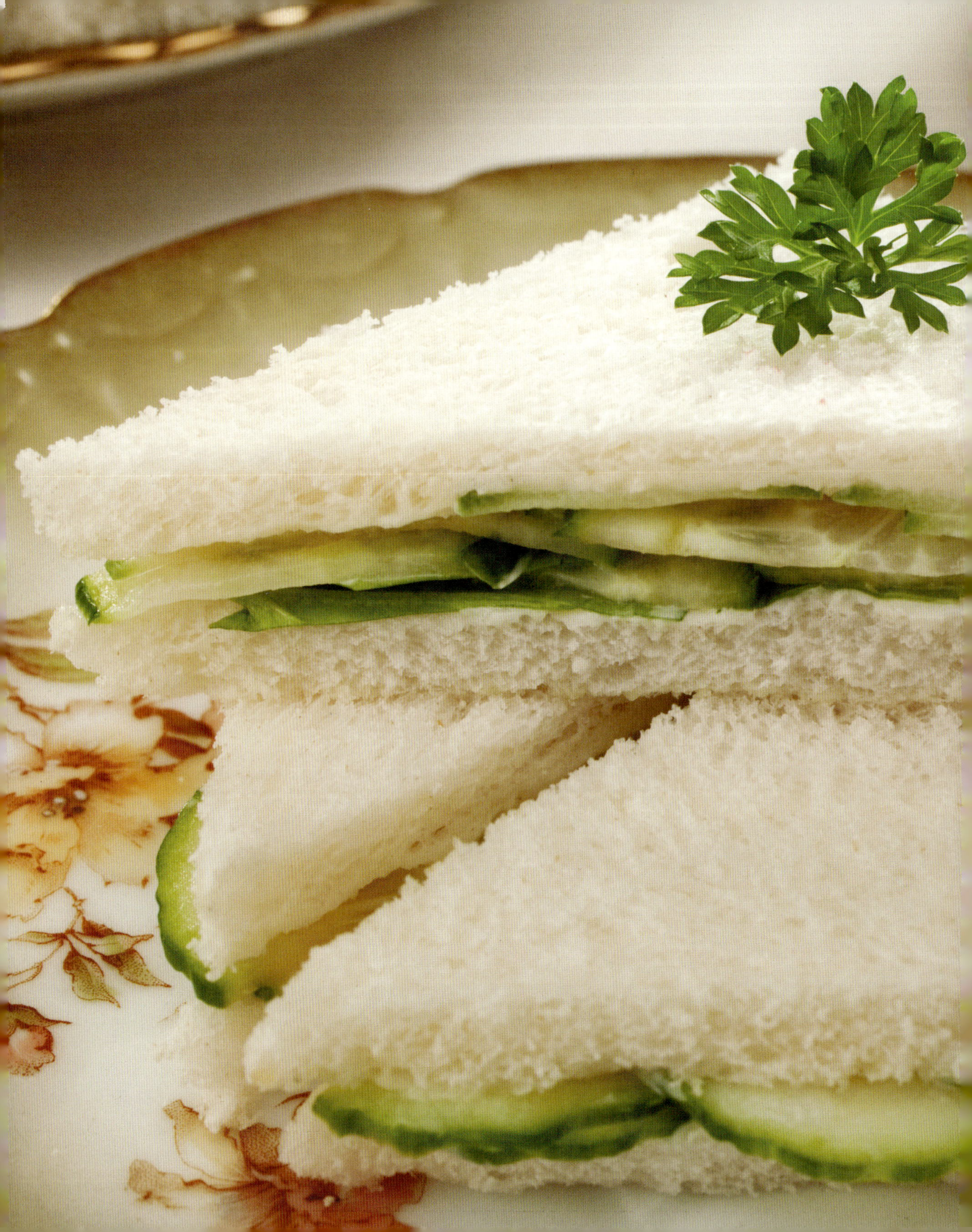

SANDWICHES

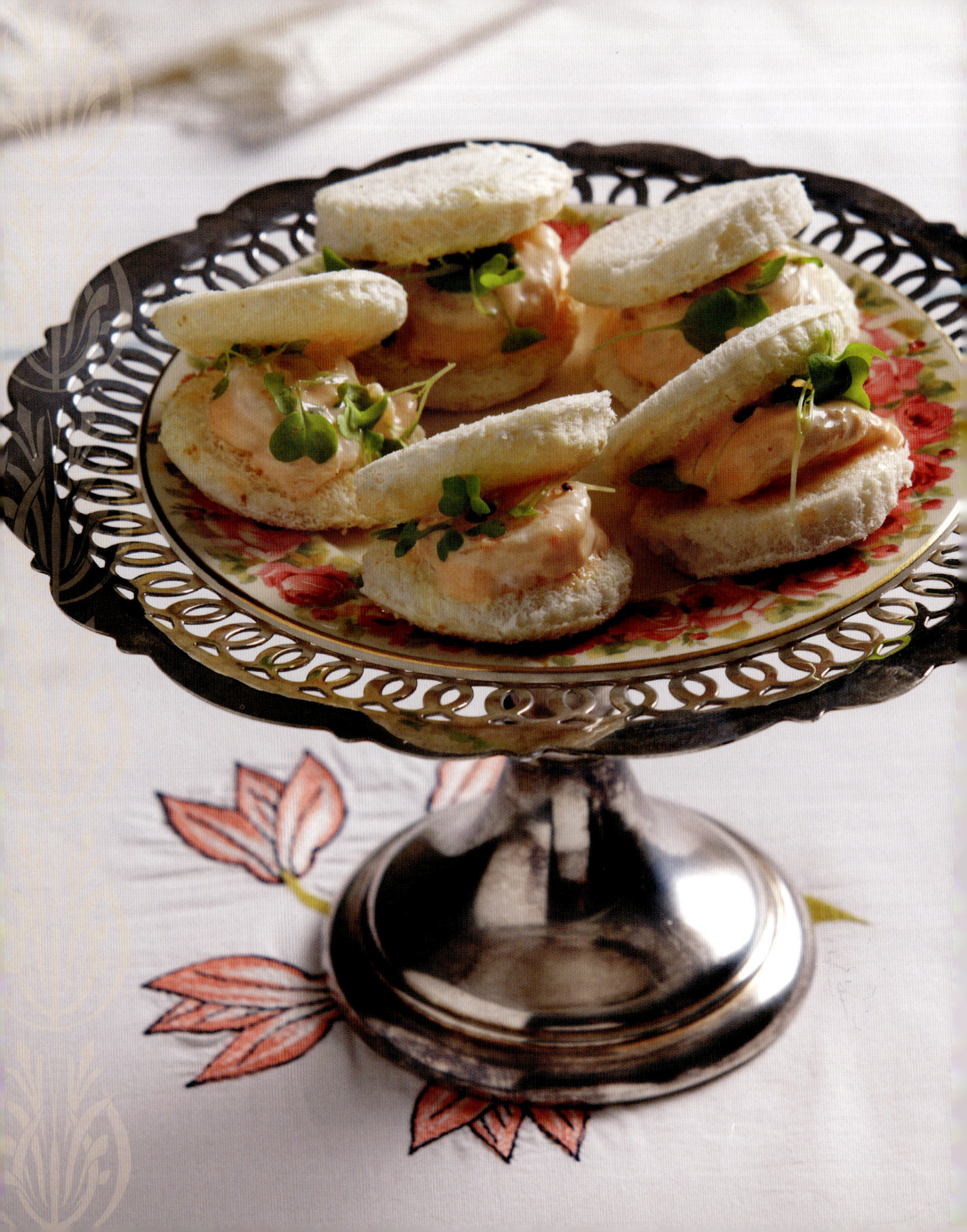

Dainty Seafood Circles

INGREDIENTS:

2 tablespoons mayonnaise
2 teaspoons tomato sauce
a dash Worcestershire Sauce
salt and black pepper
200 g (6½ oz) fresh, peeled and cooked shrimp (prawns) (roughly chopped, depending on the size)
10 slices soft white sliced fresh bread, lightly buttered
½ teaspoon paprika
watercress or mustard cress, to garnish

Makes 15

METHOD:

1. Combine mayonnaise, tomato sauce and Worcestershire Sauce. Season with salt and pepper. This mixture must be quite stiff, otherwise it will not coat the prawns and will make a soggy sandwich.
2. Add shrimp (prawns) and stir gently to coat.
3. Cut three circles out of each slice of bread using a 4cm (1½in) cookie cutter (serrated is best for a pretty edge).
4. Spread 2 teaspoons prawn mixture onto 15 circles. Sprinkle each with paprika.
5. Top with remaining fresh bread circles.
6. Arrange on a large platter, garnished with watercress or mustard cress.

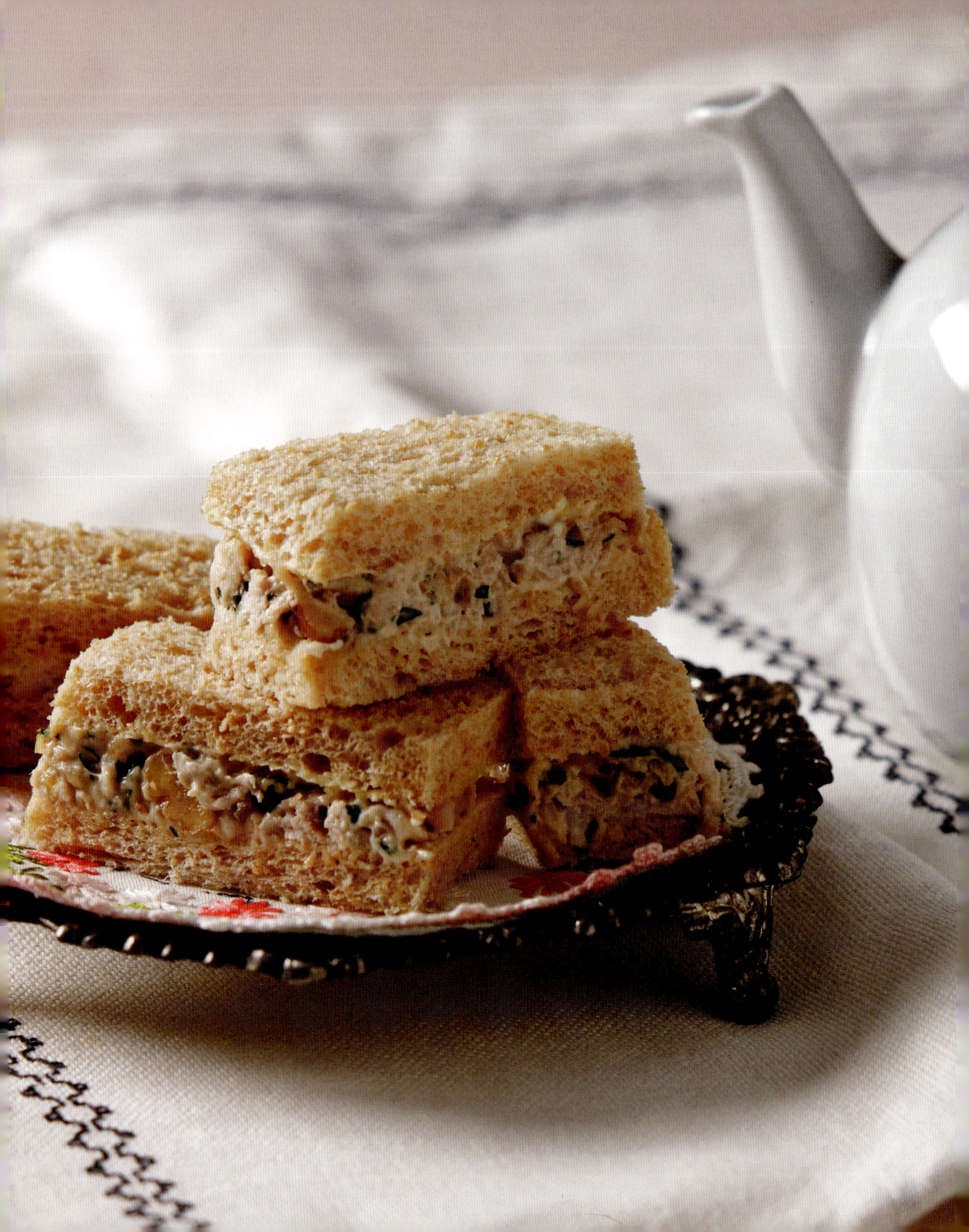

Chicken & Walnut

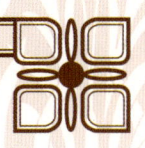

INGREDIENTS:

½ tablespoon cream cheese (softened)

½ tablespoon mayonnaise

1 tablespoon milk

a handful of walnuts, finely chopped

½ poached chicken breast (approx 100g/3½oz), shredded

1 tablespoon flat-leaf parsley, chopped

salt and black pepper

4 slices soft wholemeal fresh bread, lightly buttered

Makes 6

METHOD:

1 Mix the cream cheese and mayonnaise together. If a more liquid consistency is needed to coat the chicken, add a small quantity of milk.

2 Stir the walnuts into the mayonnaise mixture.

3 Add the shredded chicken and chopped parsley, and mix to combine. Season to taste.

4 Divide the mixture onto two slices of fresh bread and top with the other slices.

5 Trim crusts off sandwich and cut into three fingers, then cut each finger in half.

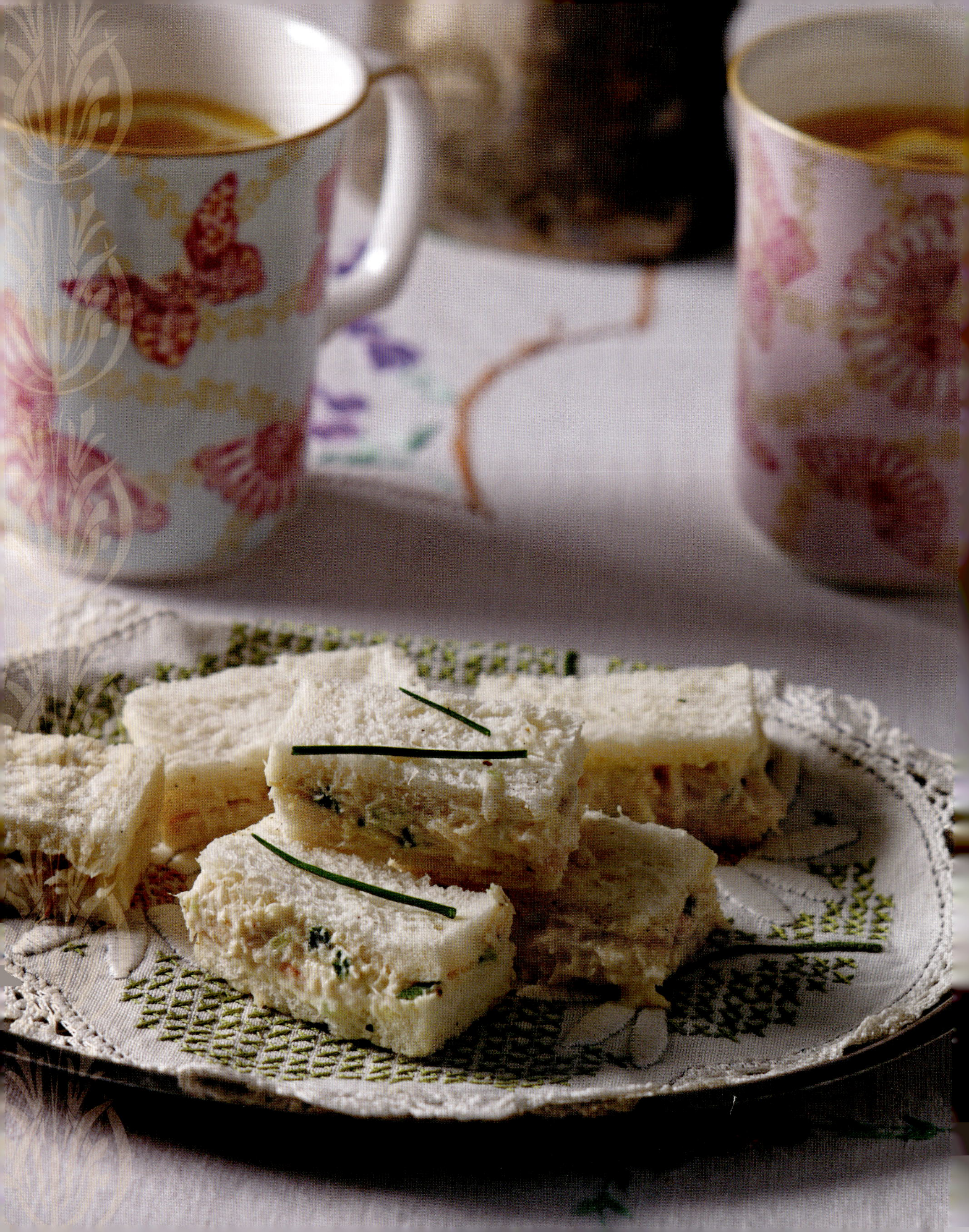

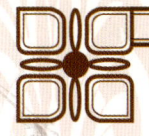

Crab, Chives & Celery

INGREDIENTS:

¼ stick celery, very finely chopped

½ tablespoon crème fraiche

2 garlic chives (or ordinary chives), finely chopped

70 g (2½ oz) crabmeat

salt and black pepper

4 slices soft white bread, lightly buttered

Makes 6

METHOD:

1. Mix the celery with the crème fraiche and chives.
2. Add the crabmeat, gently stirring to combine. Season well with salt and pepper.
3. Spread the mixture onto two slices of fresh bread.
4. Top with second slice of bread.
5. Trim the crusts and cut into three fingers, then cut each finger in half.

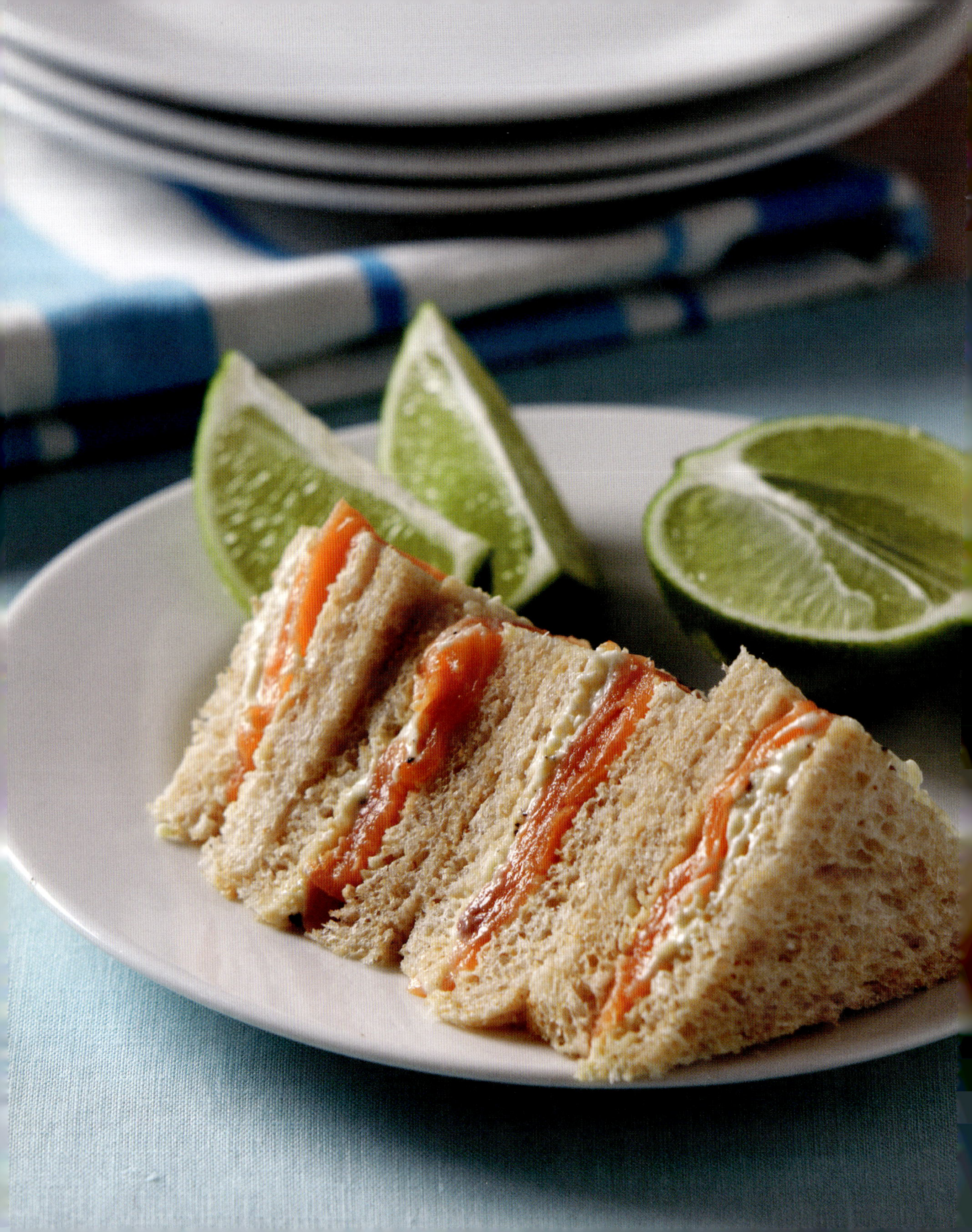

Smoked Trout with Lime

INGREDIENTS:

1 tablespoon softened cream cheese
2 teaspoons whole egg mayonnaise
½ lime
salt and black pepper
4 slices soft wholemeal fresh bread, lightly buttered
50–100 g (1½–3½ oz) smoked ocean trout

Makes 8

METHOD:

1 Combine the cream cheese and mayonnaise.
2 Add the juice and grated peel of ½ lime. The mixture needs to be quite stiff, so do not add all the lime juice if this makes it runny.
3 Season with salt and pepper to taste.
4 Spread quite thickly onto two slices of fresh bread.
5 Top with slices of ocean trout and second slice of fresh bread.
6 Trim the crusts and cut each into four neat triangles.

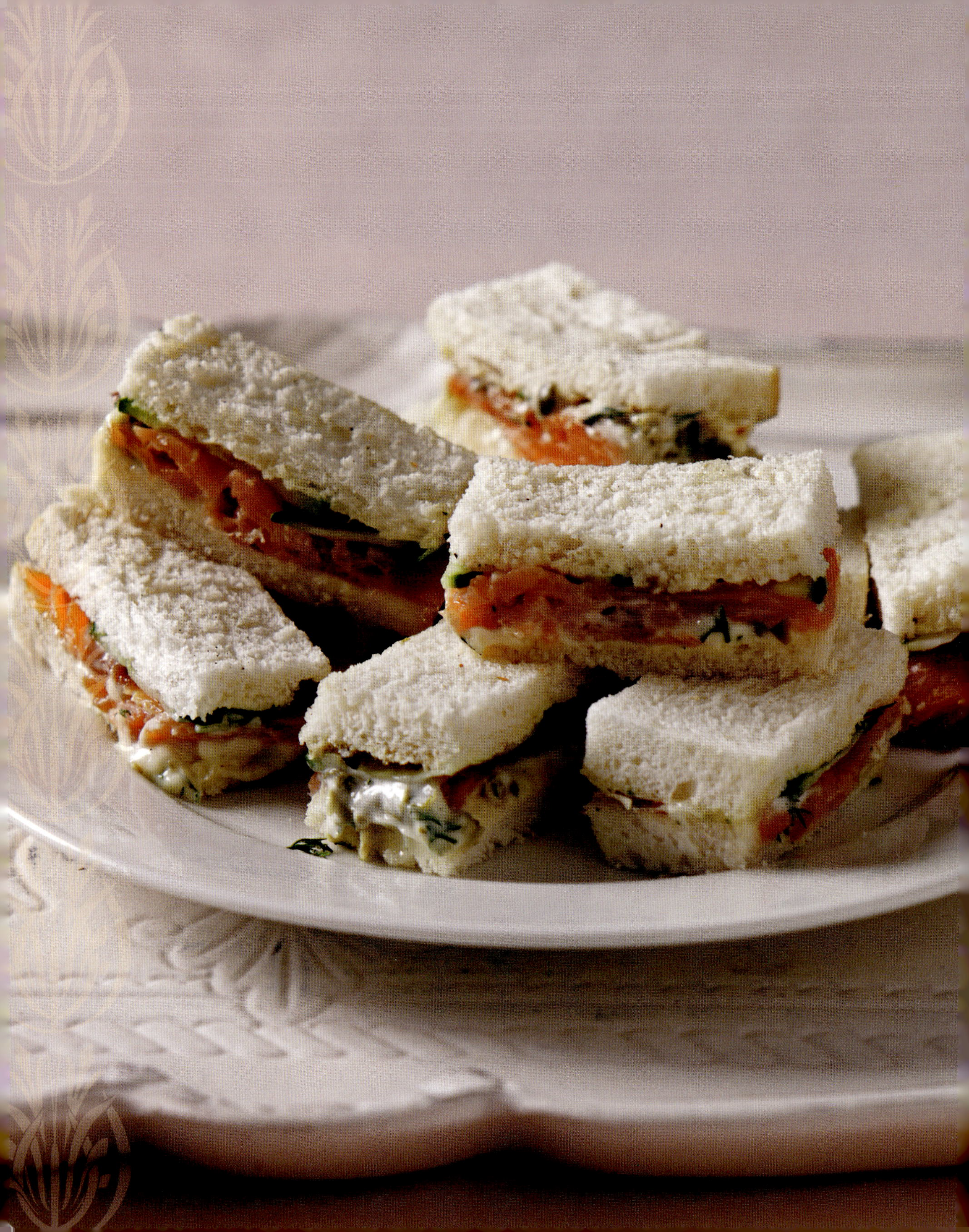

Smoked Salmon & Cucumber

INGREDIENTS:

1 tablespoon whole egg mayonnaise

2 teaspoons (approx. 16) baby capers, chopped

1 teaspoon chopped fresh dill

4 slices soft white fresh bread, lightly buttered

50–100 g (1½–3½ oz) smoked salmon (or smoked trout)

¼ small or English cucumber, finely sliced

black pepper

Makes 6

METHOD:

1. Combine the mayonnaise, chopped capers and dill and spread on the two slices of fresh bread.
2. Place the smoked salmon generously on top.
3. Overlap nine thin slices of cucumber until they are covering the salmon.
4. Season with freshly ground black pepper.
5. Top with second slice of fresh bread.
6. Trim crusts off sandwich and cut into three fingers, then cut each finger in half.

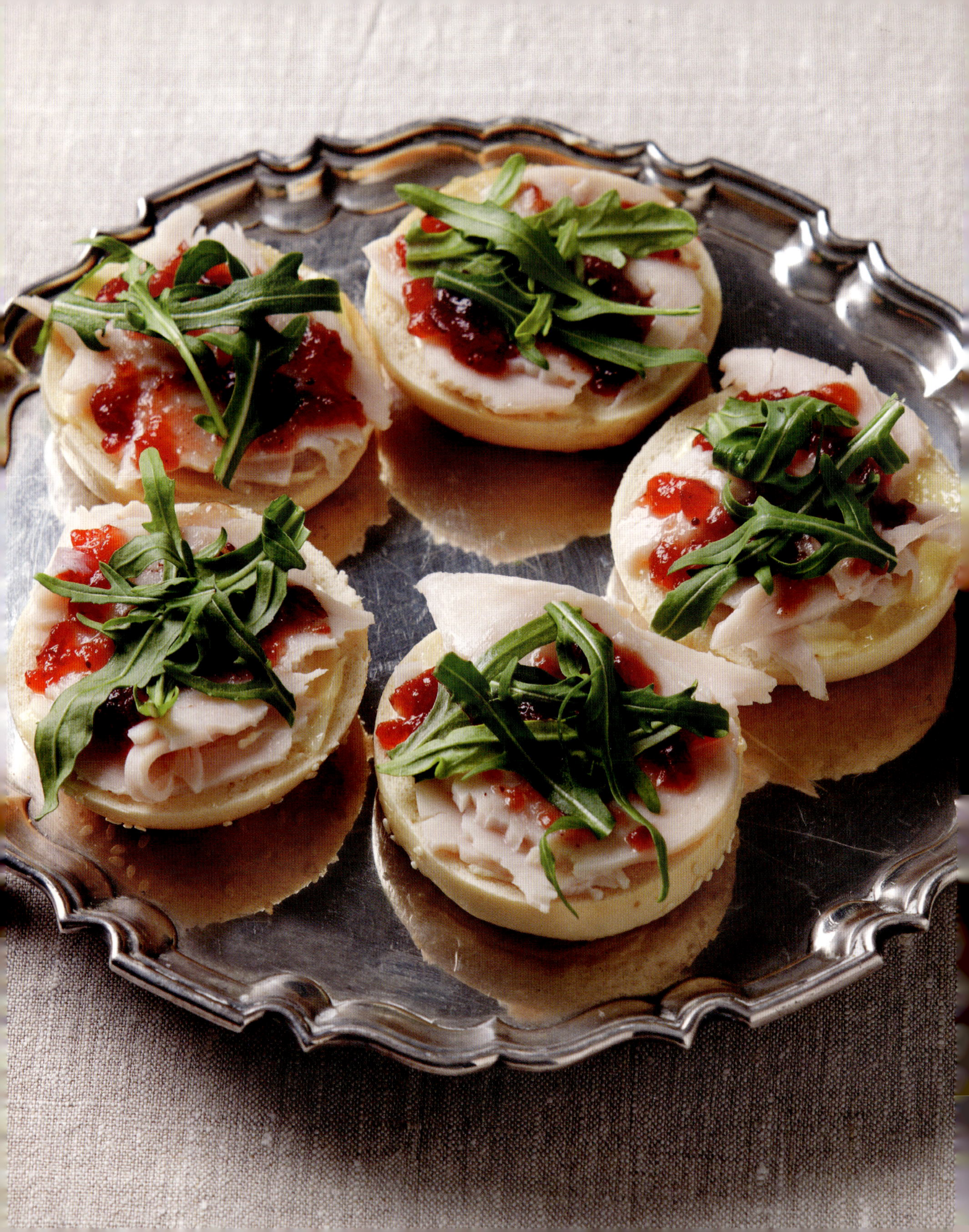

Smoked Turkey Open Sandwich

INGREDIENTS:

1 tablespoon whole egg mayonnaise

12 slices (approx 200 g/6½ oz) smoked turkey

6 mini bagels, halved

salt and black pepper

2 tablespoons cranberry jelly

a handful of baby rocket leaves

Makes 12

METHOD:

1. Spread the mayonnaise evenly on each bagel half.
2. Put a slice of folded turkey on each bagel.
3. Season well with salt and black pepper.
4. Smear a teaspoon of cranberry jelly across the turkey.
5. Top with a few leaves of rocket (about 5 on each).
6. Serve on a large platter.

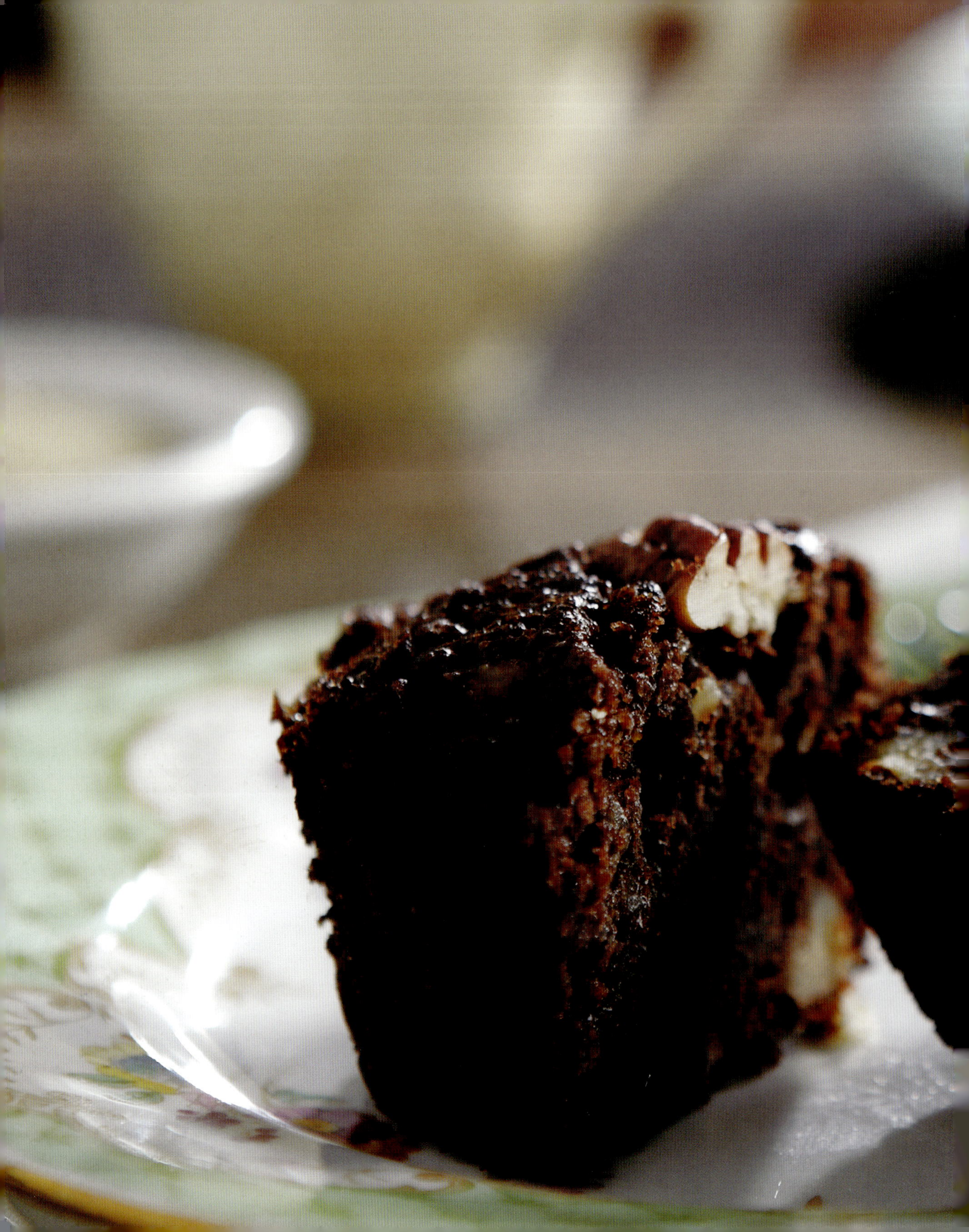

SCONES & MUFFINS

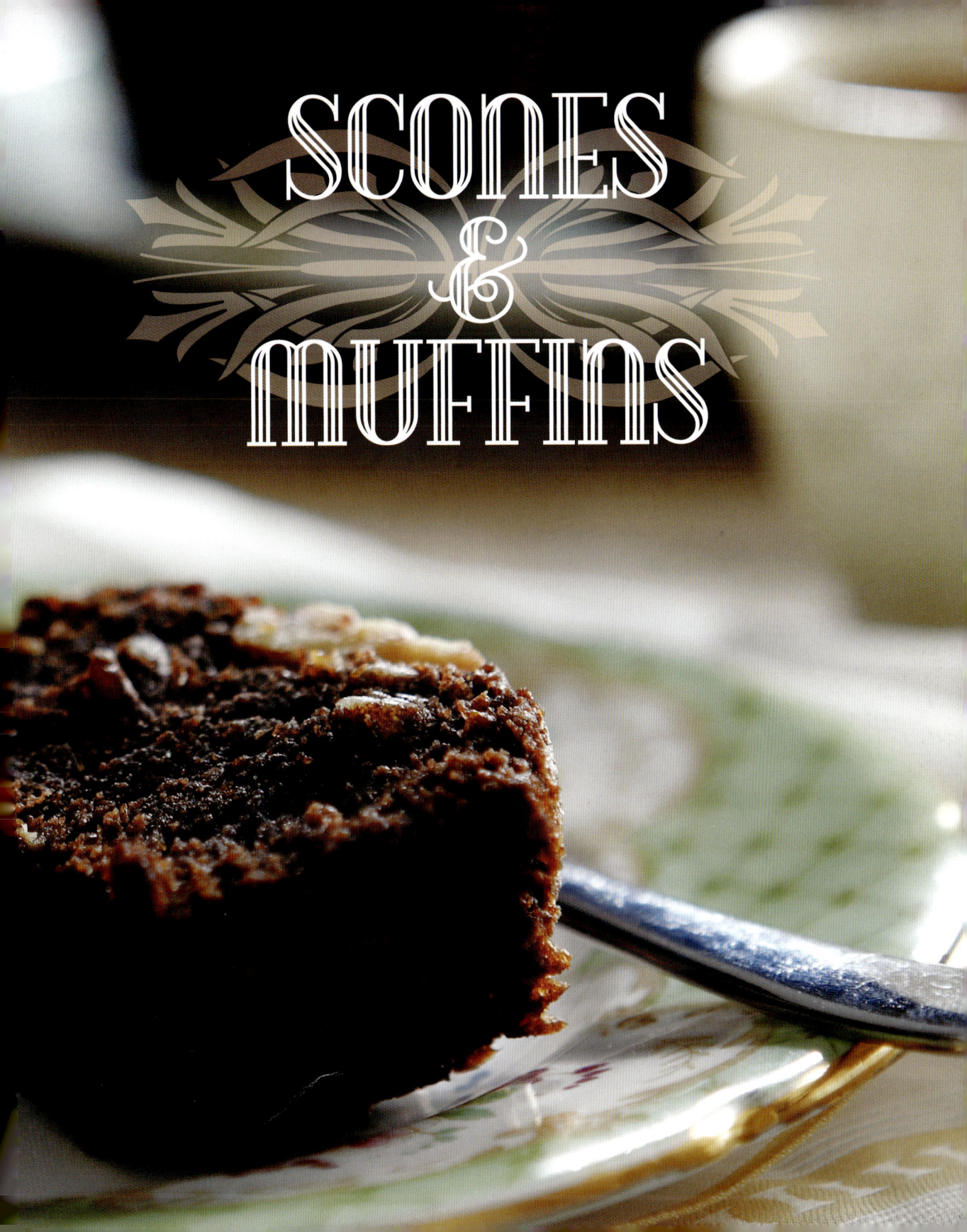

Coffee & Walnut Surprises

INGREDIENTS:

250g (9oz) butter, at room temperature
½ cup sugar
2 eggs
2 tablespoons Baileys Irish Cream
1 cup chopped walnuts
2 tablespoons instant coffee powder
1½ cups self-raising flour
icing sugar

SAUCE
½ cup caster sugar
1 cup thickened cream
1 tablespoon instant coffee powder

Makes 12

METHOD:

1. Preheat oven to 180°C/350°F.
2. Beat butter and sugar until light and fluffy, stir in eggs, Baileys and walnuts. Sift in coffee and flour and mix to combine.
3. Divide mixture evenly into a lightly buttered 12-hole muffin or friand tin.
4. Bake for 15–20 minutes or until risen and firm.
5. Leave to cool for 10 minutes, then remove from tin. Pour over sauce. Serve with tea or coffee and Irish cream liqueur.

Sauce

1. Heat sugar and ¼ cup water in saucepan until mixture is boiling and sugar dissolves. Reduce heat, simmer until golden. Add cream and coffee. Bring to the boil and simmer until toffee dissolves and sauce thickens.

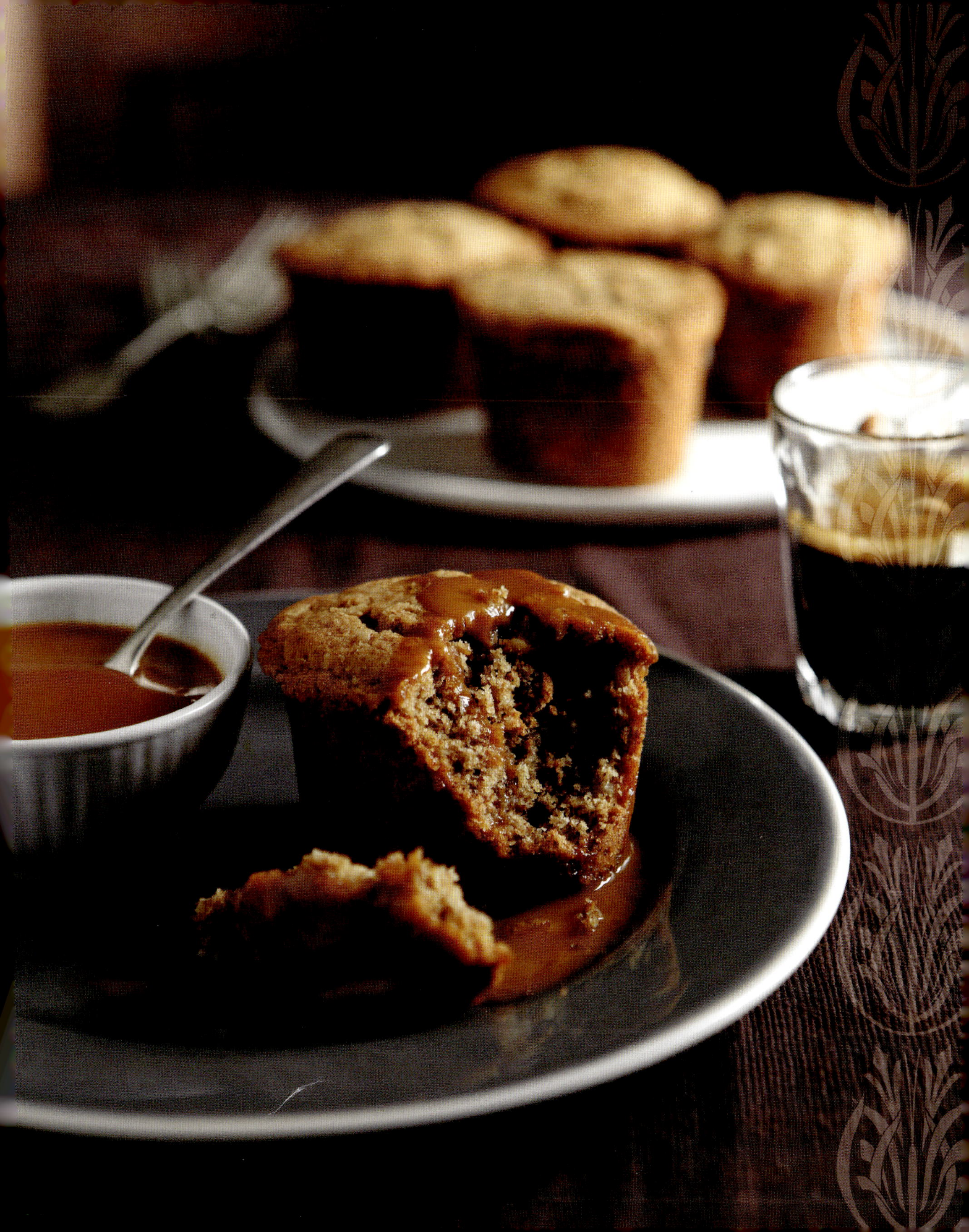

Traditional Scones

INGREDIENTS:

2 cups self-rising (self-raising) flour
1 teaspoon baking powder
2 teaspoons sugar
45 g (1½ oz) butter
1 egg
½ cup milk

Makes 12

METHOD:

1. Preheat oven to 220°C/420°F.
2. Sift flour and baking powder into a large bowl. Stir in sugar, then rub in butter using fingertips until mixture resembles coarse breadcrumbs.
3. Whisk together egg and milk. Make a well in centre of flour mixture, pour in egg mixture and mix to form a soft dough. Turn out onto a lightly floured surface and knead lightly.
4. Press dough out to a 25mm (1in) thickness using the palm of your hand. Cut out scones using a floured 5cm (2in) cutter. Avoid twisting the cutter, or the scones will rise unevenly.
5. Arrange scones close together on a buttered and lightly floured baking tray or in a shallow 20cm (8in) round cake tin. Brush with a little milk and bake for 12–15 minutes or until golden.

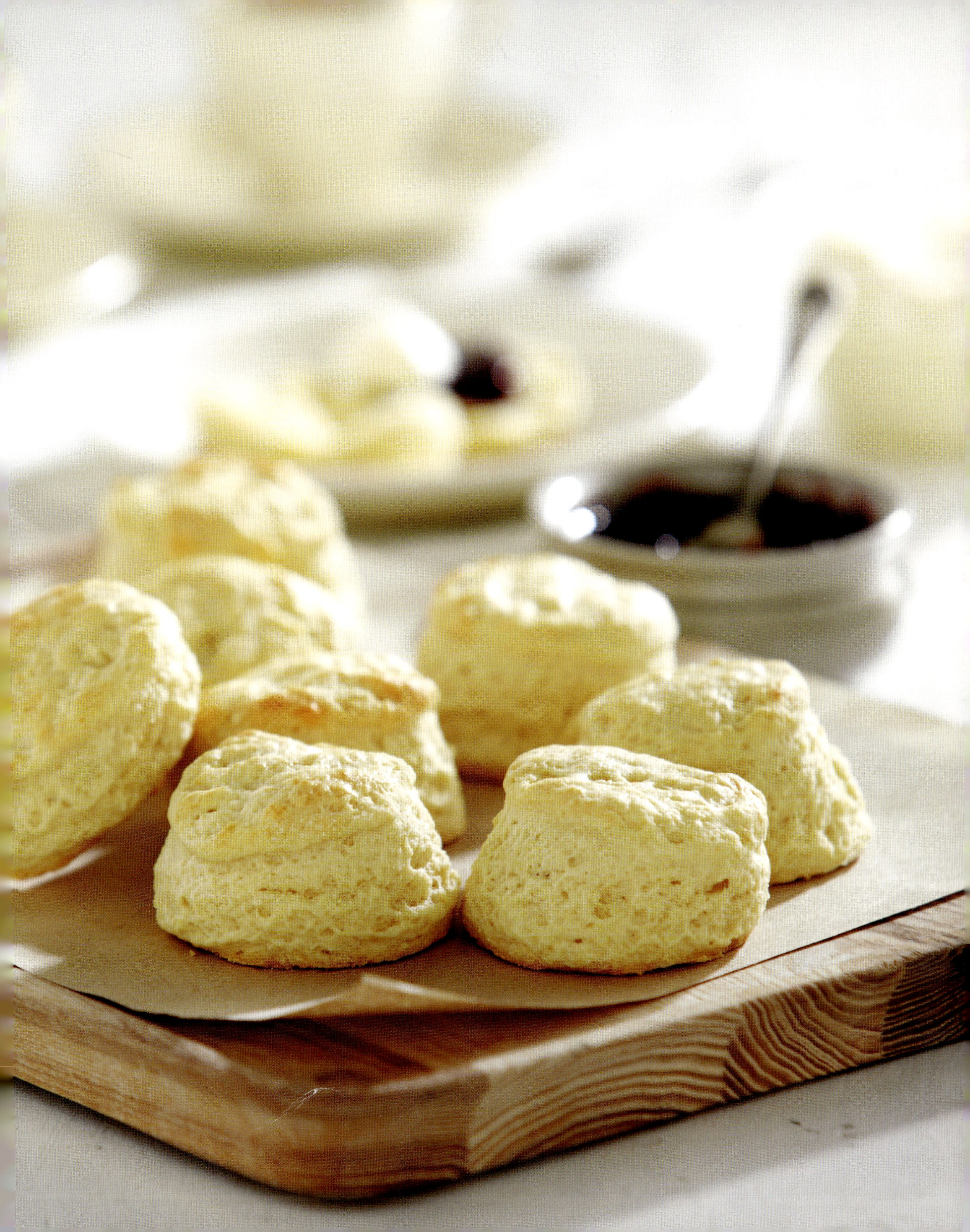

Cheese Scones

INGREDIENTS:

500 g (1 lb) self-rising (self-raising) flour
¼ teaspoon Cayenne pepper
1 teaspoon salt
60 g (2 oz) butter
1 tablespoon finely chopped onion
60 g (2 oz) Cheddar cheese, grated
1 egg
¼ cup parsley, finely chopped
2 cups milk
1 egg, beaten
¼ cup milk

Makes 12–16

METHOD:

1 Preheat oven to 230°C/450°F.
2 Sift flour, pepper and salt then, using fingertips, rub butter into the flour mixture. Add onion, cheese, egg and parsley. Make a well in the centre and add the milk all at once, stirring quickly and lightly to a soft dough.
3 Turn out onto a lightly floured board and knead just enough to make a smooth surface. Pat into 12–18mm (½–¾in) thickness and, using a small scone cutter, cut into rounds.
4 Place on a floured baking tray. Brush tops with combined beaten egg and milk and then bake for about 10 minutes.

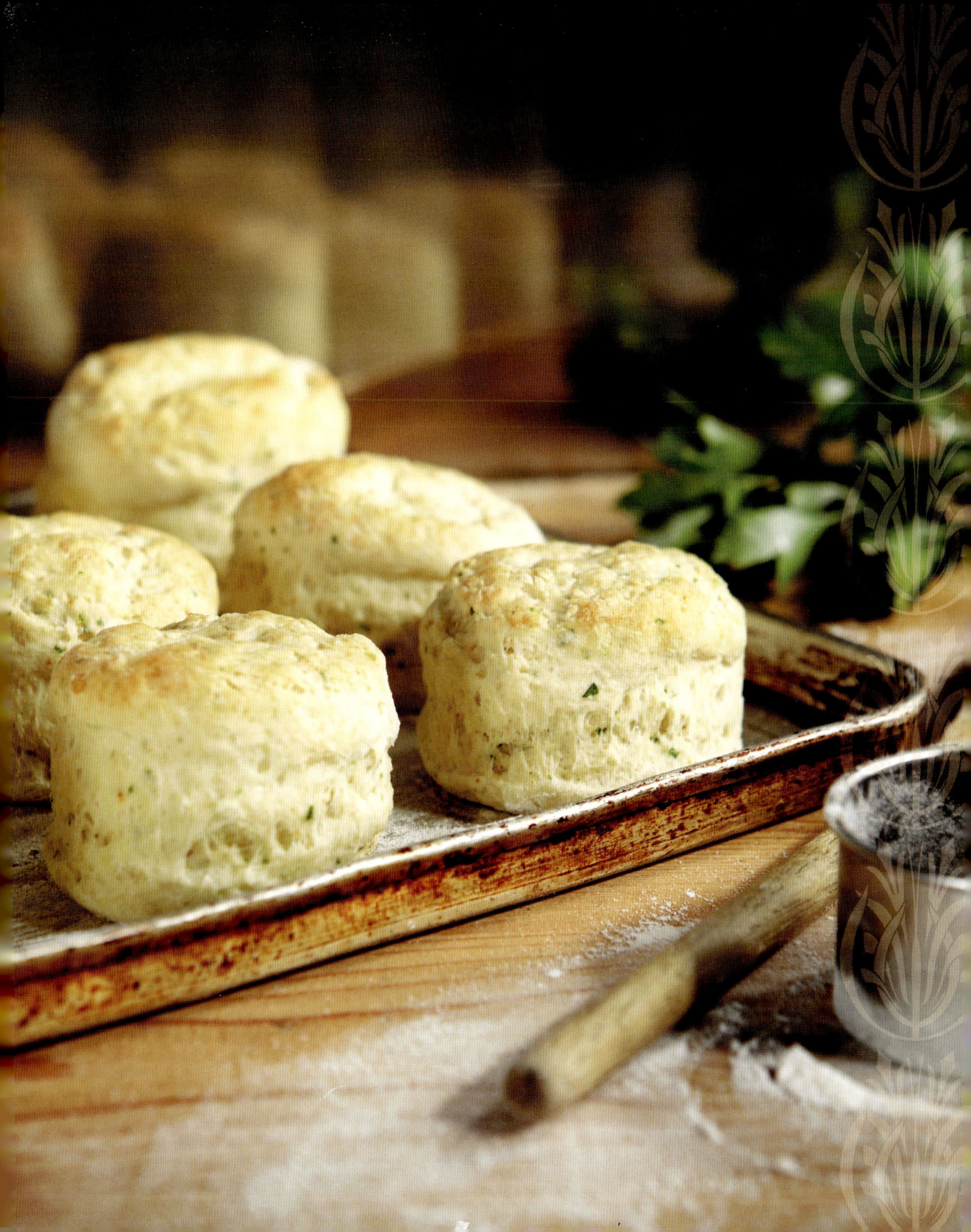

Date Scones

INGREDIENTS:

500 g (1 lb) self-rising (self-raising) flour
1 teaspoon salt
2 teaspoons ground cinnamon
60 g (2 oz) butter
125 g (4 oz) chopped dates
30 g (1 oz) sugar
2 cups milk
1 egg
¼ cup milk

Makes 12–16

METHOD:

1. Preheat oven to 230°C/450°F.
2. Sift flour, salt and cinnamon then, using fingertips, rub butter into the flour mixture. Add dates and sugar. Make a well in the centre and add the milk all at once, stirring quickly and lightly to a soft dough.
3. Turn onto a lightly floured board and knead just enough to make a smooth surface. Pat into 12–18mm (½–¾in) thickness and, using a small scone cutter, cut into rounds.
4. Place on a floured baking tray. Brush tops with combined beaten egg and milk and then bake for about 10 minutes.

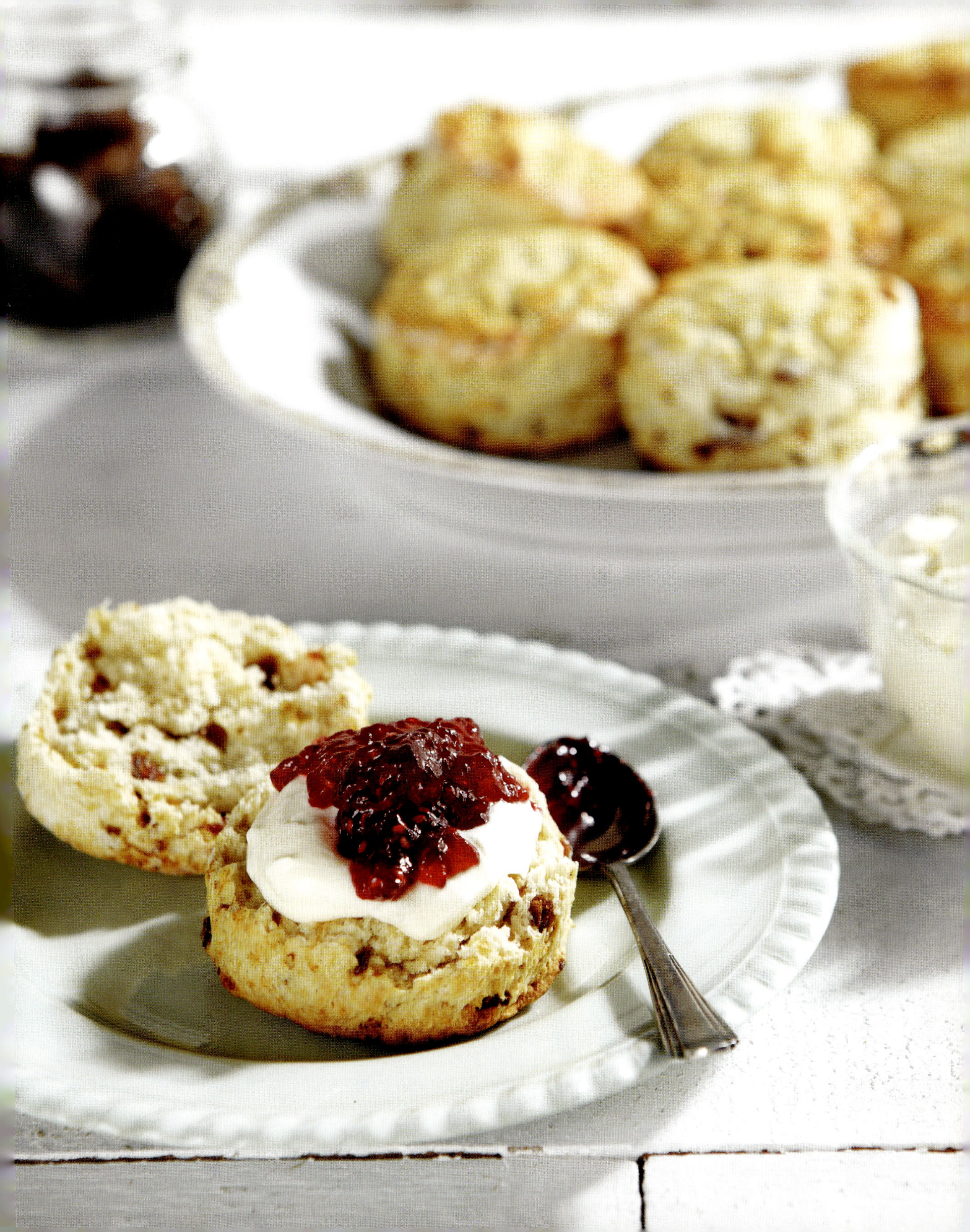

Raspberry Muffins

INGREDIENTS:

- 1 cup wholemeal self-rising (self-raising) flour
- 1 cup white self-rising (self-raising) flour
- ½ cup bran
- ½ teaspoon baking soda
- 1 teaspoon ground ginger
- ¾ cup buttermilk
- ⅓ cup orange juice concentrate
- 2 eggs
- ⅔ cup fresh, or frozen, partly thawed, raspberries

Makes 10

METHOD:

1. Preheat oven to 180°C/350°F. Sift dry ingredients into a bowl. Return any bran to the bowl.
2. Beat together buttermilk, orange juice and eggs. Pour into dry ingredients, all at once. Add raspberries and mix until just combined – take care not to overmix. Spoon into buttered muffin pans.
3. Bake for 20–25 minutes or until cooked when tested with a skewer.

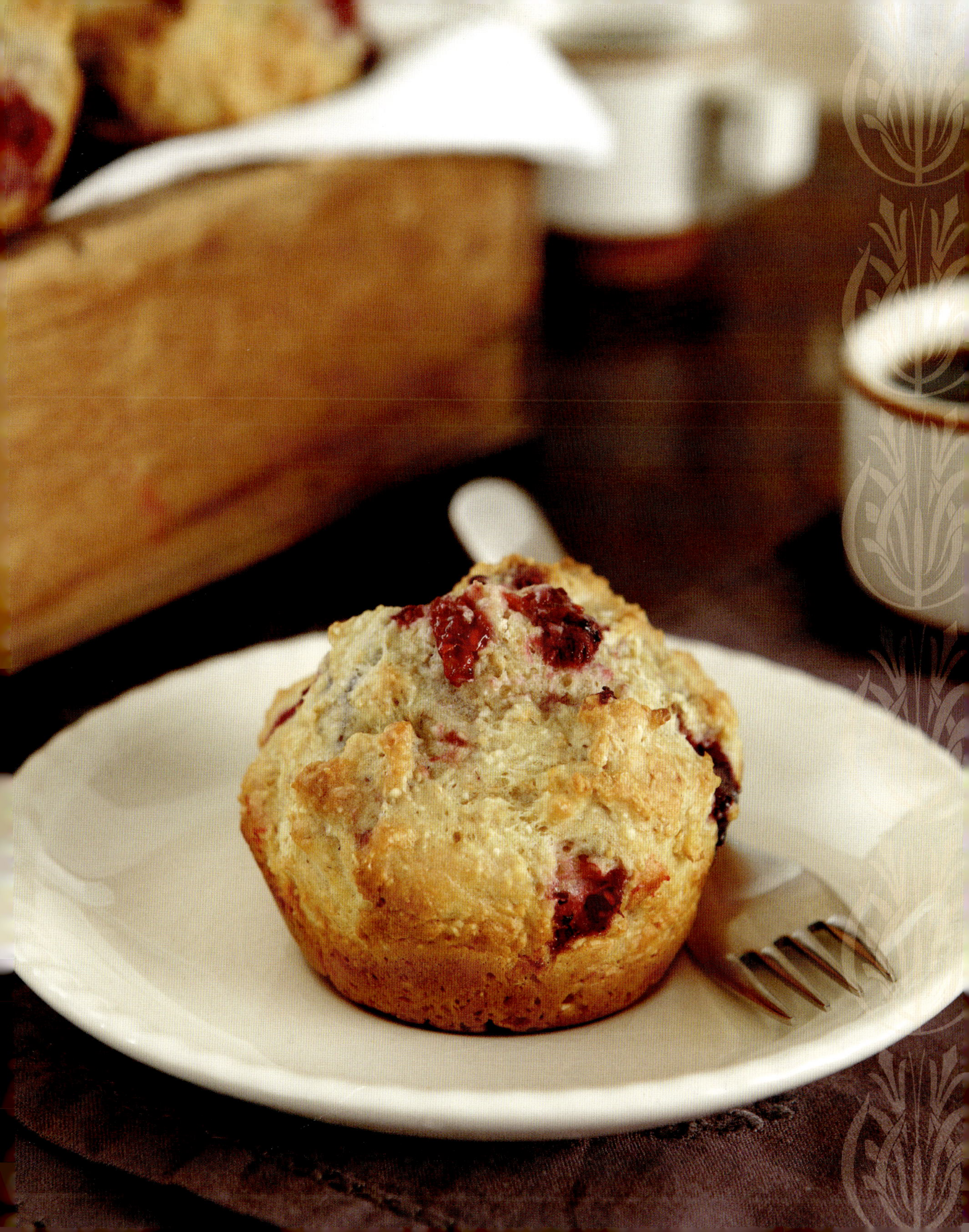

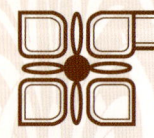

Berry Crumble Muffins

INGREDIENTS:

1 cup self-rising (self-raising) flour, sifted
1 cup plain flour, sifted
1 teaspoon baking powder
½ cup brown sugar
¾ cup milk
¼ cup canola oil
2 eggs, lightly beaten
1 cup frozen mixed berries

CRUMBLE TOPPING:

2 tablespoons plain flour
2 tablespoons brown sugar
30g (1oz) butter, cut into cubes

Makes 12

METHOD:

1. Preheat oven to 180C°C/350°F. Butter 12 medium muffin tins.
2. In a medium bowl sift together the flours and baking powder and stir in the sugar.
3. In a separate bowl, mix the milk, oil and eggs together. Make a well in the centre of the dry ingredients and pour in the milk mixture.
4. Add the berries and mix until just combined.
5. To make the crumble topping, place the flour and butter in a medium bowl and rub in the butter with your fingertips until the mixture resembles breadcrumbs. Stir in the sugar and set aside.
6. Spoon the dough into muffin tins and sprinkle with the crumble mixture. Bake for 20–25 minutes or until muffins are cooked when tested with skewer. Turn out onto wire racks to cool.

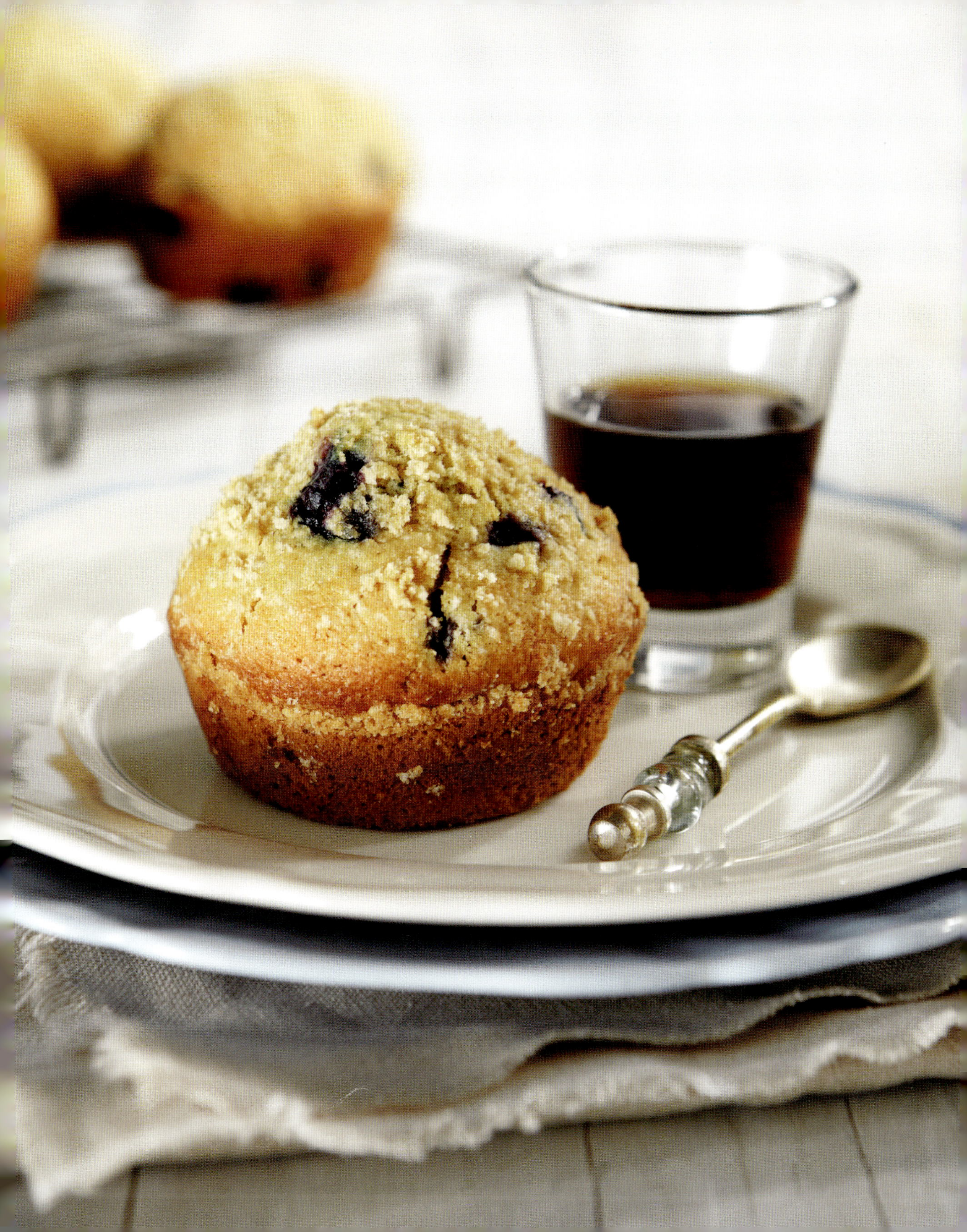

Carrot & Sesame Muffins

INGREDIENTS:

3 cups self-raising flour
½ teaspoon baking soda
1 teaspoon mixed spice
½ cup brown sugar
1 large carrot, grated
4 tablespoons toasted sesame seeds
6 oz/170 g sultanas
1 cup natural yoghurt
1 cup milk
45 g (1½ oz) butter, melted
3 egg whites, lightly beaten

Makes 24

METHOD:

1. Preheat oven to 400°F/200°C.
2. Sift baking flour, baking soda and mixed spice into a large bowl. Add sugar, carrot, sesame seeds and sultanas and mix to combine.
3. Place yoghurt, milk, butter and egg whites in a bowl and whisk to combine. Stir yoghurt mixture into flour mixture and mix until just combined. Spoon batter into lightly buttered muffin tins and bake for 20 minutes or until golden and cooked.

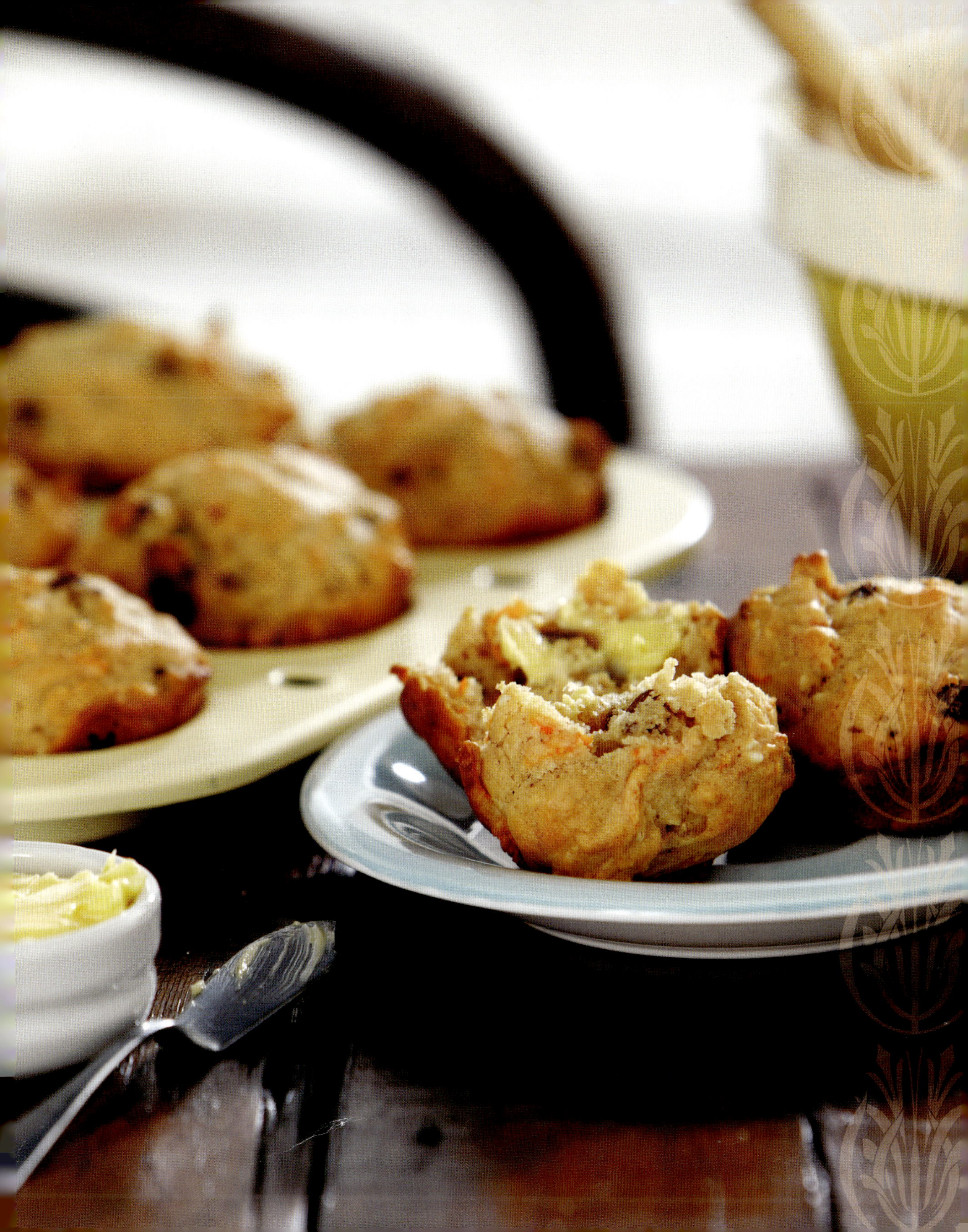

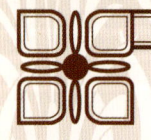

Apple Tea Cakes

INGREDIENTS:

2 cups self-rising (self-raising) flour

½ teaspoon salt

½ teaspoon ground cinnamon

½ teaspoon ground nutmeg

60 g (2 oz) butter

½ cup superfine (caster) sugar

1 egg, lightly beaten

1 apple, peeled and finely diced

¾ cup milk

extra sugar and cinnamon

1 apple, unpeeled, finely sliced

Makes 12

METHOD:

1. Preheat oven to 200°C/400°F.
2. Sift together the self-raising flour, salt, cinnamon and nutmeg. Cream butter and sugar until light and fluffy, add egg and beat well. Fold in the sifted dry ingredients alternately with the peeled apple slices and sufficient milk to make a dropping consistency.
3. Spoon mixture into paper-lined deep patty pans. Top with unpeeled apple slices. Sprinkle each with a little extra sugar and cinnamon. Bake in the upper half of the oven for 15–20 minutes. Serve with butter.

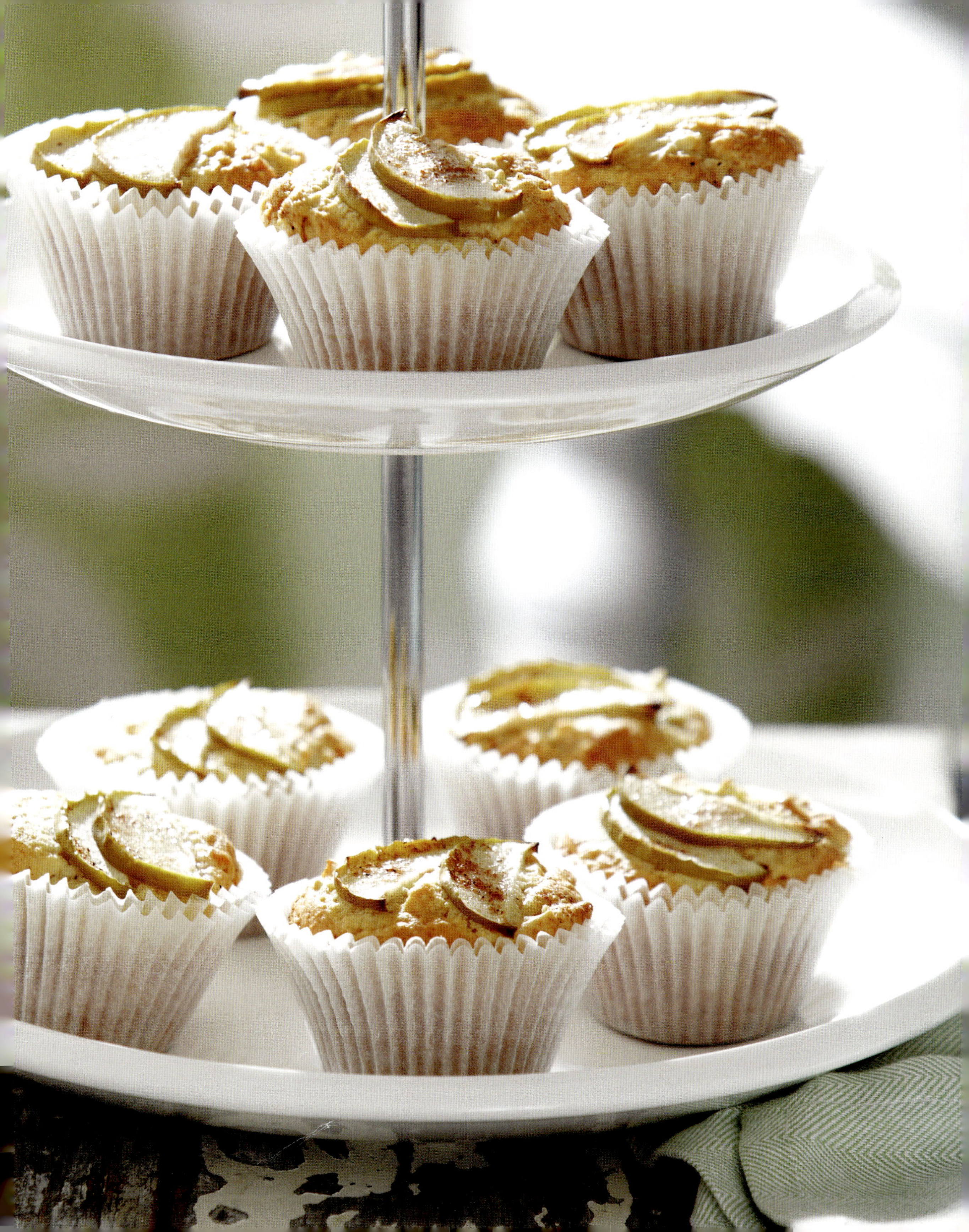

Jaffa Pecan Muffins

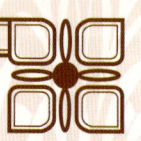

INGREDIENTS:

100 g (3½ oz) dark chocolate, chopped
125 g (4oz) butter
2 eggs, beaten
2 tablespoons orange-flavoured liqueur
finely grated zest of 1/2 orange
1/4 cup caster sugar
60 g (2 oz) pecans, chopped
1/2 cup plain flour, sifted
18 pecan halves

Makes 18

METHOD:

1. Preheat oven to 360°F/180°C.
2. Place chopped chocolate and butter in a heatproof bowl set over a saucepan of simmering water and cook, stirring, until chocolate and butter melt and mixture is combined. Remove bowl from heat and set aside to cool slightly.
3. Stir eggs, liqueur, orange zest, sugar and chopped pecans into chocolate mixture and mix to combine. Fold in flour.
4. Spoon batter into patty tins lined with paper cake cases, top with a pecan half and bake for 20 minutes or until cakes are cooked when tested with a skewer. Remove cakes from patty tins and allow to cool on wire racks.

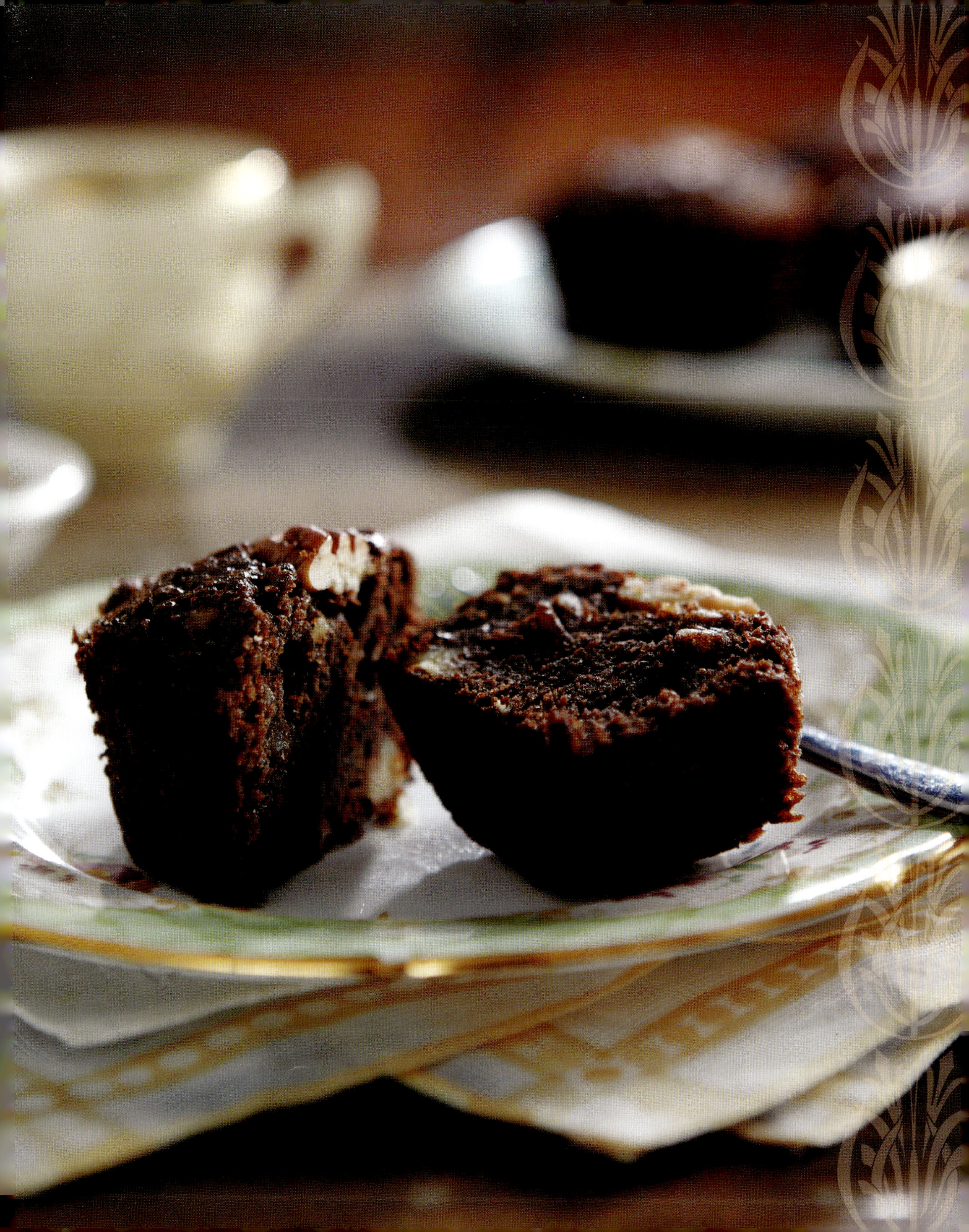

Chocolate Rum Pudding

INGREDIENTS:

¾ cup sultanas
1 tablespoon rum
200 g (7 oz) dark chocolate-covered biscuits
1½ cups self-raising flour
125 g (4oz) butter, melted
2 eggs
¾ cup milk

Serves 6–8

METHODS:

1. Soak sultanas in rum for 30 minutes. Place biscuits into food processor, process until fine. Combine with flour in a bowl, making a well in the centre.

2. Beat together melted butter, eggs and milk. Pour into centre of well with sultanas and rum mixture. Stir until just mixed through. Spoon into eight greased muffin or brioche pans. Bake at 180°C/360°F oven for 25–30 minutes. Serve plain, or warm with cream, custard and/or chocolate sauce.

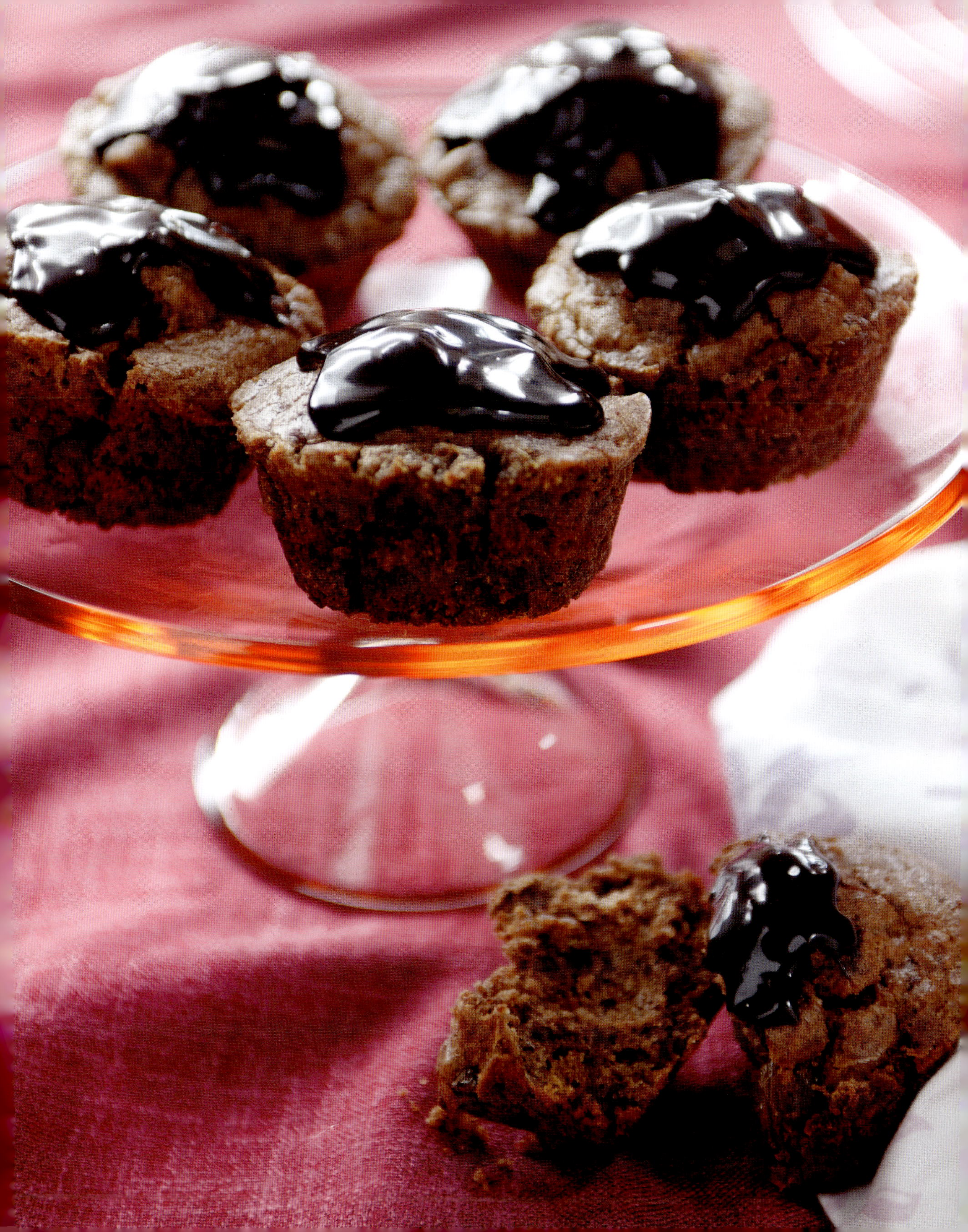

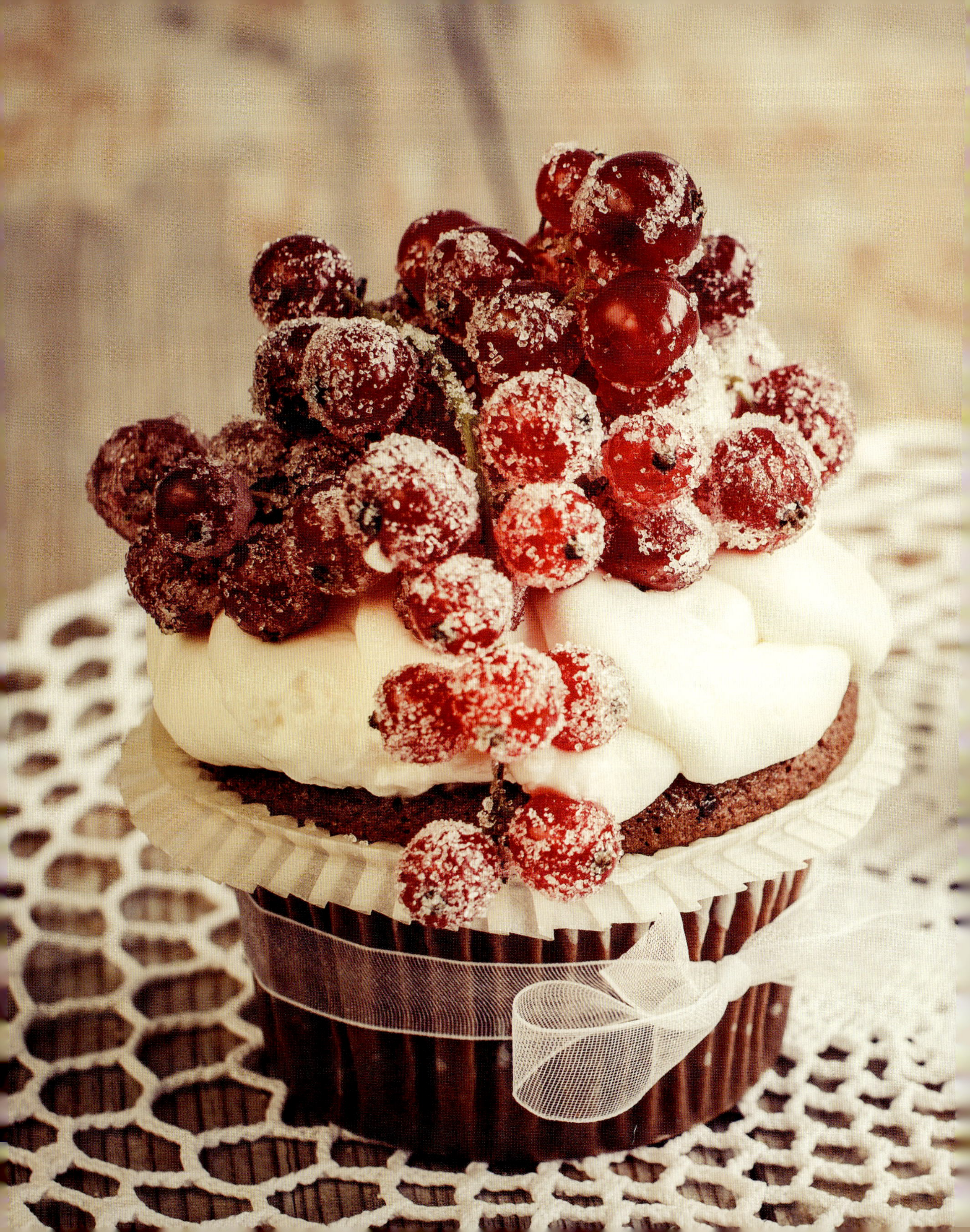

CUPCAKES

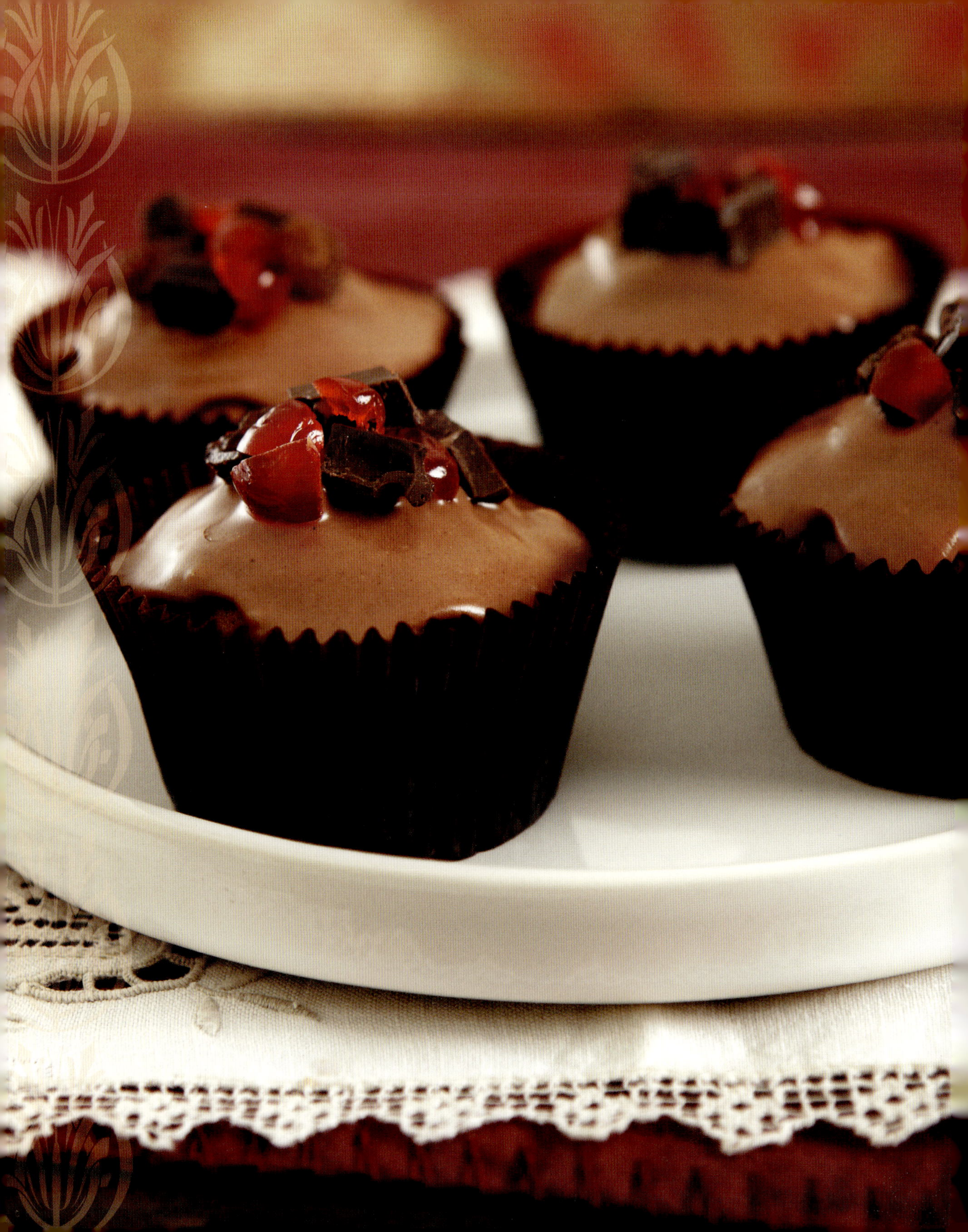

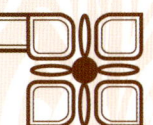

Choc Fruity Mini Cupcakes

INGREDIENTS:

125 g (4½ oz) butter
115 g (4 oz) sugar
2 eggs, lightly beaten
225 g (8 oz) self-raising (self-rising) flour
115 g (4 oz) unsweetened cocoa powder
120 ml (4 fl oz) milk
175 g (6 oz) sultanas (golden raisins), plus extra to decorate
85 g (3 oz) glacé cherries, chopped, plus extra to decorate
40 g (1½ oz) chocolate chips, chopped, plus extra to decorate

TOPPING:
175 g (6 oz) icing (confectioners') sugar
15 g (½ oz) unsweetened cocoa powder
15 g (½ oz) butter, melted
2 tablespoons milk

Makes 30

METHOD:

1 Preheat the oven to 180°C/350°F Line two trays of mini muffin tins with mini paper cases.
2 In a medium bowl beat the butter and sugar until light and fluffy. Stir in the beaten eggs.
3 Fold in the flour, cocoa and milk, then stir in the sultanas, chopped cherries and chocolate.
4 Divide the batter between the paper cases and bake for about 15 minutes until firm to the touch. Leave to set for a few minutes, then transfer to a wire rack to cool. Leave to go cold before icing.

Topping

1 Sift the icing sugar and cocoa into a bowl, add the melted butter and milk and beat until smooth.
2 Spread the icing over the cakes, then decorate with extra sultanas, cherries and chocolate.

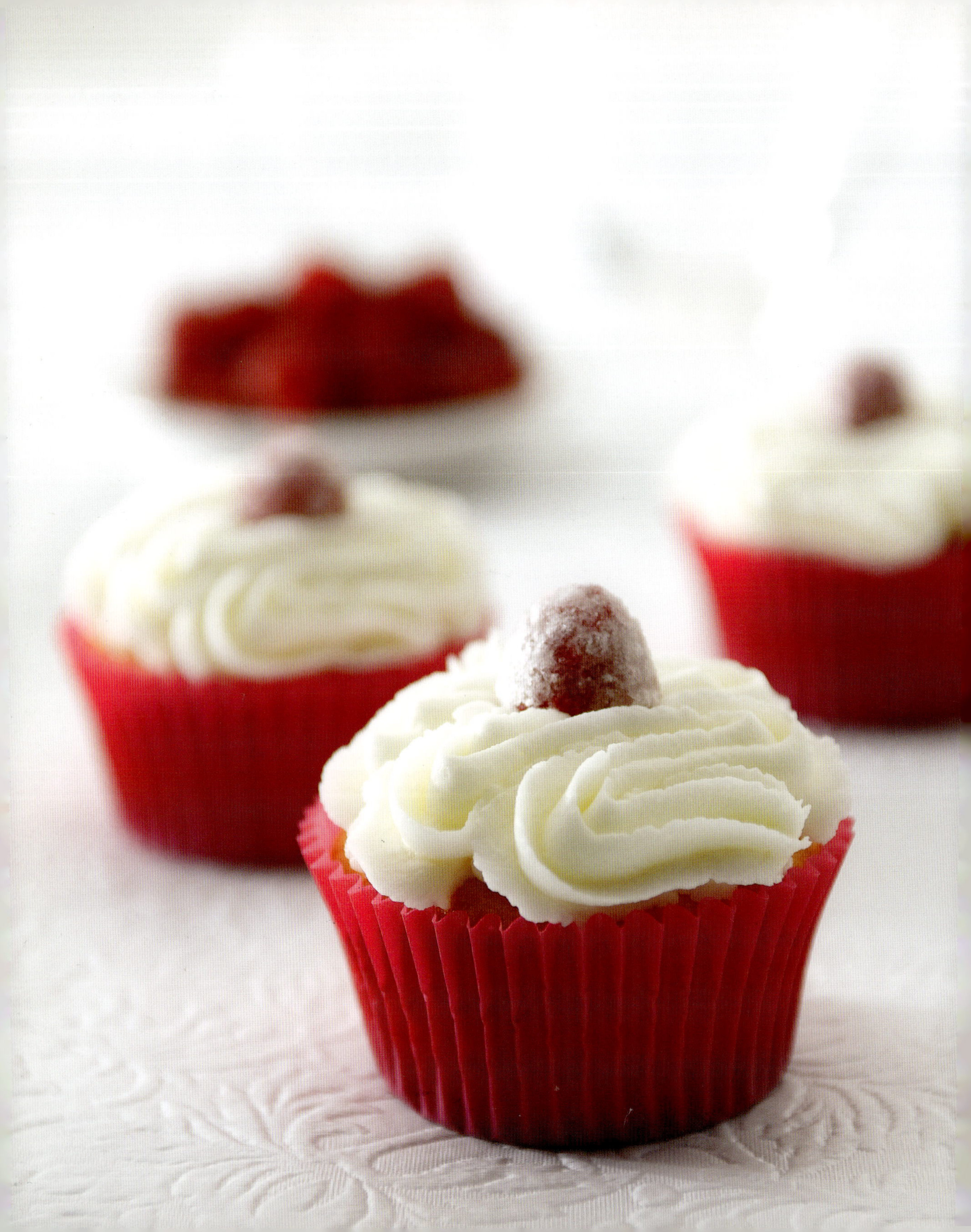

Raspberry Cupcakes

INGREDIENTS:

125 g (4½ oz) butter, softened
200 g (7 oz) caster (superfine) sugar
2 eggs, lightly beaten
120 ml (4 fl oz) milk
225 g (8 oz) self-raising (self-rising) flour, sifted
1 teaspoon vanilla extract
40 g (1½ oz) raspberries, crushed

TOPPING:

175 g (6 oz) icing (confectioners') sugar
125 g (4½ oz) butter, softened
raspberries, to decorate
egg white
caster (superfine) sugar, to decorate

Makes 12

METHOD:

1. Preheat the oven to 160°C/320°F. Line a 12-cup muffin tin with paper cases.
2. In a medium bowl, beat the butter and sugar until light and fluffy, then mix in the beaten eggs.
3. Add the milk, flour and vanilla, and stir to combine. Beat until light and creamy. Stir in the crushed raspberries.
4. Divide the batter evenly between the paper cases. Bake for 18–20 minutes until risen and firm to the touch. Allow to cool for a few minutes and then transfer to a wire rack. Allow to go cold before icing.

Topping

1. Meanwhile, combine the icing sugar and butter in a bowl, mix with a wooden spoon until well combined, then beat with a whisk until light and fluffy.
2. Spoon the mixture into a piping bag fitted with a medium-star-shaped nozzle. Pipe icing onto each cupcake.
3. To coat the raspberries in sugar, brush each lightly with beaten egg white and dust with caster sugar. Add one to the top of each cupcake.

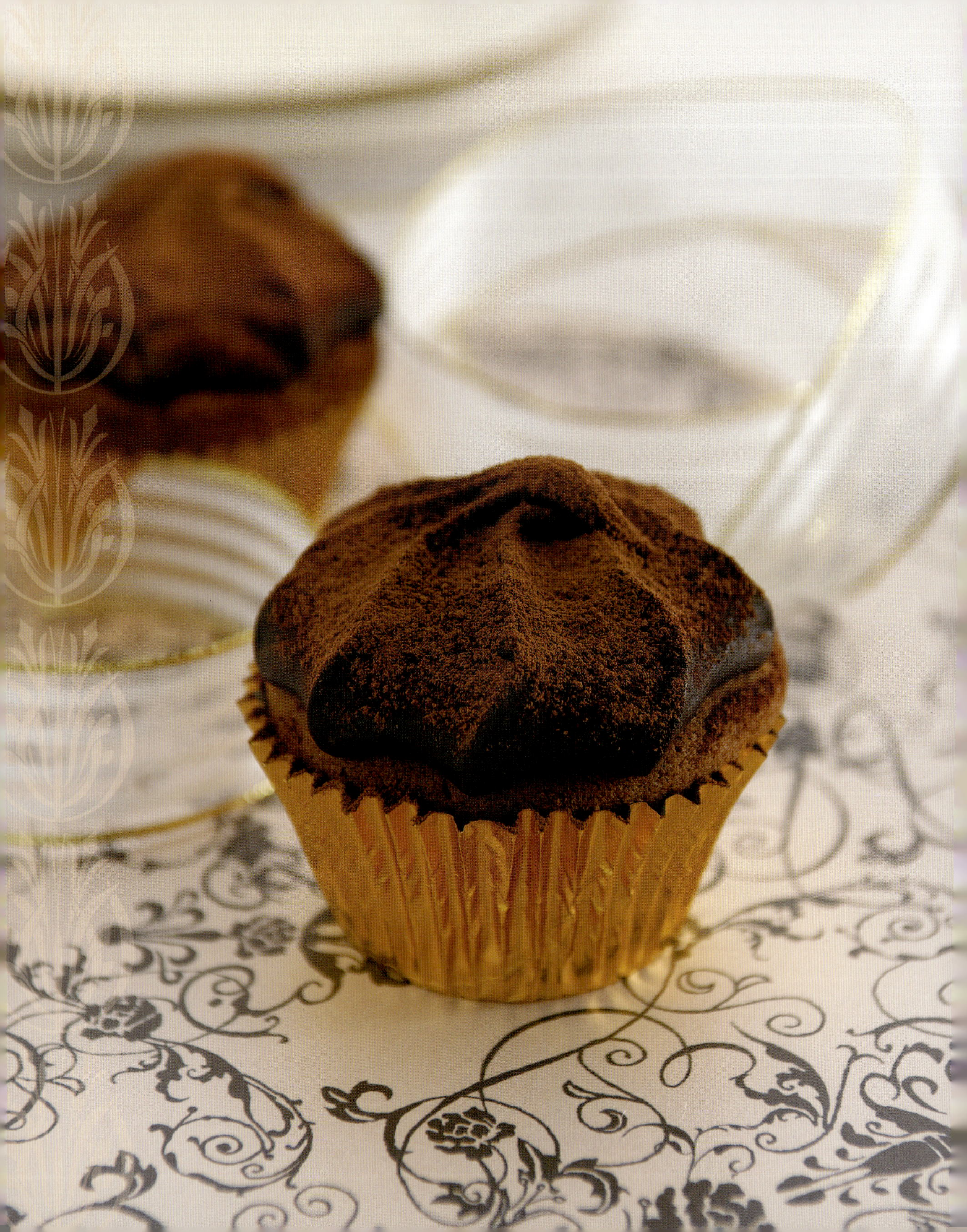

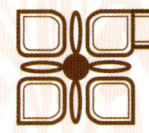

Dark Choc Truffle Cupcakes

INGREDIENTS:

125 g (4½ oz) butter, softened
200 g (7oz) caster (superfine) sugar
2 eggs, lightly beaten
120 ml (4 fl oz) vanilla yogurt
225 g (8 oz) self-raising (self-rising) flour, sifted
15 g (½ oz) unsweetened cocoa powder
100 g (3½ oz) dark (bittersweet) chocolate pieces

TOPPING:

100 g (3½ oz) dark (bittersweet) chocolate
20 g (¾ oz) butter
75 ml (2½ fl oz) double (heavy) cream
unsweetened cocoa powder, for dusting

Makes 12

METHOD:

1 Preheat the oven to 160°C/320°F. Line a 12-cup muffin tin with paper cases.
2 In a medium bowl, beat the butter and sugar until light and fluffy, then mix in the beaten eggs.
3 Add the yogurt, flour and cocoa, and beat until light and fluffy. Stir in the dark chocolate.
4 Divide the batter evenly between the paper cases. Bake for 18–20 minutes until risen and firm to the touch. Allow to cool for a few minutes, and then transfer to a wire rack. Allow to go cold before icing.

Topping

1 Meanwhile, combine the chocolate and butter in a pan over a medium heat, stirring constantly, until melted. Remove from the heat, add the cream, and stir. Set aside for 10 minutes until firm and velvety in consistency.
2 Half-fill a piping bag fitted with a star nozzle and pipe the mixture onto the cupcakes. Dust heavily with cocoa.

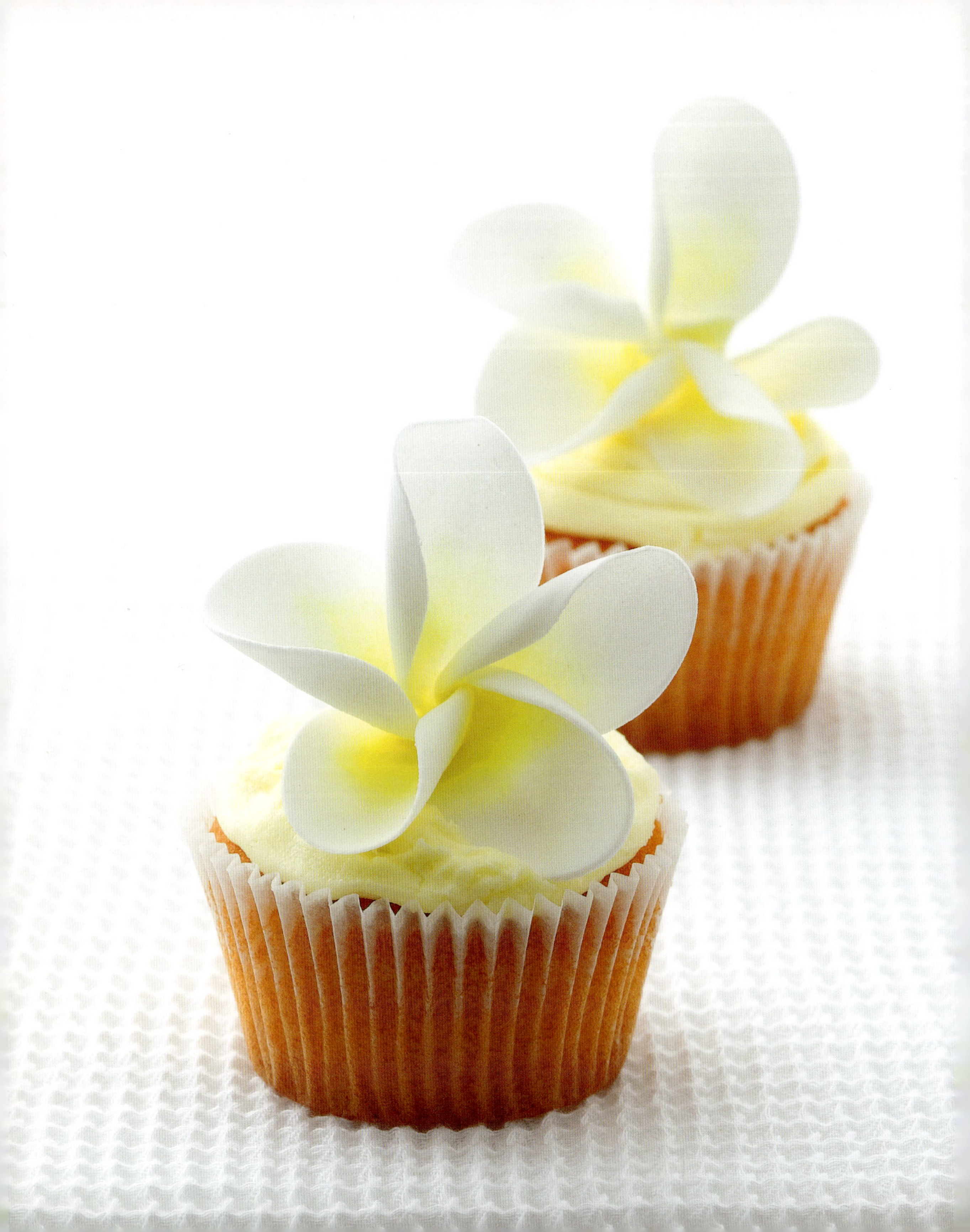

White Chocolate Cupcakes

INGREDIENTS:

115 g (4 oz) butter, softened
200 g (7 oz) caster (superfine) sugar
3 eggs, lightly beaten
120 ml (4 fl oz) buttermilk
175 g (6 oz) self-raising (self-rising) flour, sifted
1 teaspoon vanilla extract

TOPPING:

100 g (3½ oz) white chocolate, coarsely grated (shredded)
15 g (½ oz) butter, softened
75 ml (2½ fl oz) double (heavy) cream, thickened
candied frangipani flowers

Makes 12

METHOD:

1. Preheat the oven to 320°F/160°C. Line a 12-cup muffin tin (pan) with paper cases.
2. In a medium bowl, beat the butter and sugar until light and fluffy, then mix in the beaten eggs.
3. Add the buttermilk, flour and vanilla and stir to combine until light and creamy.
4. Divide the batter evenly between the paper cases. Bake for 18–20 minutes until risen and firm to the touch. Allow to cool for a few minutes and then transfer to a wire rack. Allow to go cold before icing.

Topping

1. Meanwhile, combine the chocolate and butter in a small saucepan over a gentle heat. As the mixture begins to melt, add the cream slowly, then reduce the heat to low, stirring constantly, until mixture thickens. Remove from heat and allow to cool.
2. Spread evenly onto the cupcakes, then top with frangipani decorations.

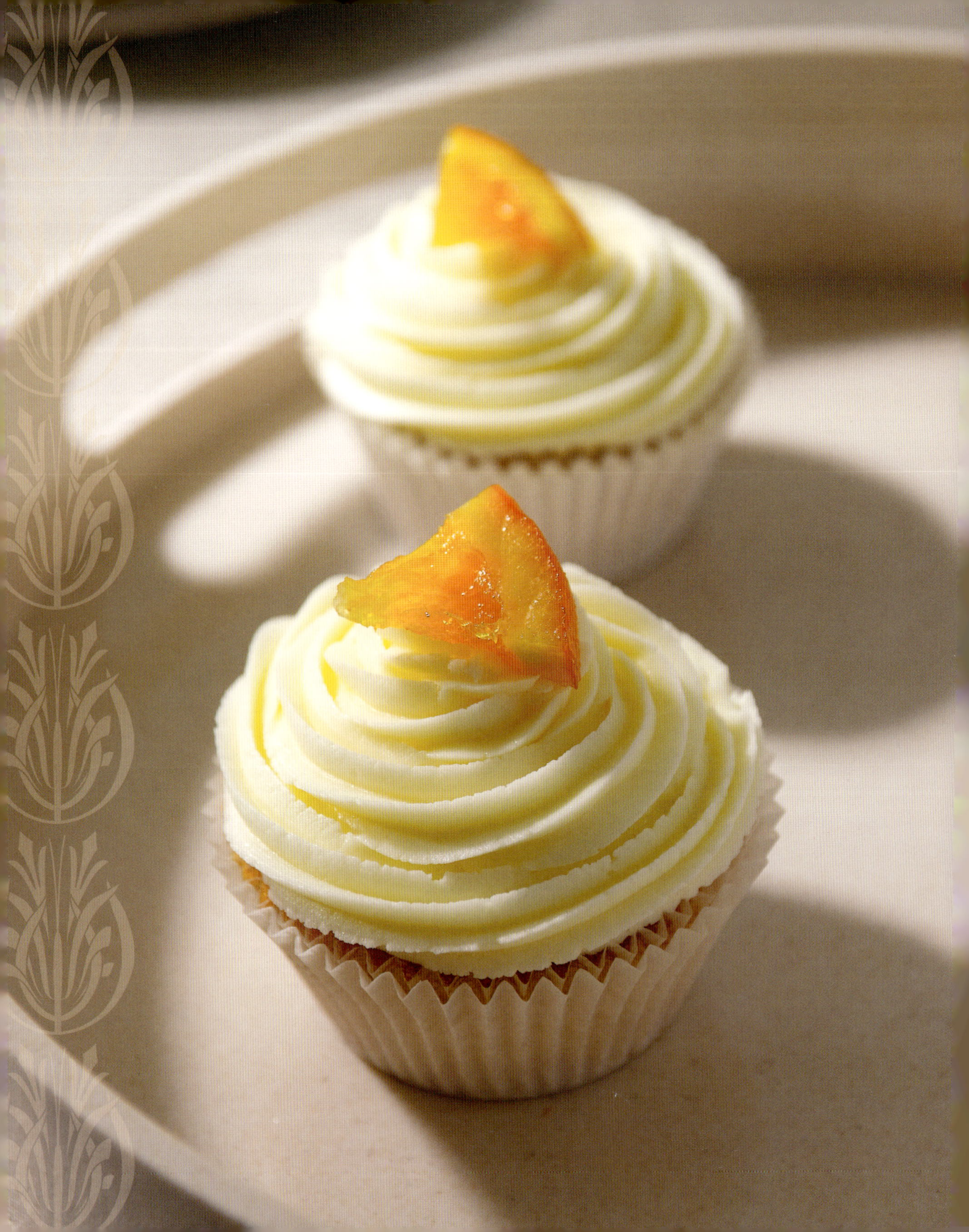

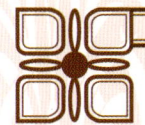

Orange Blossom Cupcakes

INGREDIENTS:

125 g (4½ oz) butter, softened
200 g (7 oz) caster (superfine) sugar
2 eggs, lightly beaten
120 ml (4 fl oz) milk
225 g (8 oz) self-raising (self-rising) flour, sifted
1 teaspoon vanilla extract
6 drops orange blossom water

TOPPING:

175 g (6 oz) icing (confectioners') sugar
125 g (4½ oz) butter, softened
6 drops orange blossom water
candied orange, to decorate

Makes 12

METHOD:

1. Preheat the oven to 320°F/160°C/Gas 3. Line a 12-cup muffin tin (pan) with paper cases.
2. In a medium bowl, beat the butter and sugar until light and fluffy, then mix in the beaten eggs.
3. Add the milk, flour, vanilla and orange blossom, and stir to combine. Beat until light and creamy.
4. Divide the batter evenly between the paper cases. Bake for 18–20 minutes until risen and firm to the touch. Allow to cool for a few minutes and then transfer to a wire rack. Allow to go cold before icing.

Topping

1. Meanwhile, combine all the topping ingredients except the candied orange in a small bowl, mix with a wooden spoon until light and fluffy.
2. Half fill a piping bag fitted with a star-shaped nozzle with the mixture and pipe onto all cupcakes. Top with candied orange.

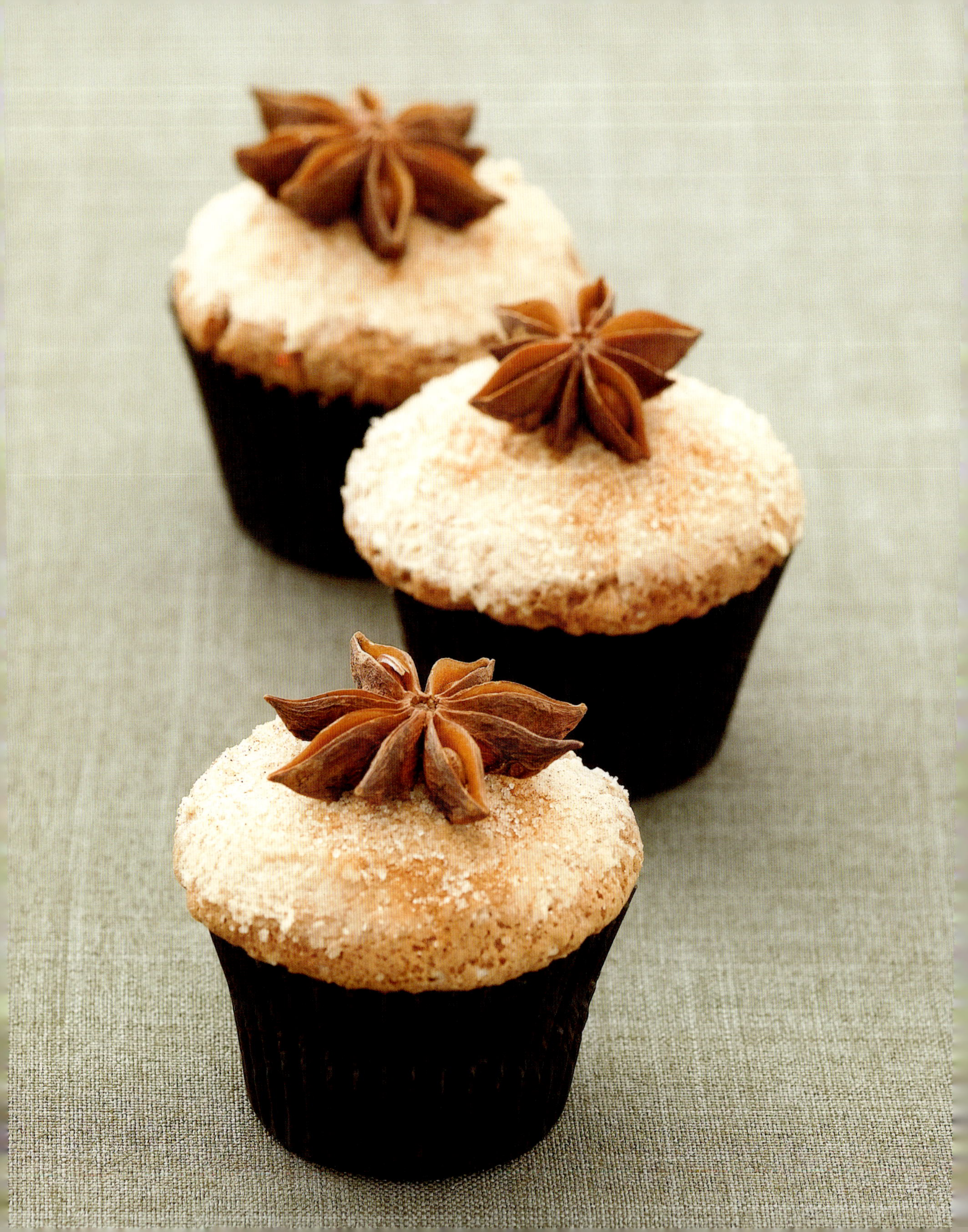

Chai Cupcakes

INGREDIENTS:

115 g (4 oz) butter, softened
200 g (7 oz) caster (superfine) sugar
3 eggs, lightly beaten
60 ml (2 fl oz) milk
175 g (6 oz) self-raising (self-rising) flour, sifted
60 ml (2 fl oz) chai tea
1 teaspoon ground cinnamon
1 teaspoon ground nutmeg

TOPPING:

55 g (2 oz) molasses (raw) sugar
2 tablespoons warm water
cinnamon sugar, to decorate, made by mixing 3 teaspoons of sugar with 1 teaspoon of ground cinnamon
12 star anises, to decorate

Makes 12

METHOD:

1. Preheat the oven to 320°F/160°C. Line a 12-cup muffin tin with paper cases.
2. In a medium bowl, beat the butter and sugar until light and fluffy, then mix in the beaten eggs.
3. Add the milk and flour, and stir to combine. Add remaining ingredients. Beat until light and creamy.
4. Divide the batter evenly between the paper cases. Bake for 18–20 minutes until risen and firm to the touch. Allow to cool for a few minutes and then transfer to a wire rack. Allow to go cold before icing.

Topping

1. Meanwhile, combine the sugar and water in a small bowl, mix with a wooden spoon, spoon onto cupcakes and sprinkle with cinnamon sugar. Decorate each cupcake with a single star anise.

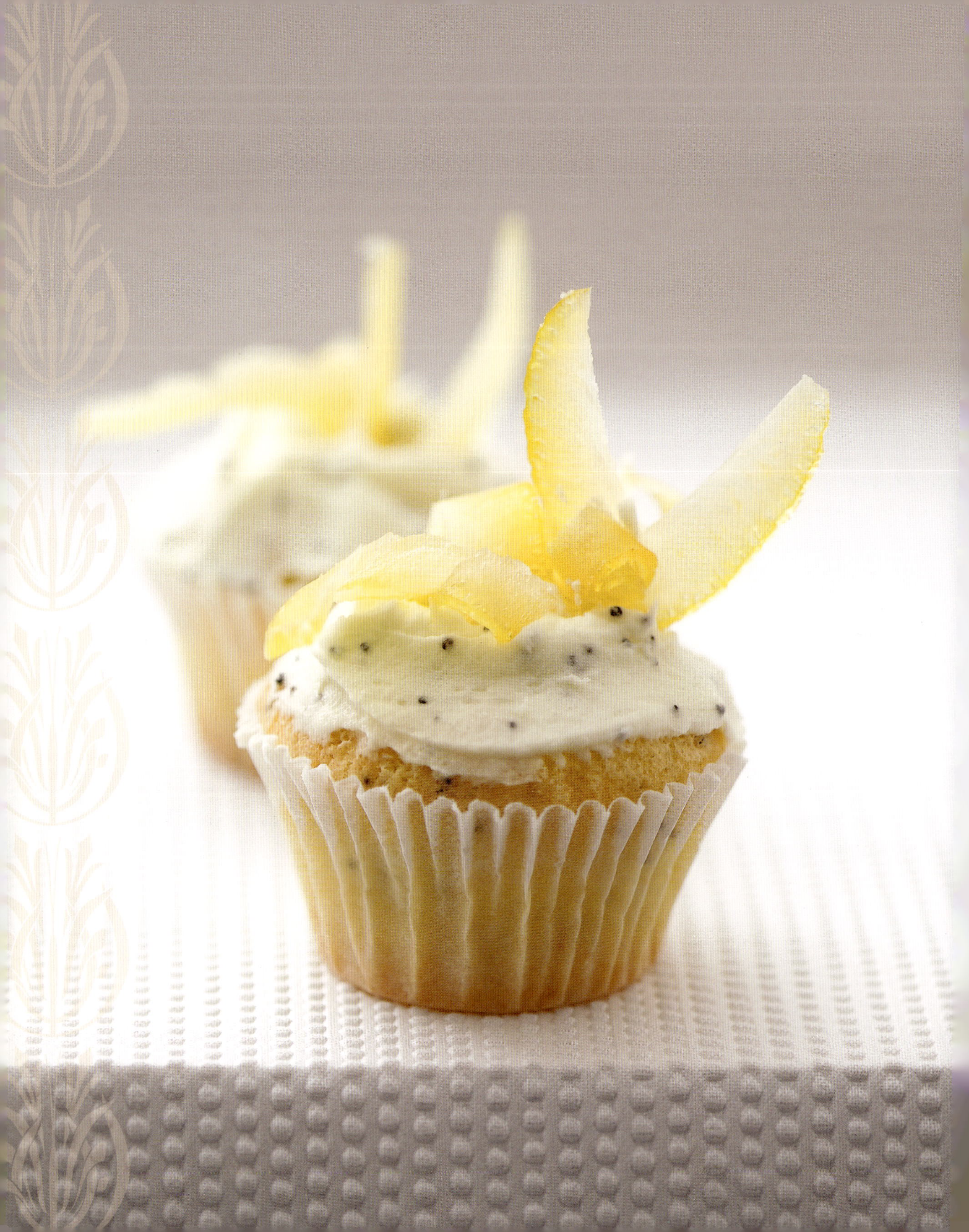

Orange Poppy Cupcakes

INGREDIENTS:

115 g (4 oz) butter, softened
200 g (7 oz) caster (superfine) sugar
3 eggs, lightly beaten
120 ml (4 fl oz) buttermilk
175 g (6 oz) self-raising (self-rising) flour, sifted
zest of 1 orange
juice of ½ orange
1 teaspoon poppy seeds

TOPPING:

175 g (6 oz) icing (confectioners') sugar
115 g (4 oz) butter, softened
juice of ½ orange
½ teaspoon poppy seeds
zest of 1 orange
candied orange pieces, cut into thin slivers

Makes 12

METHOD:

1 Preheat the oven to 320°F/160°C. Line a 12-cup muffin tin (pan) with paper cases.
2 In a medium bowl, beat the butter and sugar until light and fluffy, then mix in the beaten eggs.
3 Add the buttermilk and flour, and stir to combine. Beat until light and creamy. Add the orange zest, juice and poppy seeds, and mix through with a wooden spoon.
4 Divide the batter evenly between the paper cases. Bake for 18–20 minutes until risen and firm to the touch. Allow to cool for a few minutes and then transfer to a wire rack. Allow to go cold before icing.

Topping

1 Meanwhile, combine all the topping ingredients except for the candied orange, and mix with a wooden spoon. Spoon onto the cakes. Top with candied orange pieces.

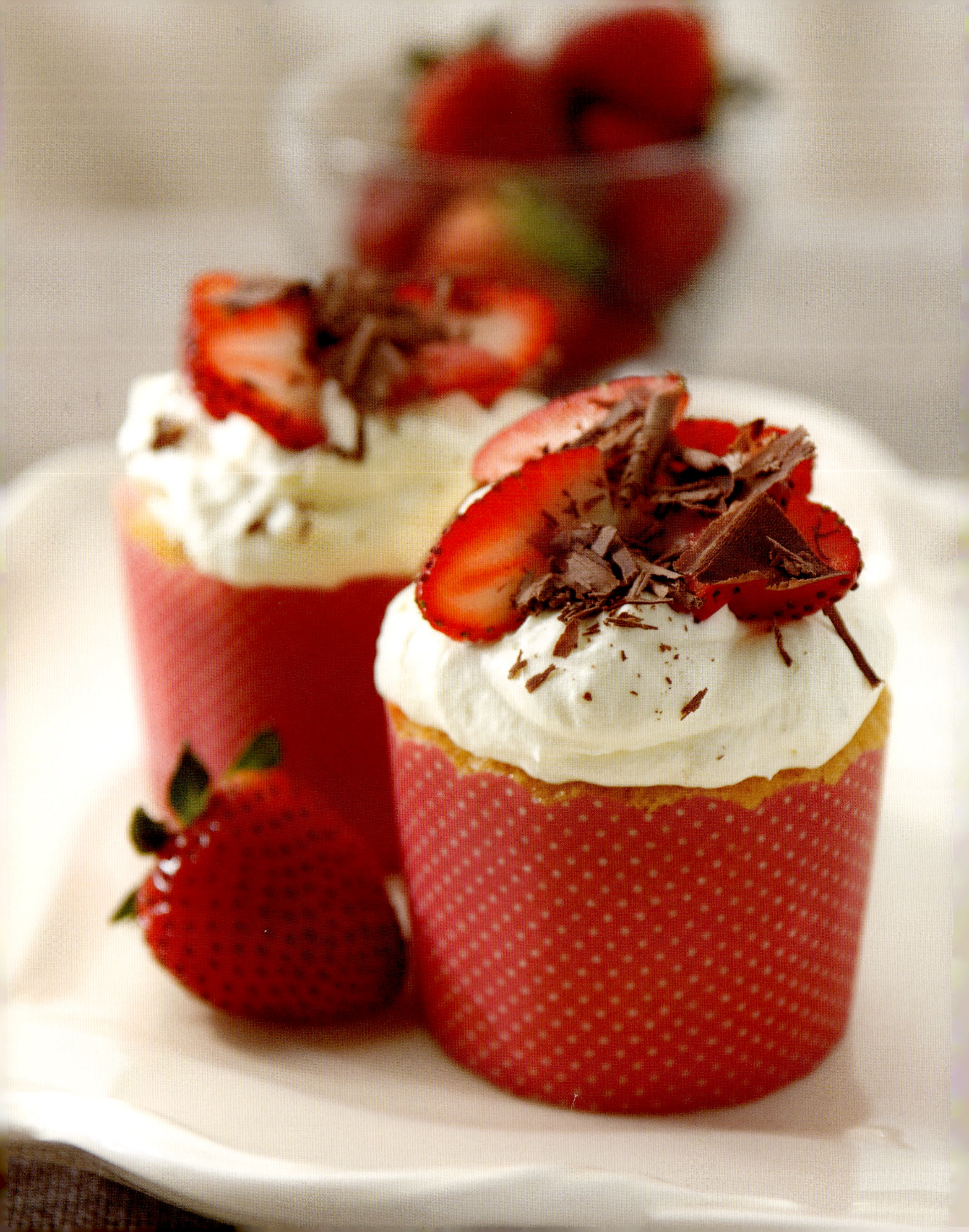

Choc Strawberry Mini Cupcakes

INGREDIENTS:

125 g (4½ oz) butter, softened

200 g (7 oz) caster (superfine) sugar

2 eggs, lightly beaten

8 oz (225 g) self-raising (self-rising) flour, sifted

120 ml (4 fl oz) milk

30 g (1 oz) unsweetened cocoa powder, sifted

55 g (2 oz) strawberries chopped

TOPPING:

225 ml (8 fl oz) double (heavy) cream, whipped

strawberries, sliced, to decorate

dark (bittersweet) chocolate, grated (shredded), to decorate

Makes 24

METHOD:

1 Preheat the oven to 320°F/160°C. Line a mini cupcake tin with 24 mini paper cases.

2 In a medium bowl, cream the butter and sugar until light and fluffy. Add the eggs and mix well.

3 Add the flour, milk and cocoa, and beat until creamy. Stir in strawberries.

4 Divide the batter evenly between the paper cases. Bake for 10–15 minutes until well risen and firm to the touch. Allow to cool for a few minutes and then transfer to a wire rack. Allow to go cold before icing.

Topping

1 Top the cupcakes with whipped cream and decorate with strawberries and chocolate.

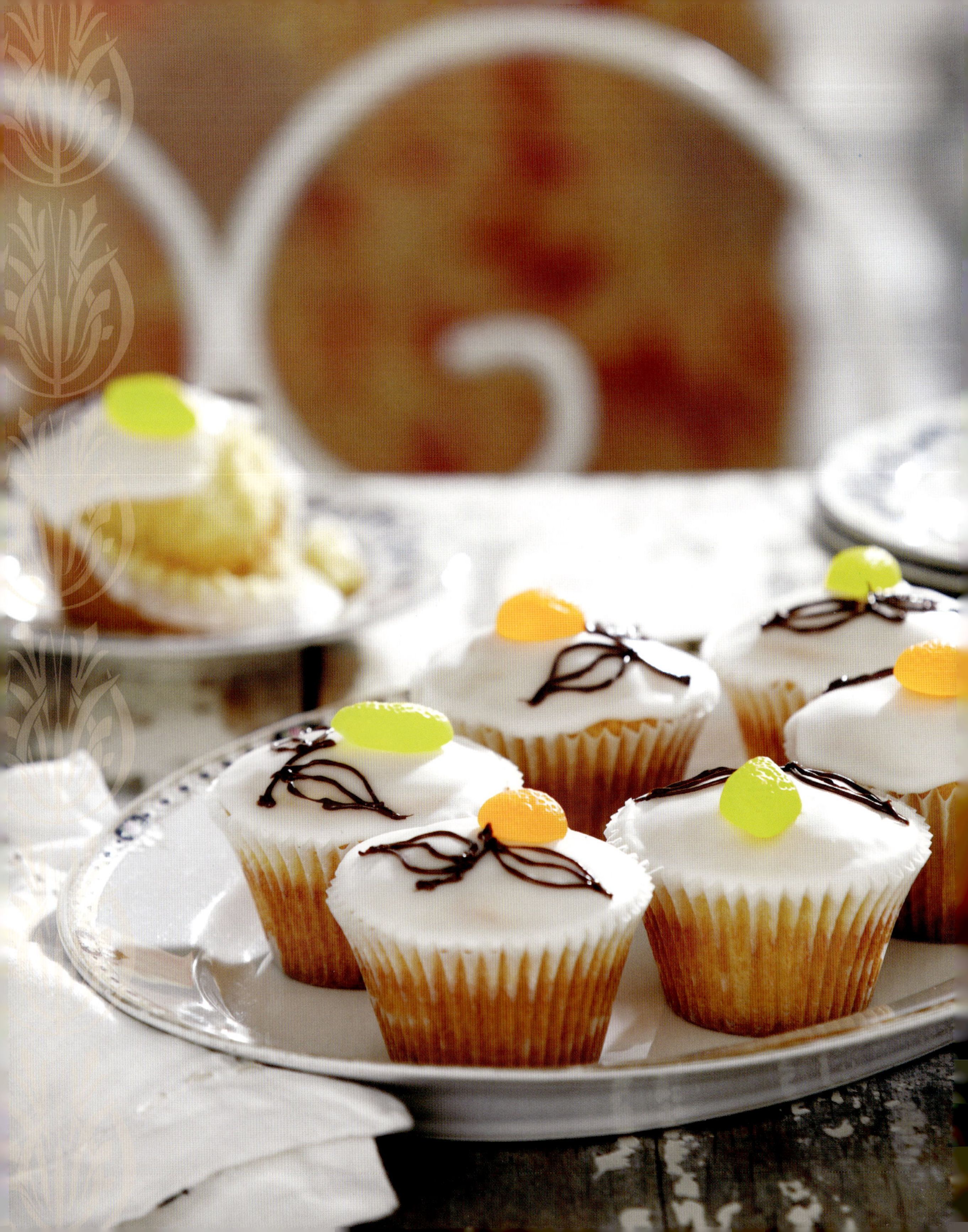

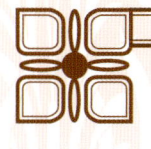

One-step Patty Cakes

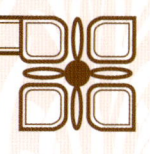

INGREDIENTS:

60g (2 oz) butter, melted
1¼ cups self-raising flour
1/2 cup sugar
2 eggs
2½ tablespoons milk
1 teaspoon vanilla extract
white glacé icing (see below), to decorate
melted chocolate, to decorate
orange and lemon jubes, to decorate

White glacé icing
2 cups icing sugar
vanilla extract to taste

Makes about 18

METHOD:

1. Preheat oven to 200°C/400°F.
2. Place all ingredients into a bowl and beat until well blended. Pour into paper-lined patty tins and bake in the upper half of the oven for 12–15 minutes. Allow to cool.
3. Place the icing sugar in a bowl and, stirring continuously, add enough water or fruit juice to make a creamy consistency. Add vanilla and stir, and if adding food colouring, add a drop at a time until desired colour is achieved.
4. Ice the cakes with the icing then decorate with orange and lemon jubes and drizzled melted chocolate.

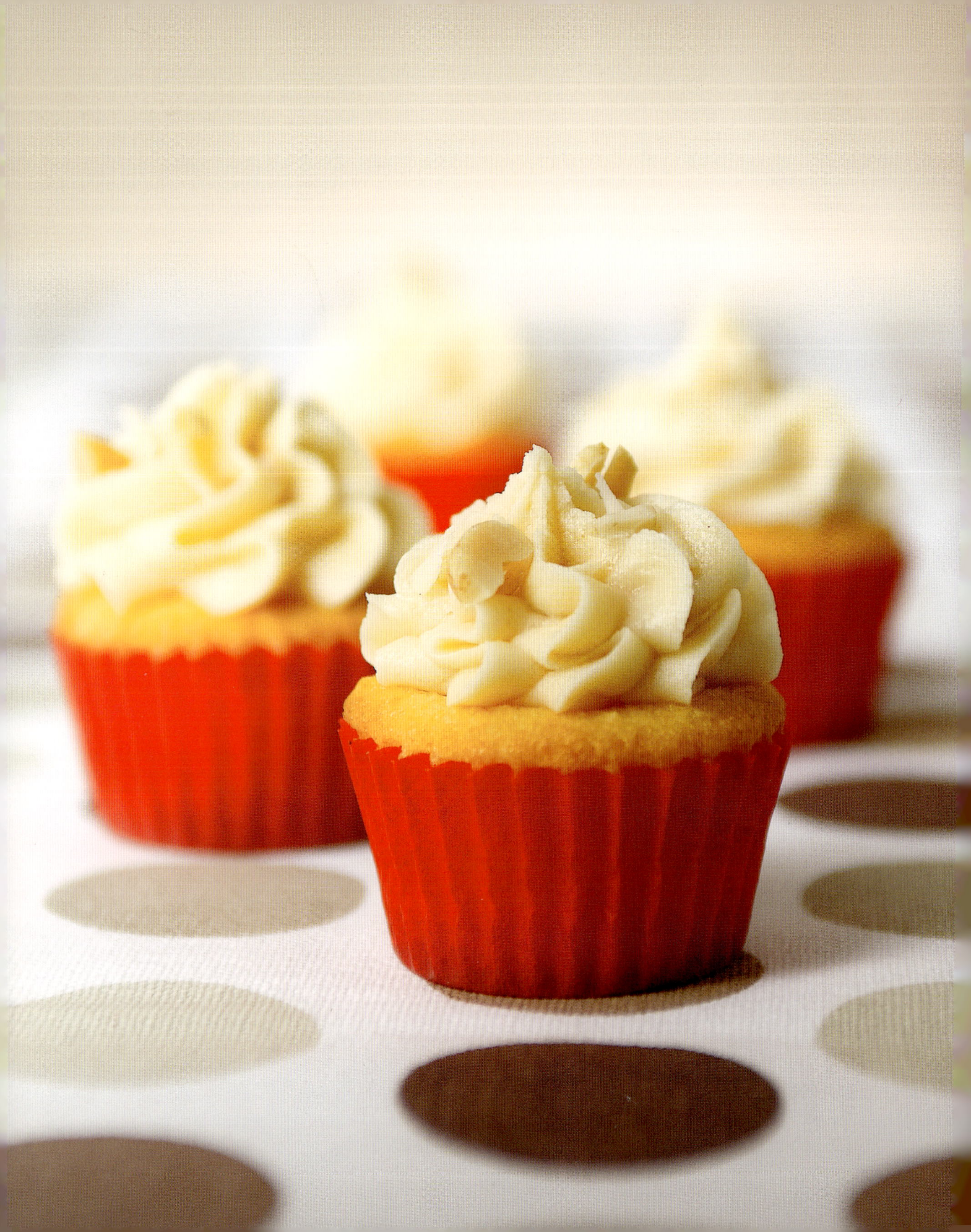

Peanut Butter Mini Cupcakes

INGREDIENTS:

85 g (3 oz) butter, softened
100 g (3½ oz) caster (superfine) sugar
1 egg
225 g (8 oz) self-raising (self-rising) flour, sifted
75 ml (2½ fl oz) milk
55 g (2 oz) peanut butter

TOPPING:

85 g (3 oz) butter, softened
225 g (8 oz) icing (confectioners') sugar
55 g (2 oz) crunchy peanut butter
roasted peanuts, chopped, to decorate

Makes 24

METHOD:

1 Preheat the oven to 320°F/160°C. Line a mini cupcake tin (pan) with 24 mini paper cases.
2 In a medium bowl, cream the butter and sugar until light and fluffy. Add the egg and mix well.
3 Add the flour and milk, and beat until well combined. Stir in the peanut butter.
4 Divide the batter evenly between the paper cases. Bake for 10–15 minutes until well risen and firm to the touch. Allow to cool for a few minutes and then transfer to a wire rack. Allow to go cold before icing.

Topping

1 In a bowl, beat the butter and icing sugar until light and creamy, then stir in the peanut butter. Use to half-fill a piping bag fitted with a star nozzle and pipe onto the cupcakes. Decorate with roasted peanuts.

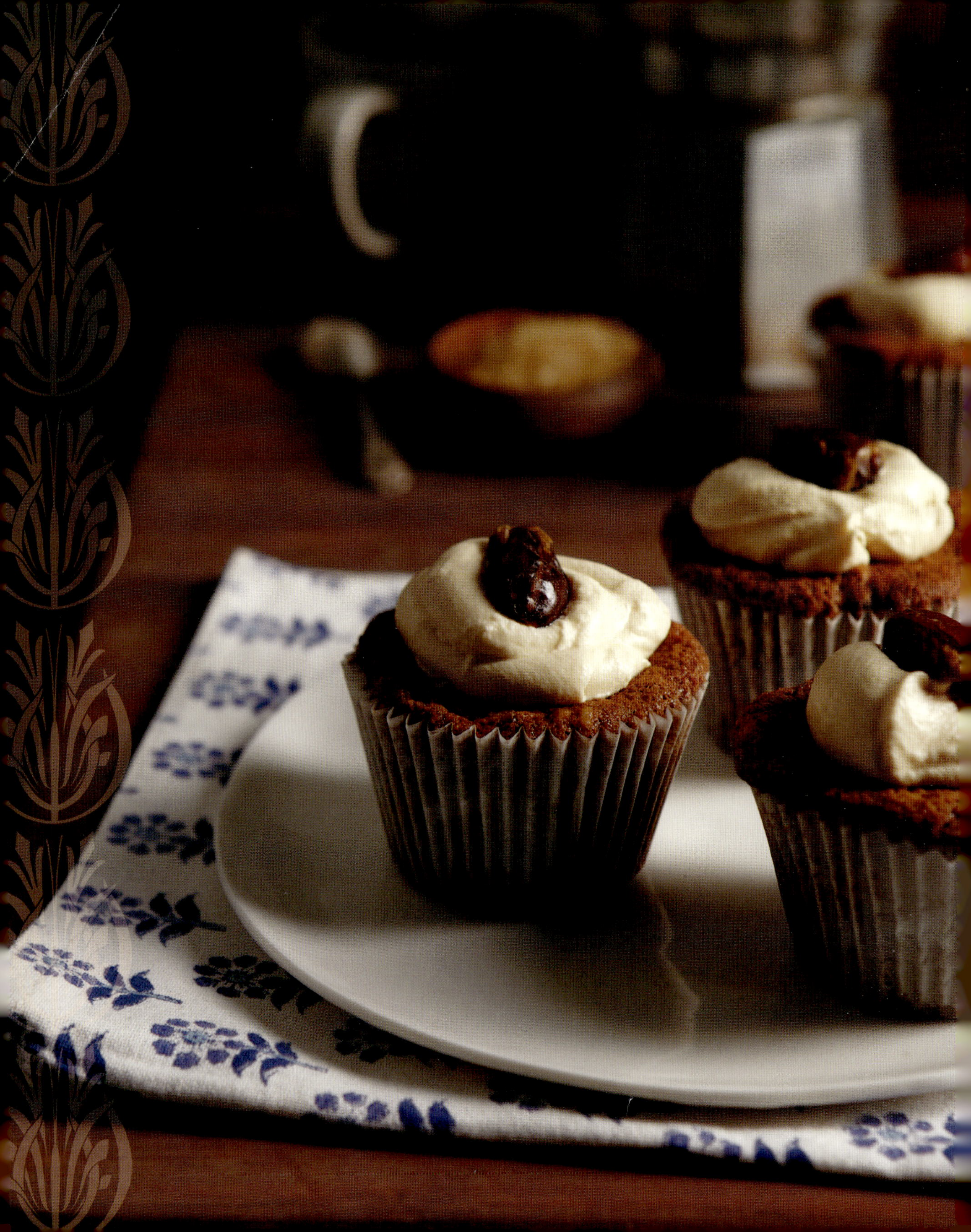

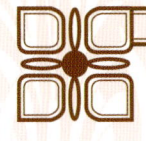

Sticky Date Cupcakes

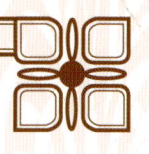

INGREDIENTS:

2 eggs
135 g (4½ oz) butter, at room temperature
¾ cup caster sugar
1 cup self-raising flour, sifted
400 g (14 oz) dates, chopped
2 teaspoons instant coffee powder
1 teaspoon baking soda
1 teaspoon vanilla extract
1 cup ground almond flour
½ cup walnuts, finely chopped

TOPPING:

1 cup light-brown sugar, firmly packed
60 g (2 oz) unsalted butter
1 teaspoon vanilla extract
1 cup whipped cream
12 dates

Makes 12

METHOD:

1. Preheat the oven to 160°C/320°F. Line a 12-cupcake pan with cupcake papers. In a medium bowl, lightly beat the eggs, add the butter and sugar, then mix until light and fluffy.
2. Add ¾ cup water and the flour, and stir to combine. Add remaining ingredients. Mix with a wooden spoon for 2 minutes, until light and creamy.
3. Divide the mixture evenly between the cake papers. Bake for 18–20 minutes until risen and firm to touch. Allow to cool for a few minutes and then transfer to a wire rack. Allow to cool fully before icing.

Topping

1. Meanwhile, combine sugar, butter, vanilla and 1 tablespoon water in a saucepan. Bring to a simmer over medium-low heat, stirring constantly. Without stirring again, simmer for 1 minute. Remove from heat and allow to cool. Fold through whipped cream. Spoon onto cupcakes and top with dates.

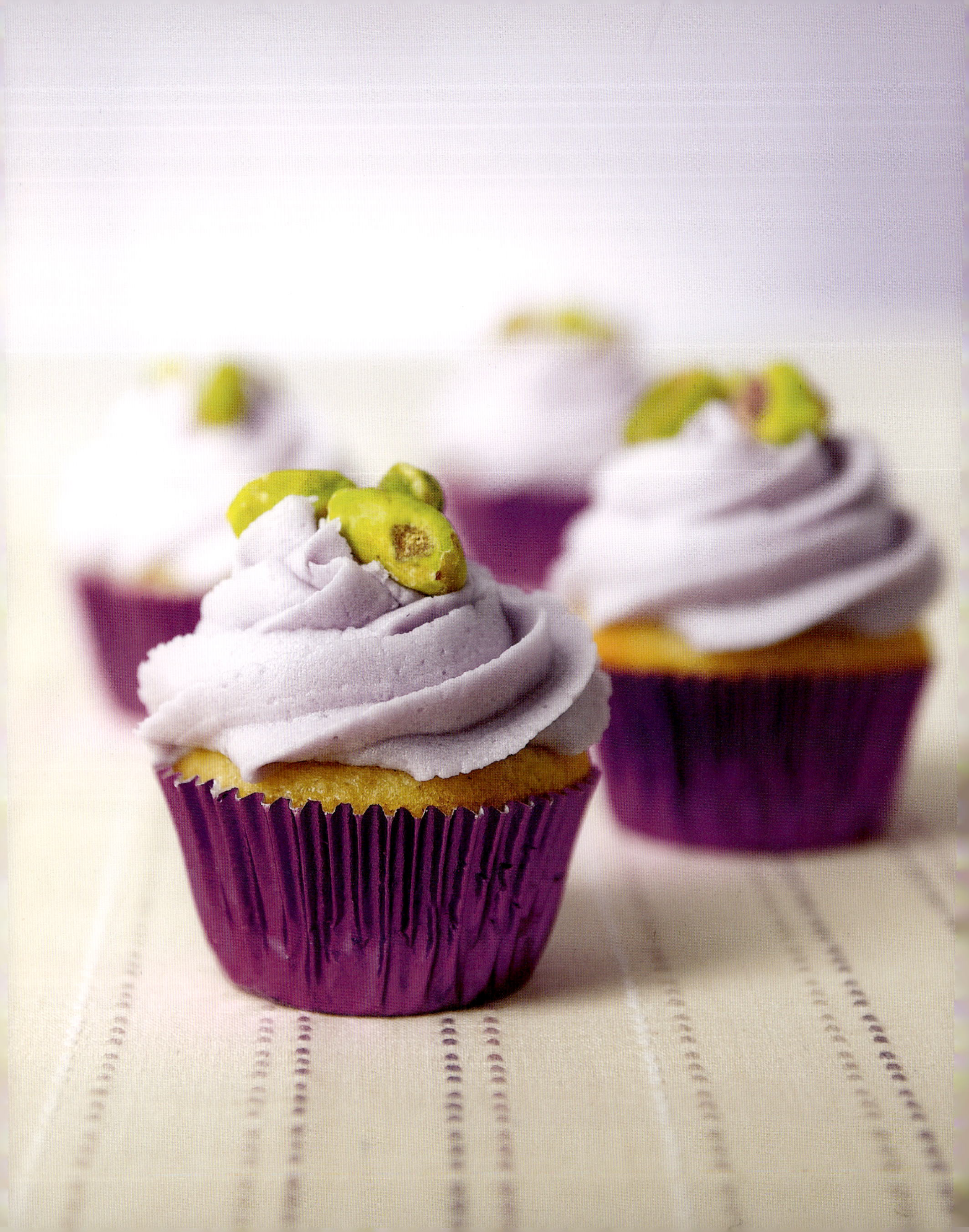

Pistachio Mini Cupcakes

INGREDIENTS:

85 g (3 oz) butter, softened
100 g (3½ oz) caster (superfine) sugar
1 egg
225 g (8 oz) self-raising (self-rising) flour, sifted
75 ml (2½ fl oz) milk
½ teaspoon vanilla extract
55 g (2 oz) pistachios, chopped

TOPPING:

85 g (3 oz) butter, softened
225 g (8 oz) icing (confectioners') sugar
purple food colouring
whole pistachios, to decorate

Makes 24

METHOD:

1. Preheat the oven to 160°C/320°F. Line a mini cupcake tin (pan) with 24 mini paper cases.
2. In a medium bowl, cream the butter and sugar until light and fluffy. Add the egg and mix well.
3. Add the flour, milk and vanilla, and beat until well combined. Stir through pistachios.
4. Divide the batter evenly between the paper cases. Bake for 10–15 minutes until well risen and firm to the touch. Allow to cool for a few minutes and then transfer to a wire rack. Allow to go cold before icing.

Topping

1. In a bowl, eat the butter and icing sugar until light and fluffy. Tint the icing light purple. Use to half-fill a piping bag fitted with a star nozzle to pipe the icing onto the cupcakes. Decorate with pistachios.

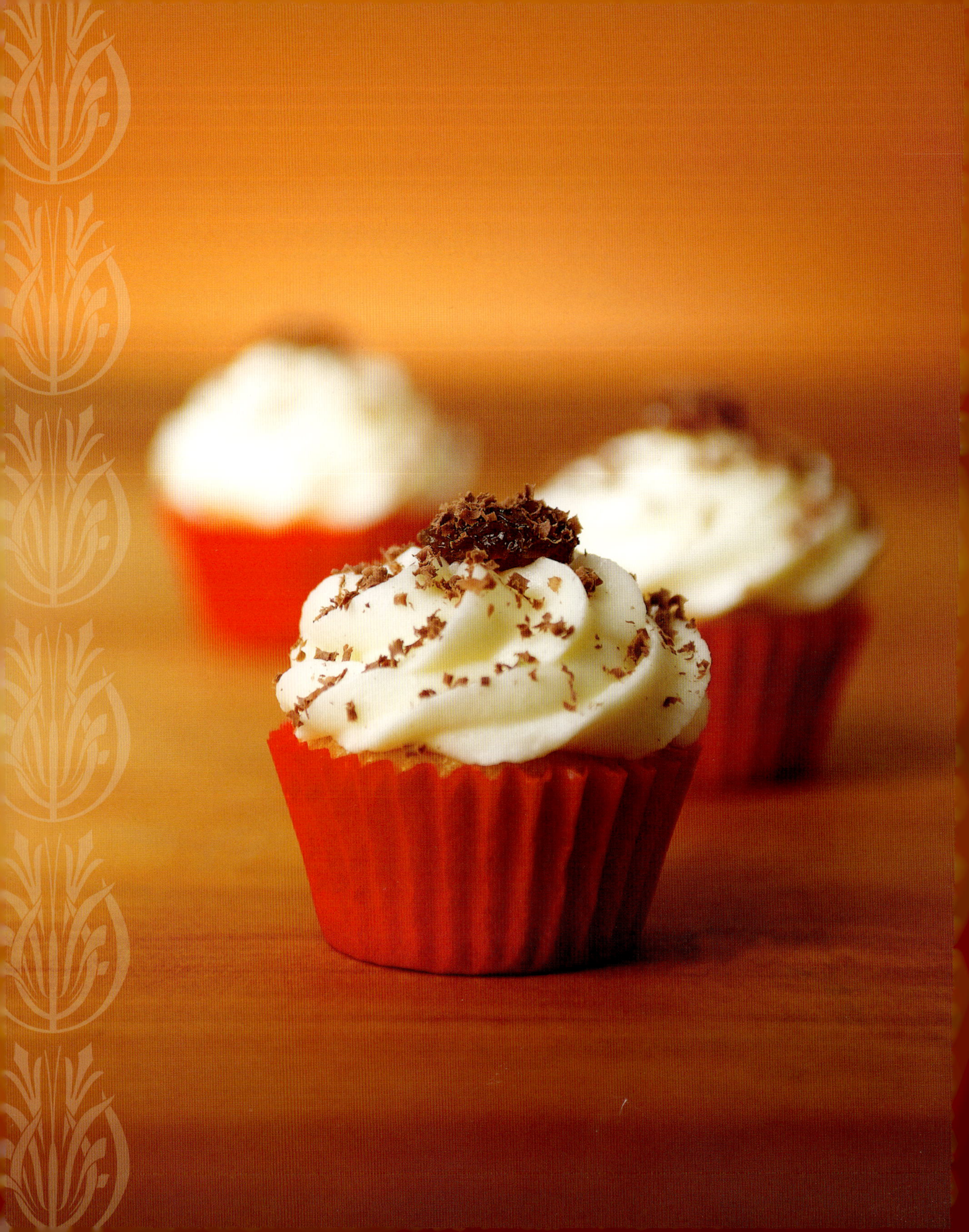

Rum & Raisin Mini Cupcakes

INGREDIENTS:

85 g (3 oz) butter, softened
100 g (3½ oz) caster (superfine) sugar
1 egg
225 g (8 oz) self-raising (self-rising) flour, sifted
75 ml (2½ fl oz) milk
65 g (2½ oz) raisins, soaked in 2 tablespoons rum

TOPPING:

85 g (3 oz) butter, softened
225 g (8 oz) icing (confectioners') sugar
1 tablespoon dark rum
raisins, to decorate
dark (bittersweet) chocolate, grated (shredded), to decorate

Makes 24

METHOD:

1 Preheat the oven to 160°C/320°F. Line a mini cupcake tin (pan) with 24 mini paper cases.
2 In a medium bowl, cream the butter and sugar until light and fluffy. Add the egg and mix well.
3 Add the flour and milk and beat until well combined. Stir through the rum-soaked raisins.
4 Divide the batter evenly between the paper cases. Bake for 10–15 minutes until well risen and firm to the touch. Allow to cool for a few minutes and then transfer to a wire rack. Allow to go cold before icing.

Topping

1 In a bowl, beat the butter, icing sugar and rum until light and fluffy. Use to half-fill a piping bag fitted with a star nozzle and pipe the icing onto the cupcakes. Decorate with raisins and chocolate.

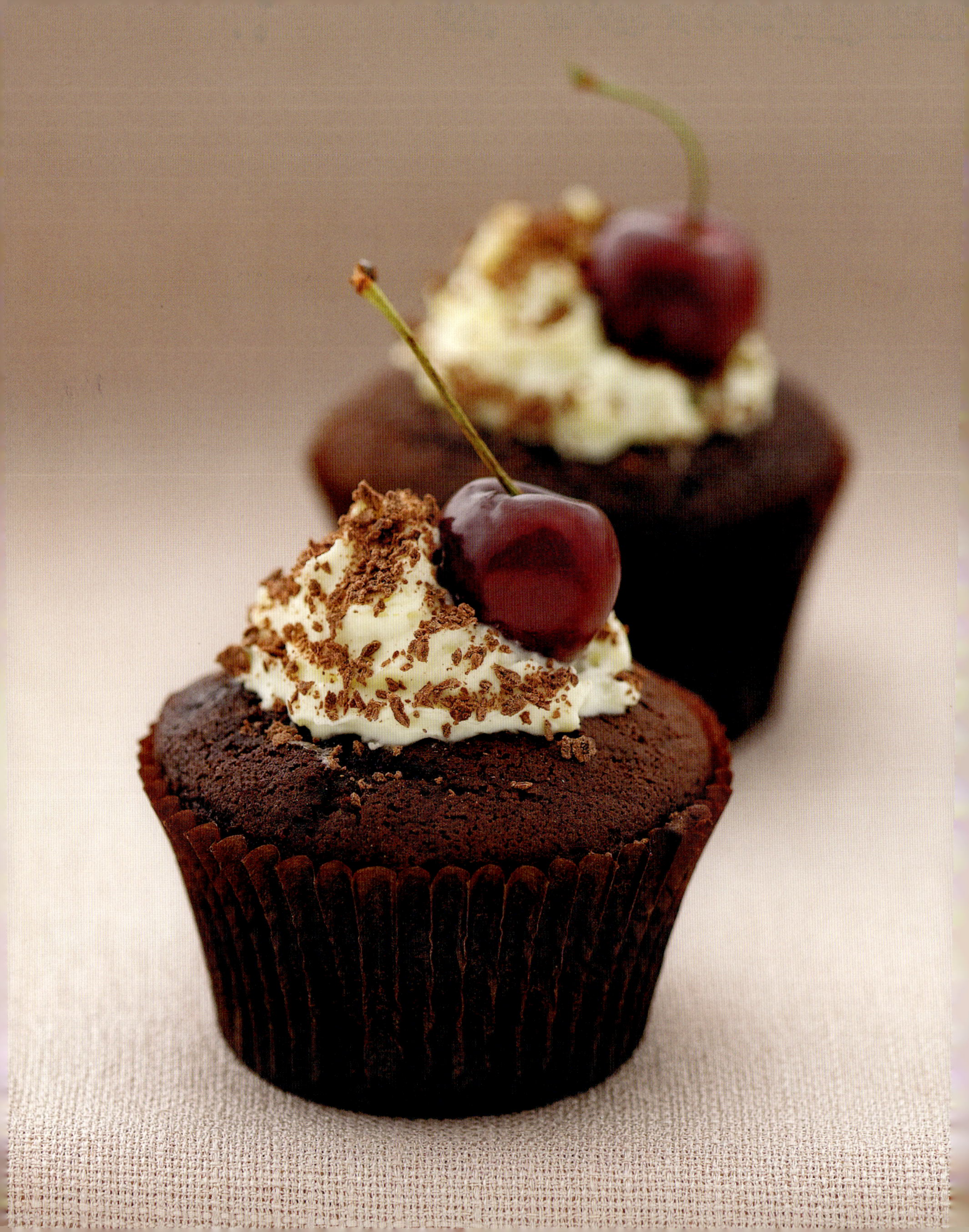

Black Forest Cupcakes

INGREDIENTS:

115 g (4 oz) butter, softened
200 g (7 oz) caster (superfine) sugar
3 eggs, lightly beaten
120 ml (4 fl oz) milk
175 g (6 oz) self-raising (self-rising) flour, sifted
55 g (2 oz) unsweetened cocoa powder
1 tablespoon kirsch liqueur

TOPPING:

100 ml (3½ fl oz) double (heavy) cream
12 fresh cherries
40 g (1½ oz) milk chocolate, grated

Makes 12

METHOD:

1. Preheat the oven to 160°C/320°F. Line a 12-cup muffin tin (pan) with paper cases.
2. In a medium bowl, beat the butter and sugar until light and fluffy, then mix in the beaten eggs.
3. Add milk, flour and cocoa powder, and stir to combine. Beat until light and creamy, then fold through kirsch liqueur.
4. Divide the batter evenly between the paper cases. Bake for 18–20 minutes until risen and firm to the touch. Allow to cool for a few minutes and then transfer to a wire rack. Allow to go cold before icing.

Topping

1. Meanwhile, in a small bowl, whip the cream until stiff peaks form, then top each cake with a dollop of cream, a sprinkle of chocolate shavings and a fresh cherry.

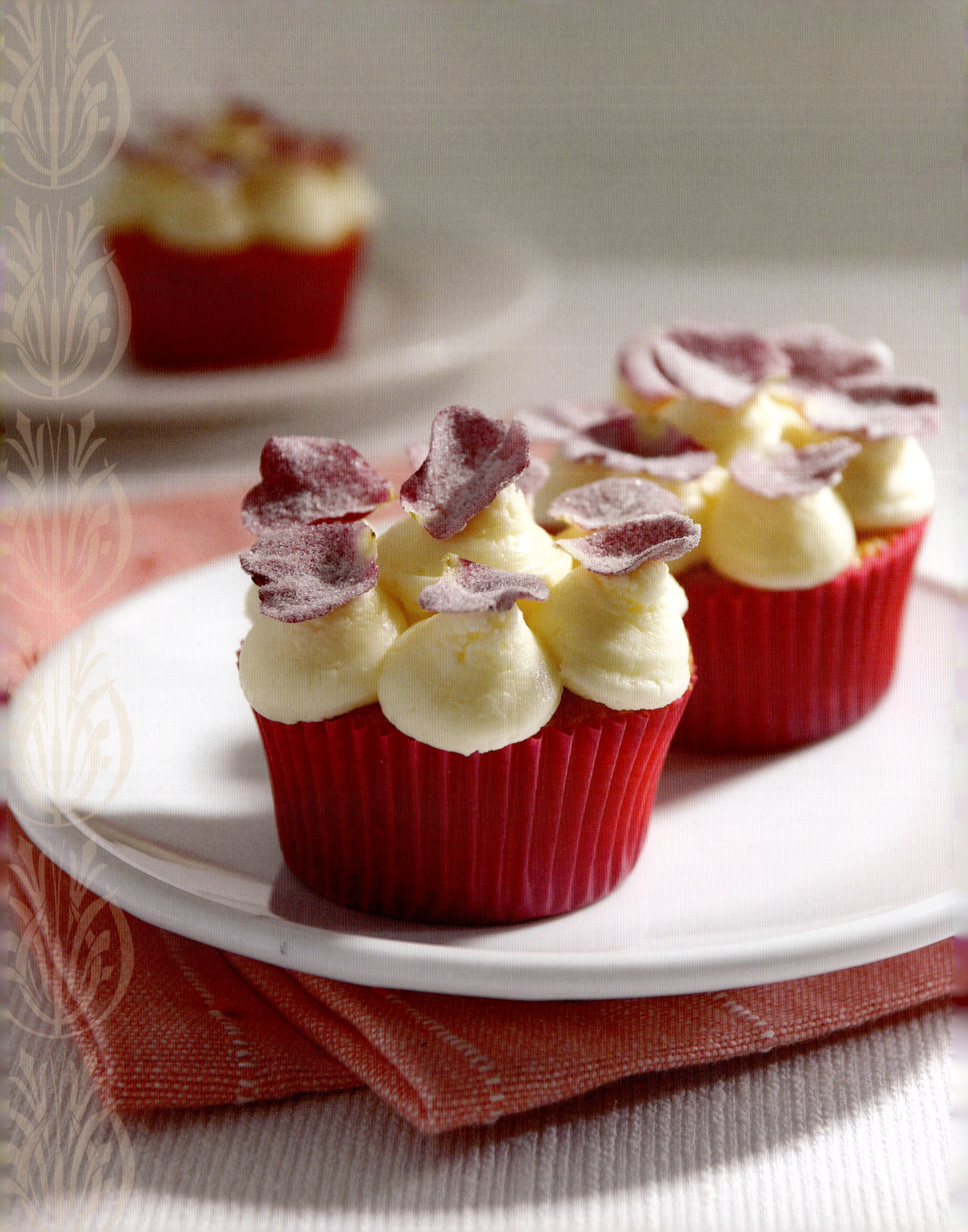

Vanilla Rose Petal Cupcakes

INGREDIENTS:

2 eggs
125 g (4 oz) butter, softened
1 cup superfine (caster) sugar
½ cup milk
2 cups self-rising (self-raising) flour, sifted
1 teaspoon vanilla extract

TOPPING

1½ cups confectioners' (icing) sugar
1 teaspoon rose water
125 g (4 oz) butter, softened
6 drops vanilla extract
candied rose petals (available from cake decoration stores)

Makes 12

METHOD:

1. Preheat the oven to 160°C/325°F. Line a 12-cupcake pan with cupcake papers. In a medium-sized bowl, lightly beat the eggs, add butter and sugar, then mix until light and fluffy.
2. Add milk, flour and vanilla, and stir to combine. Beat with an electric mixer for 2 minutes, until light and creamy.
3. Divide the mixture evenly between the cake papers. Bake for 18–20 minutes until risen and firm to touch. Allow to cool for a few minutes and then transfer to a wire rack. Allow to cool fully before icing.

Topping

1. Meanwhile, combine half of all the topping ingredients except roses, mix with a wooden spoon, add remaining ingredients and beat with the spoon until light and fluffy.
2. Place mixture into a piping bag with a plain nozzle and pipe onto cupcakes. Decorate with rose petals.

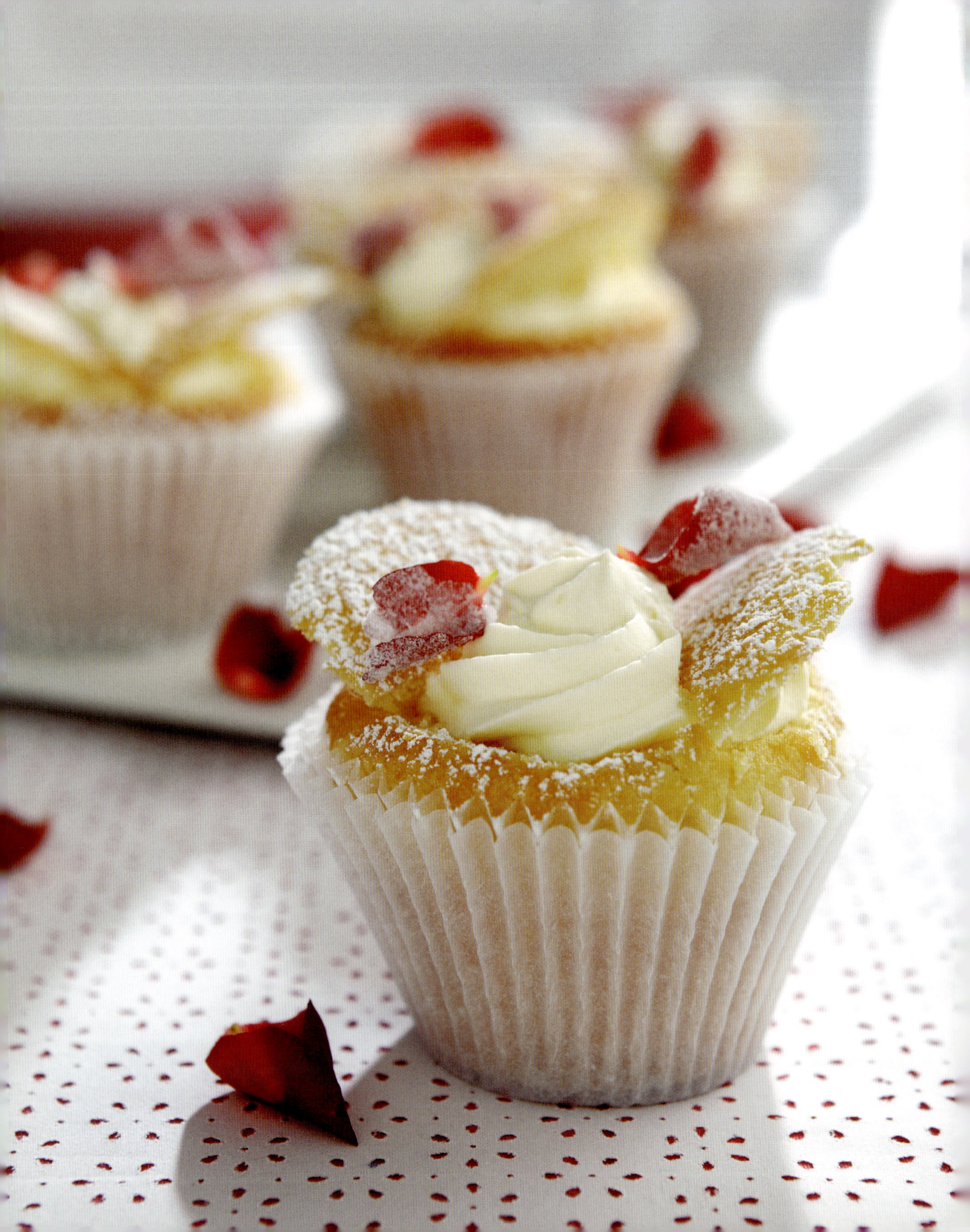

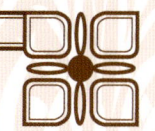

Butterfly Cupcakes

INGREDIENTS:

125 g (4 oz) butter or margarine
1 teaspoon vanilla extract
¾ cup superfine (caster) sugar
2 eggs
2 cups self-rising (self-raising) flour
pinch of salt
⅔ cup milk

FILLING

1¼ cups thickened cream
½ teaspoon vanilla extract
2 tablespoons confectioners' (icing) sugar
crystallised rose petals
confectioners' (icing) sugar, extra

Makes 24

METHOD:

1. Preheat oven to 200°C/400°F.
2. Beat butter, vanilla extract and sugar together in a bowl until light and fluffy. Add eggs one at a time, beating well after each addition.
3. Sift flour and salt together and add to creamed mixture alternately with milk. Stir until mixture is smooth and all ingredients are well combined.
4. Spoon about 1 tablespoon of mixture into each paper patty case or buttered patty pans. Bake in the oven for 15 minutes or until golden brown. Cool on a wire rack.
5. To make the filling, beat cream, vanilla extract and icing sugar together until thick.
6. When the cakes are cool, cut a slice from the top of each cake and spoon or pipe on a small amount of filling. Cut removed cake slices in half and arrange on top of cream to make butterfly wings. Dust with a little extra icing sugar and decorate with crystallised rose petals.

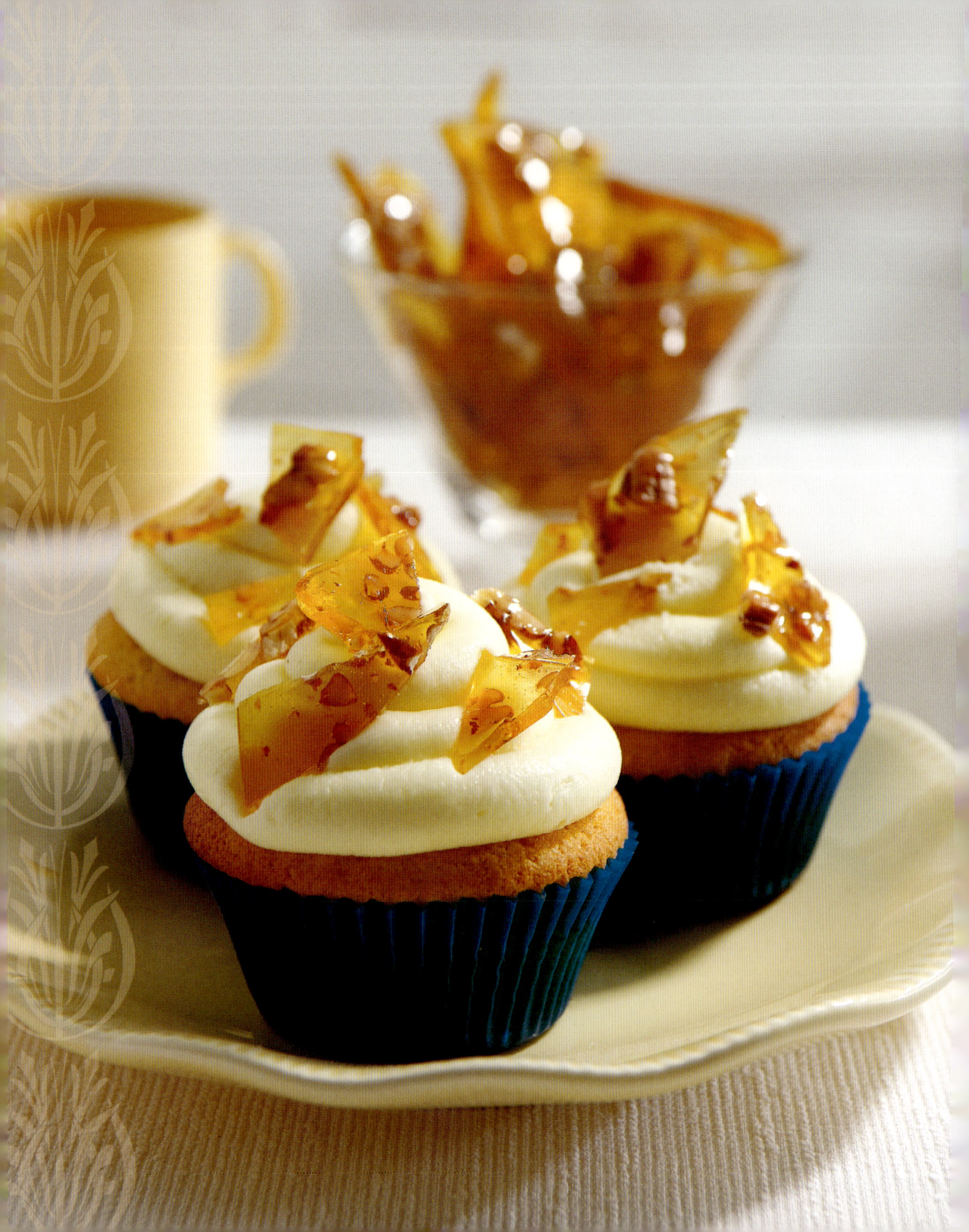

Pecan Praline Cupcakes

INGREDIENTS:

2 eggs
125 g (4 oz) butter, softened
1 cup superfine (caster) sugar
½ cup milk
2 cups self-rising (self-raising) flour, sifted
1 tablespoon espresso coffee
½ cup pecans, chopped
1 tablespoon golden syrup

TOPPING

1½ cups confectioners' (icing) sugar
125 g (4 oz) butter, softened
200 g (7 oz) sugar
100 ml (3½ fl oz) water
100 g (3½ oz) pecans, chopped

Makes 12

METHOD:

1 Preheat the oven to 160°C/325°F. Line a 12-cupcake pan with cupcake papers. In a medium-sized bowl, lightly beat the eggs, add butter and sugar, then mix until light and fluffy.
2 Add milk and flour, and stir to combine. Add remaining ingredients. Mix with a wooden spoon for 2 minutes, until light and creamy.
3 Divide the mixture evenly between the cake papers. Bake for 18–20 minutes until risen and firm to touch. Allow to cool for a few minutes, then transfer to a wire rack. Allow to cool fully before icing.

Topping

1 Meanwhile, combine sugar, butter and 100ml water in a saucepan, bring to the boil and simmer over a medium heat until the mixture becomes a golden colour. Stir in pecans and quickly pour onto an oiled tray. Allow to cool and harden before breaking into pieces.
2 Beat together icing sugar and butter until light and fluffy. Use a piping bag fitted with a plain nozzle and pipe the icing onto the cupcakes. Decorate with praline pieces.

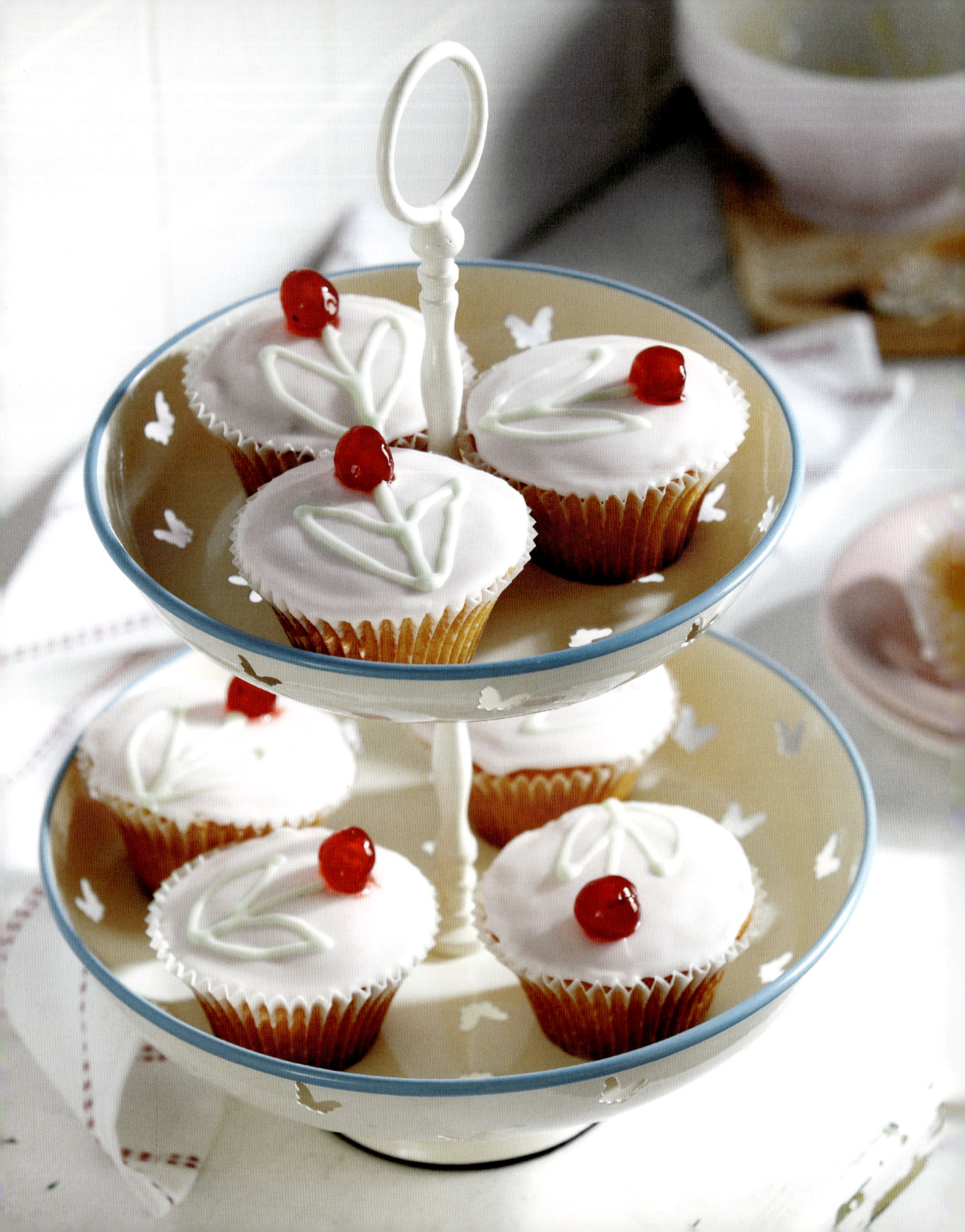

Decorated Cupcakes

INGREDIENTS

125g (4 oz) butter or margarine
1 teaspoon vanilla extract
¾ cup caster sugar
2 eggs
2 cups self-raising flour
pinch of salt
2/3 cup milk

ICING
3 cups icing sugar
green and pink food colouring
glacé cherries

Makes about 24

METHOD

1. Preheat oven to 180°C/360°F.
2. Beat butter, vanilla extract and sugar together in a bowl until light and fluffy. Add eggs one at a time, beating well after each addition.
3. Sift flour and salt together, add to the creamed mixture alternately with milk, stirring until smooth and all ingredients are well combined.
4. Spoon about 1 tablespoon of mixture into each paper patty case or buttered patty pans. Bake for 15 minutes or until golden brown. Remove from oven and cool on a wire rack.
5. To make the icing, sift icing sugar into a bowl, add sufficient hot water to make a smooth, spreadable icing. Keep a small amount aside and colour it green. Add pink colouring to the rest. Quickly spread pink icing over each cake and decorate with green icing and glacé cherries.

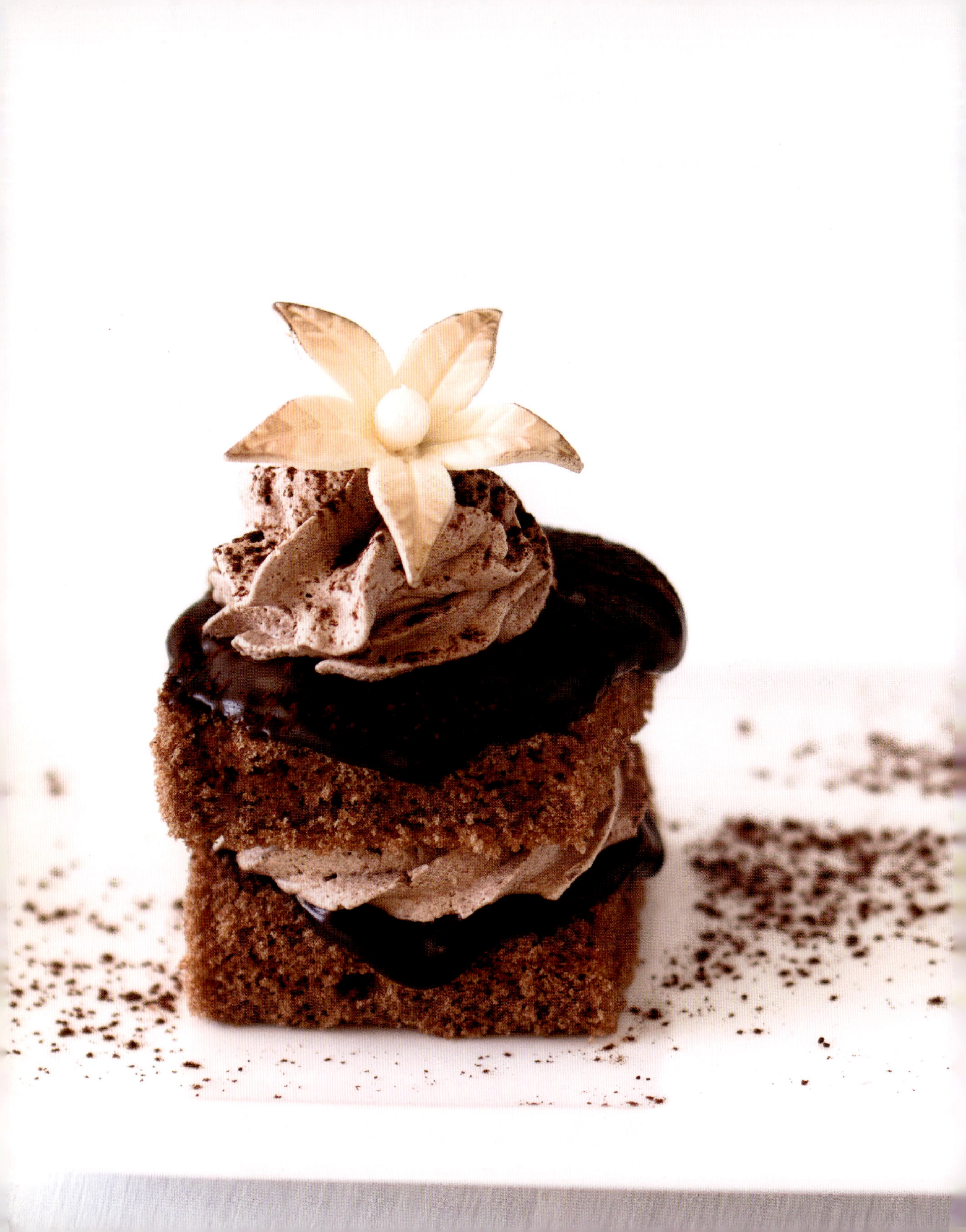

SLICES

Macadamia Coconut Squares

INGREDIENTS:

250 g (9 oz) butter
2 cups brown sugar, firmly packed
1 tablespoon instant coffee powder
½ teaspoon ground cinnamon
½ teaspoon salt
2 cups plain flour
3 eggs
2 teaspoons vanilla extract
2 cups desiccated coconut
2 cups chopped toasted macadamias

Makes 48

METHOD:

1. Preheat oven to 170°C/ 340°F.
2. Lightly butter a 22 x 33cm (8.5 x 13 in) baking pan and set aside.
3. In a large mixing bowl, beat butter, 1 cup brown sugar, instant coffee powder, ¼ teaspoon cinnamon and ¼ teaspoon salt until light and fluffy. Stir in flour half a cup at a time, blending well after each addition.
4. Spread evenly in prepared pan. Bake for 20 minutes. Cool in pan on rack for 15 minutes.
5. In a large bowl, beat eggs and vanilla with remaining 1 cup brown sugar, ¼ teaspoon cinnamon and ¼ teaspoon salt. Stir in coconut and macadamias. Spread evenly over cooled baked layer.
6. Bake for 40–50 minutes, or until golden brown and firm to the touch. Use a knife to loosen around edges while warm.
7. Cool completely in pan on a rack. Cut into 48 squares, cutting 6 strips one way and 8 strips the other way.
8. Store in an airtight container at room temperature.

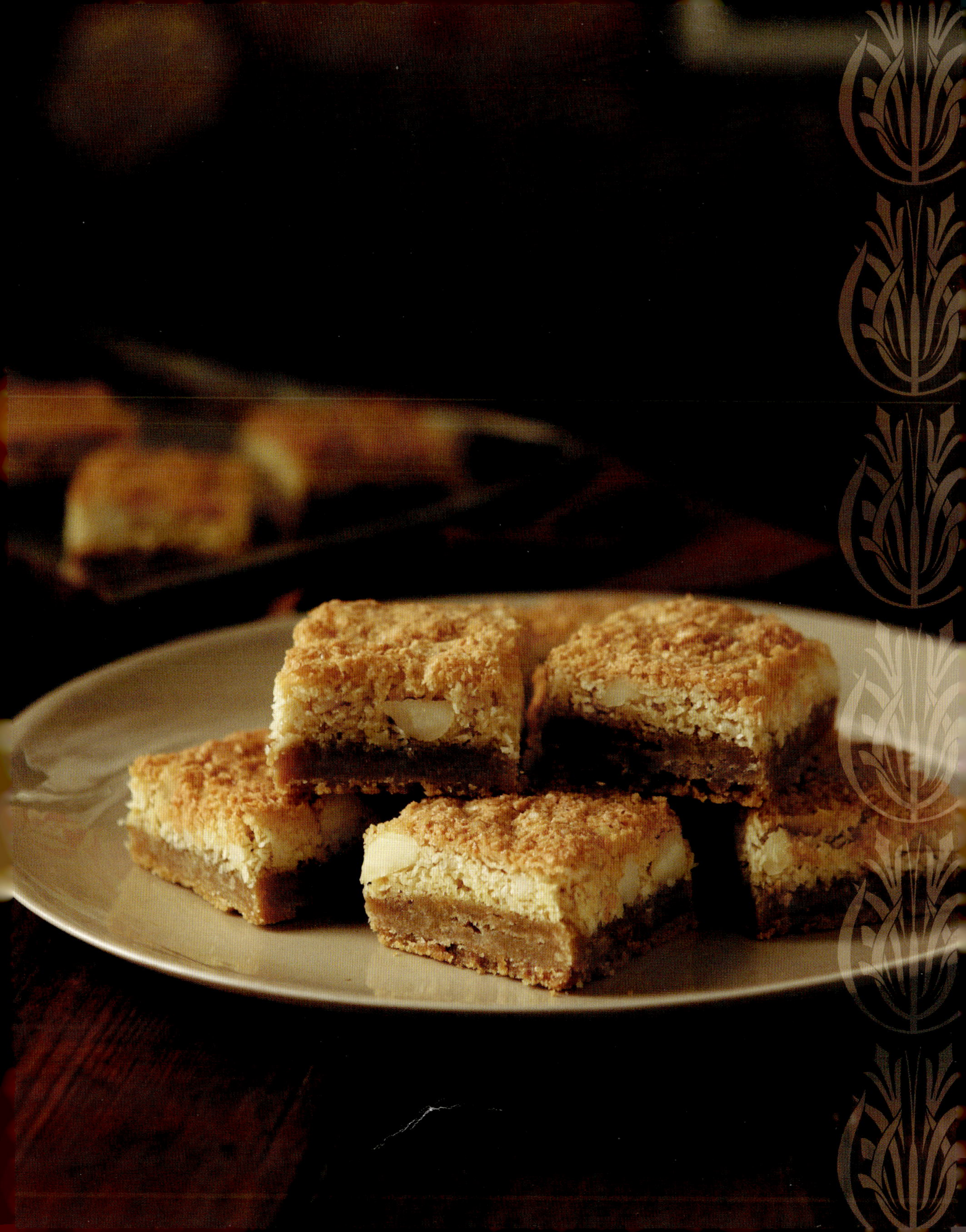

Double Fudge Blondies

These lusciously rich white brownies can double as a dinner party dessert if drizzled with melted white or dark chocolate and topped with toasted flaked almonds.

INGREDIENTS:

250 g (9 oz) butter, softened
1½ cups sugar
1 teaspoon vanilla extract
4 eggs, lightly beaten
1¾ cups plain flour
½ teaspoon baking powder
185 g (6½ oz) white chocolate, melted

CREAM CHEESE FILLING:

250 g (9 oz) cream cheese, softened
60 g (2 oz) white chocolate, melted
¼ cup maple syrup
1 egg
1 tablespoon plain flour

Makes 24

METHOD:

1. Preheat oven to 180°C/360°F. To make filling, place cream cheese, chocolate, maple syrup, egg and flour in a bowl and beat until smooth. Set aside.
2. Place butter, sugar and vanilla extract in a bowl and beat until light and fluffy. Gradually beat in eggs.
3. Sift together flour and baking powder over butter mixture. Add chocolate and mix well to combine.
4. Spread half the mixture over the base of a buttered and lined 23 cm (9 in) square cake tin. Top with filling, then remaining mixture. Bake for 40 minutes or until firm. Cool in tin, then cut into squares.

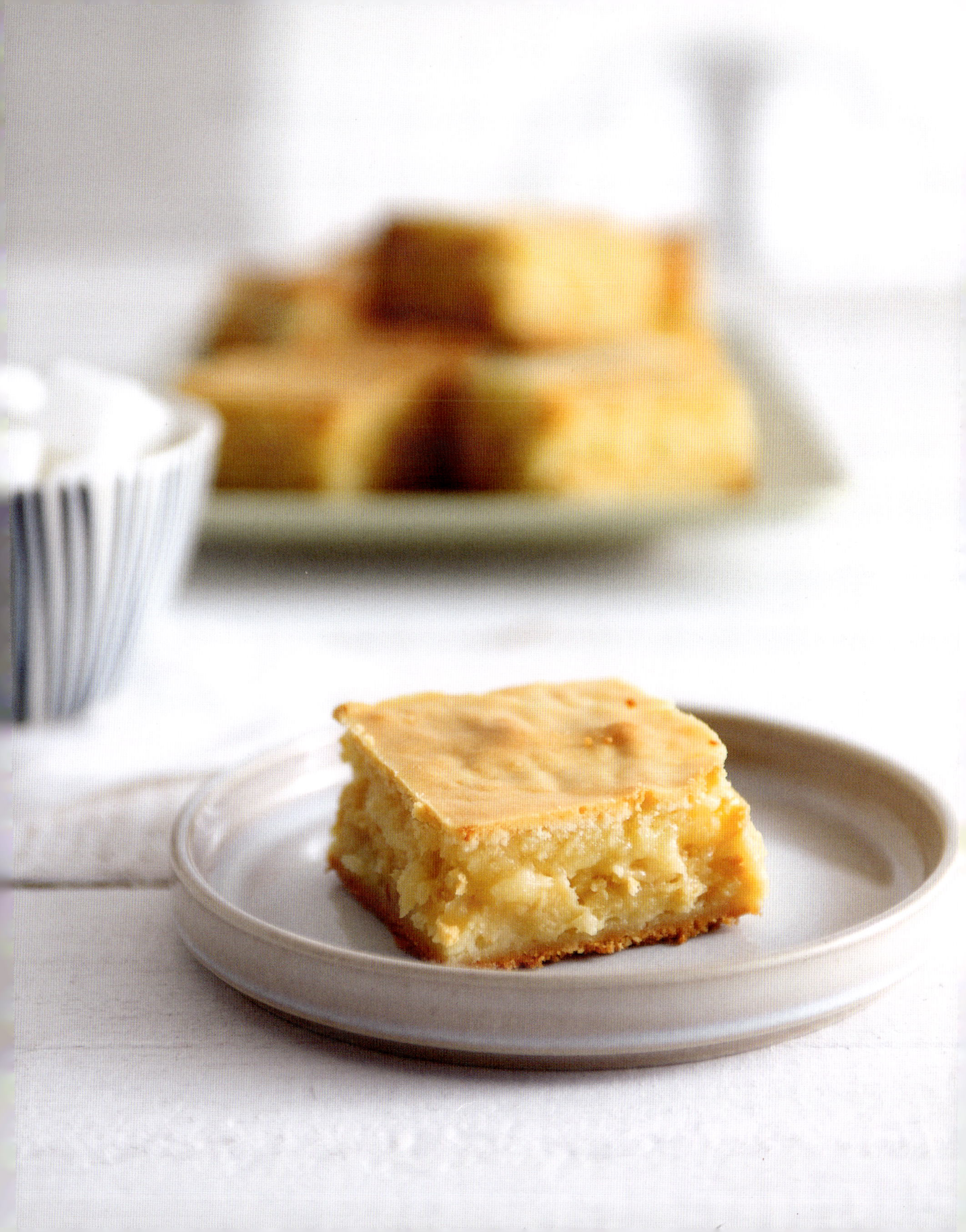

Choc-Mint Brownies

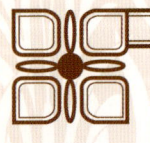

INGREDIENTS:

125 g (4 oz) butter

200 g (7 oz) dark chocolate, grated

2 eggs

¾ cup brown sugar

2 tablespoons cocoa powder

2 tablespoons oil

1 cup plain flour

ICING

1 cup confectioners' (icing) sugar

15 g (½ oz) butter

3 drops peppermint extract

Makes 20

METHOD:

1. Preheat oven to 160°C/325°F.
2. Melt butter and chocolate in a medium saucepan, stir until combined then cool slightly. Beat eggs and sugar until light and creamy. Beat in cocoa and oil, then beat in flour and cooled chocolate mixture.
3. Pour mixture into a buttered and lined 23 x 23cm (9 x 9in) square tin. Bake for 40 minutes or until cooked when tested with a skewer. Turn onto wire rack to cool.
4. To make the icing, sift icing sugar into a heatproof bowl, add butter and peppermint extract and stir over simmering water until smooth. Drizzle or pipe icing over top of brownies. Cut into squares and serve.

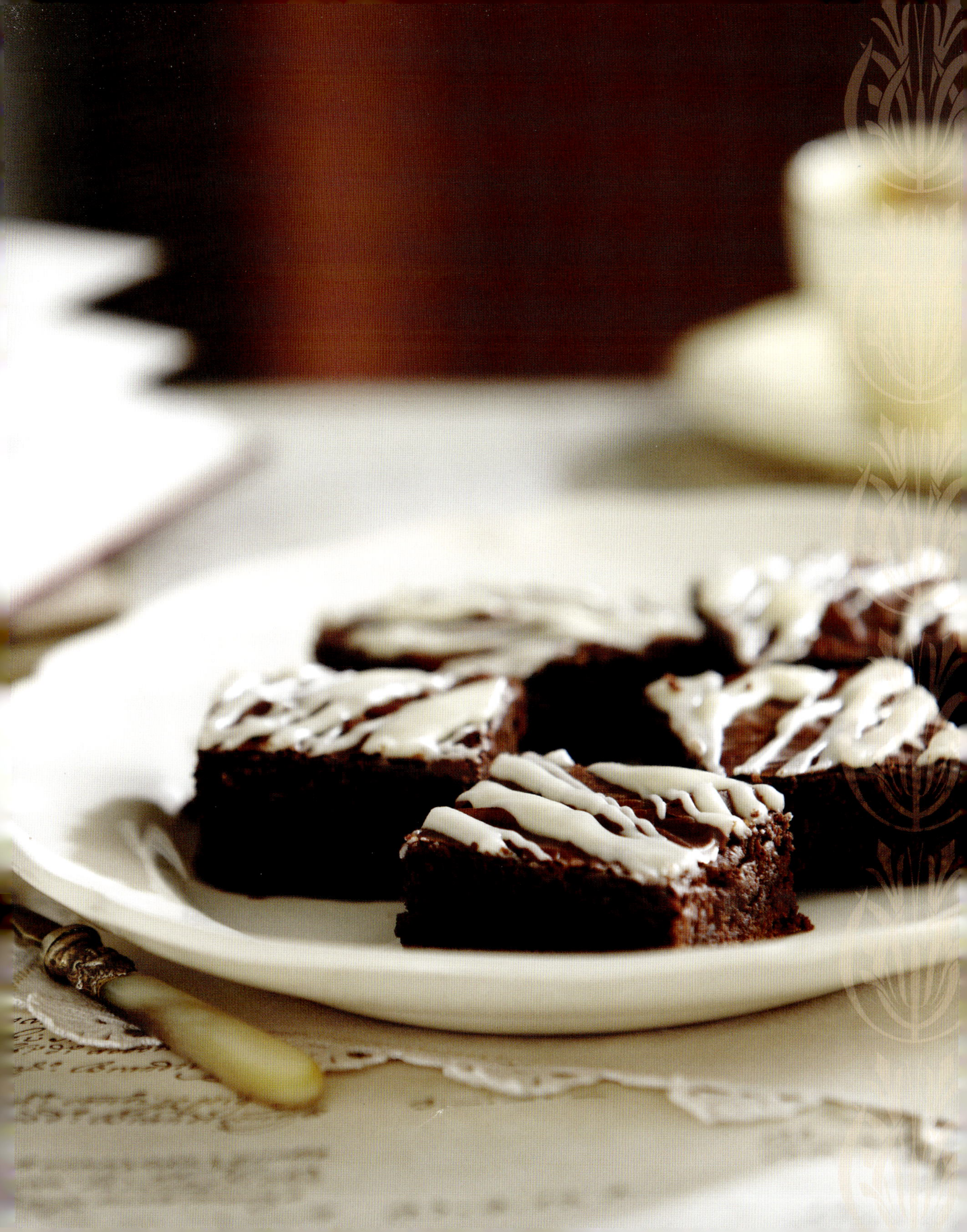

Raspberry Yoghurt Slice

INGREDIENTS:

100 g (3½ oz) butter

1 cup plain flour

¼ cup brown sugar

¾ cup rolled oats

TOPPING

125 g (4 oz) cream cheese

¾ cup raspberry-flavoured yoghurt

1 tablespoon honey

1 teaspoon lemon juice

1 teaspoon grated lemon zest

1 tablespoon gelatine

250g (8oz) frozen raspberries

¼ cup sugar

Makes 15

METHOD:

1. Preheat oven to 180°C/350°F.
2. Blend butter and flour in a food processor with sugar until dough just comes together. Fold through the oats.
3. Press into the base of a buttered and lined 28 x 18cm (11 x 7in) lamington tin. Bake for about 15–20 minutes or until a skewer comes out clean, then allow to cool.
4. Beat the cream cheese with yoghurt and honey, add lemon juice and zest. Sprinkle gelatine over ¼ cup water to soften. Heat ¾ of the thawed raspberries in a saucepan and add sugar and softened gelatine. Bring to the boil, stirring until sugar and gelatine have thoroughly dissolved. Press through a sieve and allow to cool. Then stir into the creamed cheese and yoghurt mixture with the remaining raspberries.
5. Carefully pour the yoghurt mixture over the base and refrigerate overnight. Serve with extra raspberries.

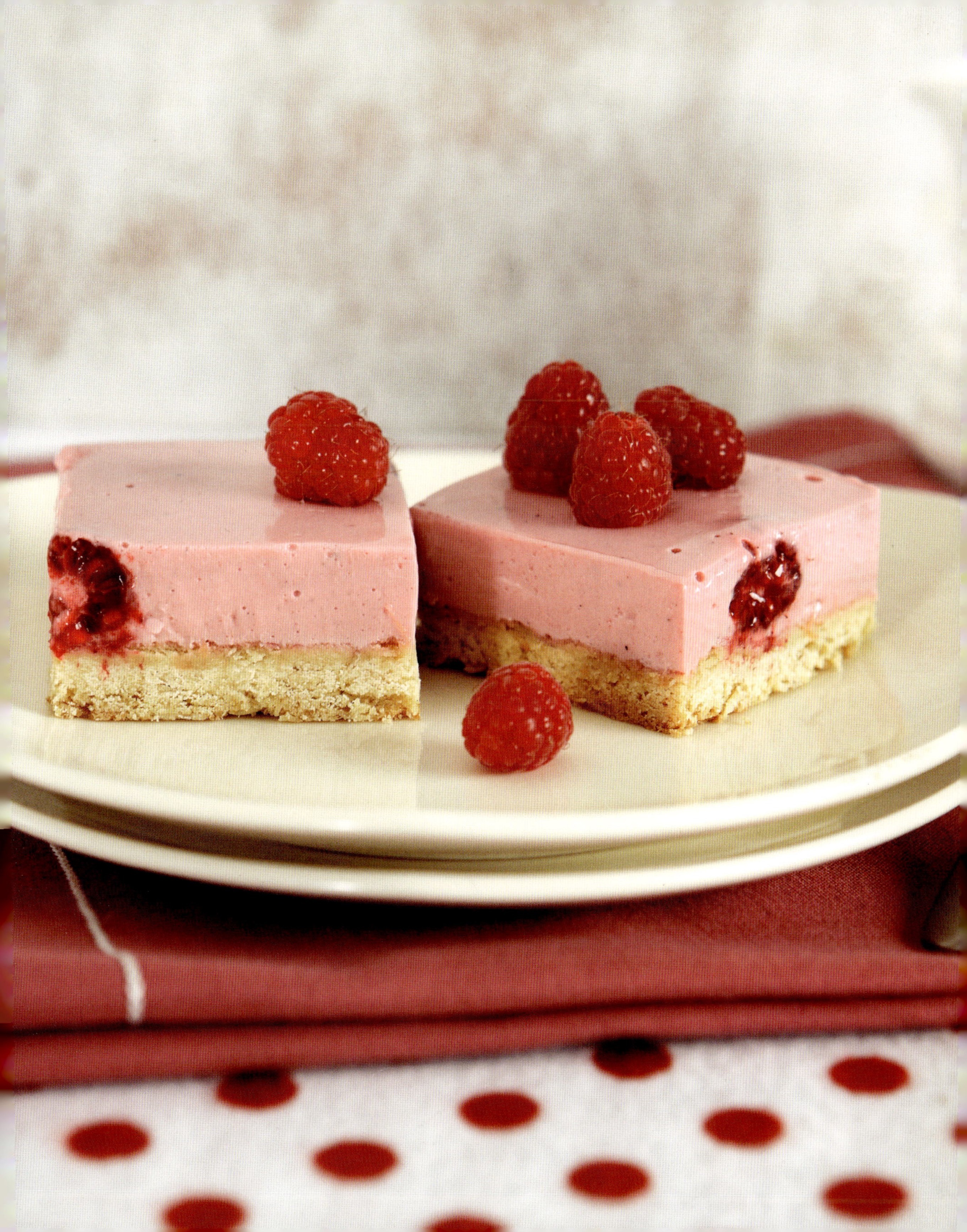

Chocolate Rum Slice

INGREDIENTS:

- 1 cup self-rising (self-raising) flour, sifted
- 1 tablespoon cocoa powder, sifted
- ½ cup superfine (caster) sugar
- 75 g (2½ oz) desiccated coconut
- 75 g (2½ oz) raisins, chopped
- 125 g (4 oz) butter, melted
- 1 teaspoon rum
- 2 tablespoons grated dark chocolate
- 2 eggs, lightly beaten

CHOCOLATE ICING

- 1 cup confectioners' (icing) sugar
- 2 tablespoons cocoa powder
- 15 g (½ oz) butter, softened

Makes 25

METHOD:

1. Preheat oven to 180°C/350°F. Place flour, cocoa powder, caster sugar, coconut and raisins in a bowl and mix to combine. Stir in butter, rum, grated chocolate and eggs. Mix well.
2. Press mixture into a buttered and lined 25cm (10 in) square cake tin and bake for 20–25 minutes or until firm. Allow to cool in tin.
3. To make icing, sift icing sugar and cocoa powder together into a bowl. Add butter and 1 tablespoon boiling water and beat to make icing of a spreadable consistency.
4. Turn slice onto a wire rack or plate, spread with icing and sprinkle with extra coconut. Refrigerate until icing is firm, then cut into squares.

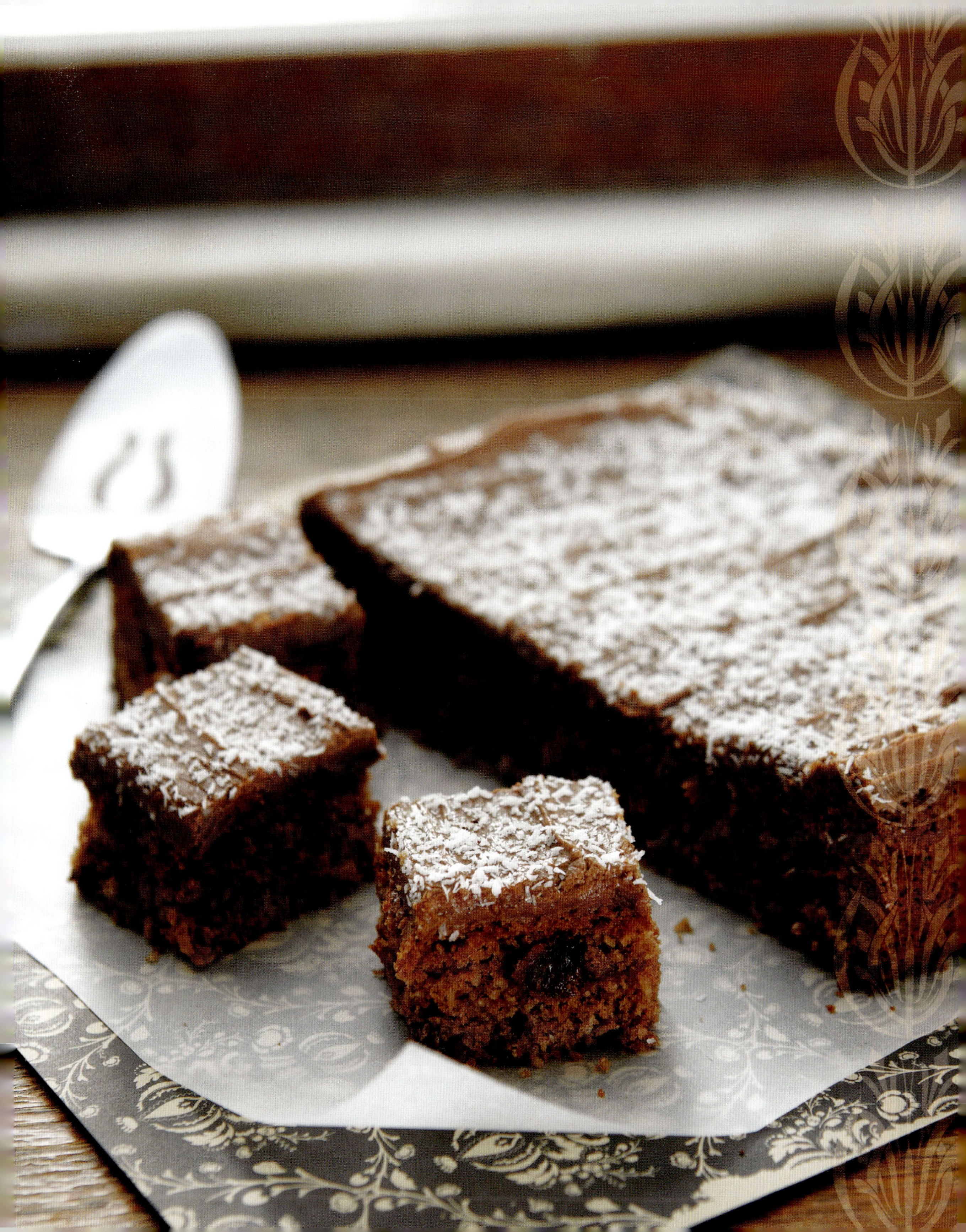

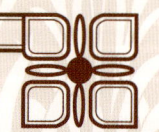

Caramel Squares

INGREDIENTS:

SHORTBREAD BASE
100 g (3½ oz) butter
3 tablespoons sugar
60 g (2 oz) cornflour, sifted
¾ cup plain flour, sifted

Caramel filling
125 g (4 oz) butter
½ cup brown sugar
2 tablespoons honey
400 g (14 oz) sweetened condensed milk
1 teaspoon vanilla extract

CHOCOLATE TOPPING
200 g (7 oz) dark chocolate, melted

Makes 24

METHOD:

1. Preheat oven to 180°C/350°F. To make base, place butter and sugar in a bowl and beat until light and fluffy. Mix in cornflour and flour, turn onto a lightly floured surface and knead briefly, then press into a buttered and lined 20 x 30cm (8 x 12in) shallow cake tin and bake for 25 minutes or until firm.

2. To make filling, place butter, brown sugar and honey in a saucepan and cook over a medium heat, stirring constantly until sugar melts and ingredients are combined. Bring to the boil and simmer for 7 minutes. Beat in condensed milk and vanilla extract, pour filling over base and bake for 20 minutes longer. Set aside to cool completely. Spread melted chocolate over filling, set aside until firm, then cut into squares.

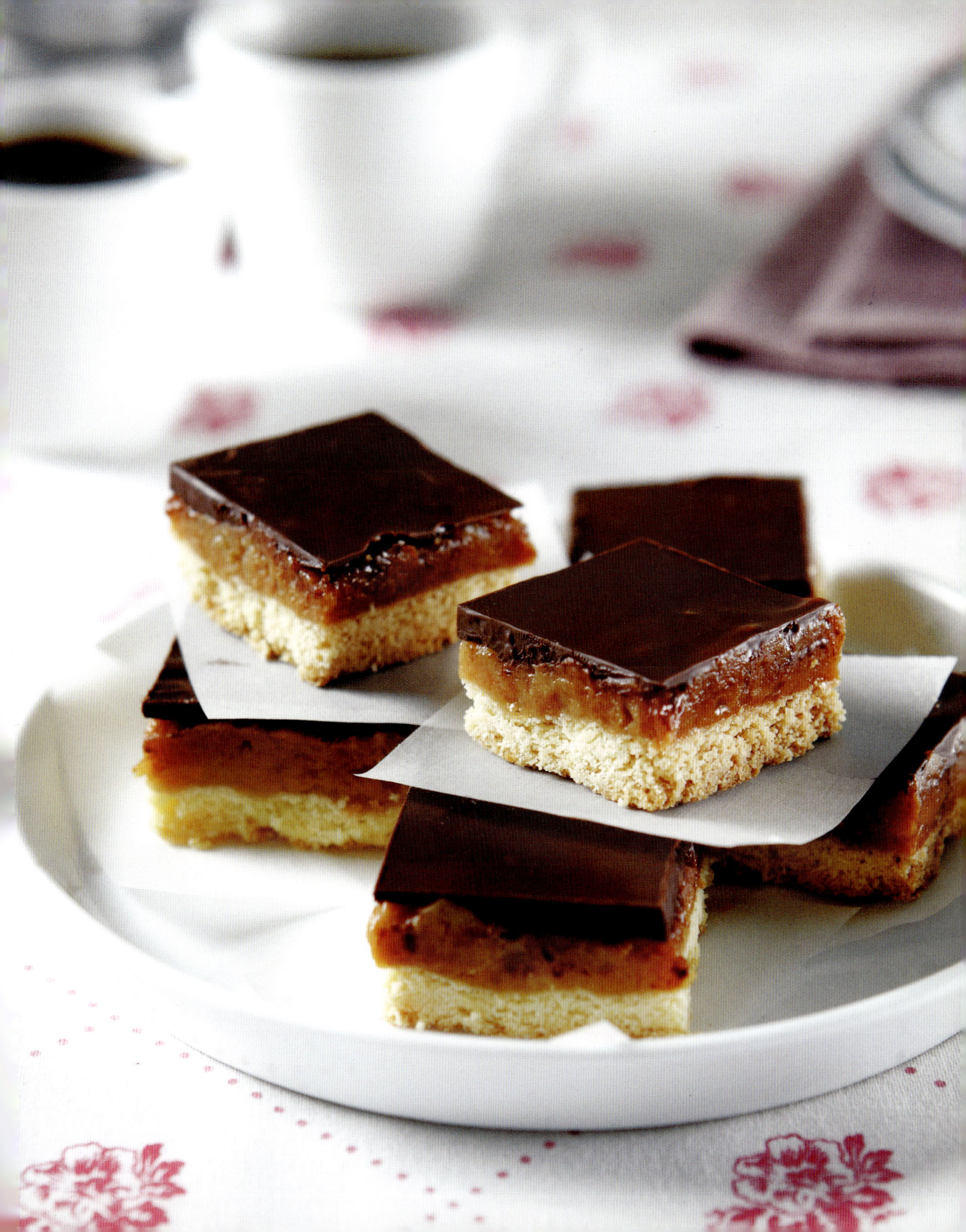

Lemon & Blueberry Shortcake Slice

INGREDIENTS:

BASE

225 g (8 oz) plain flour

100 g (3½ oz) superfine (caster) sugar

175 g (6 oz) firm butter, cut into cubes

TOPPING

3 eggs

225 g (8 oz) superfine (caster) sugar, for the base

juice (about 100 ml/3½ oz) and grated rind of 3 lemons

40 g (1½ oz) flour

75 g (2¾ oz) dried blueberries (optional)

confectioners' (icing) sugar, to serve (optional)

Makes 20

METHOD:

1. Preheat the oven to 180°C/350°F. Line the base and sides of an 18 x 27cm (7 x 10¾in) tin with baking parchment.

2. Put the flour and the first measure of sugar in a large bowl or food processor and mix to combine. Add the butter and rub together or process until the mixture resembles fine breadcrumbs. Press the crumbs evenly into the prepared tin and bake for 20–25 minutes, or until golden. Remove and reduce the temperature to 140°C/275°F.

3. While the base is cooking, whisk together the eggs and the second measure of sugar, using an electric mixer, until very thick and pale, about 8–10 minutes. Stir in the lemon juice and rind then fold in the flour. Sprinkle the blueberries evenly over the base, if using. Pour over the egg mixture and bake for 35–40 minutes, or until set. Allow to cool in the tin before cutting into bars. Serve dusted with icing sugar, if liked.

4. Try stirring fresh rather than dried blueberries into the lemon topping before baking.

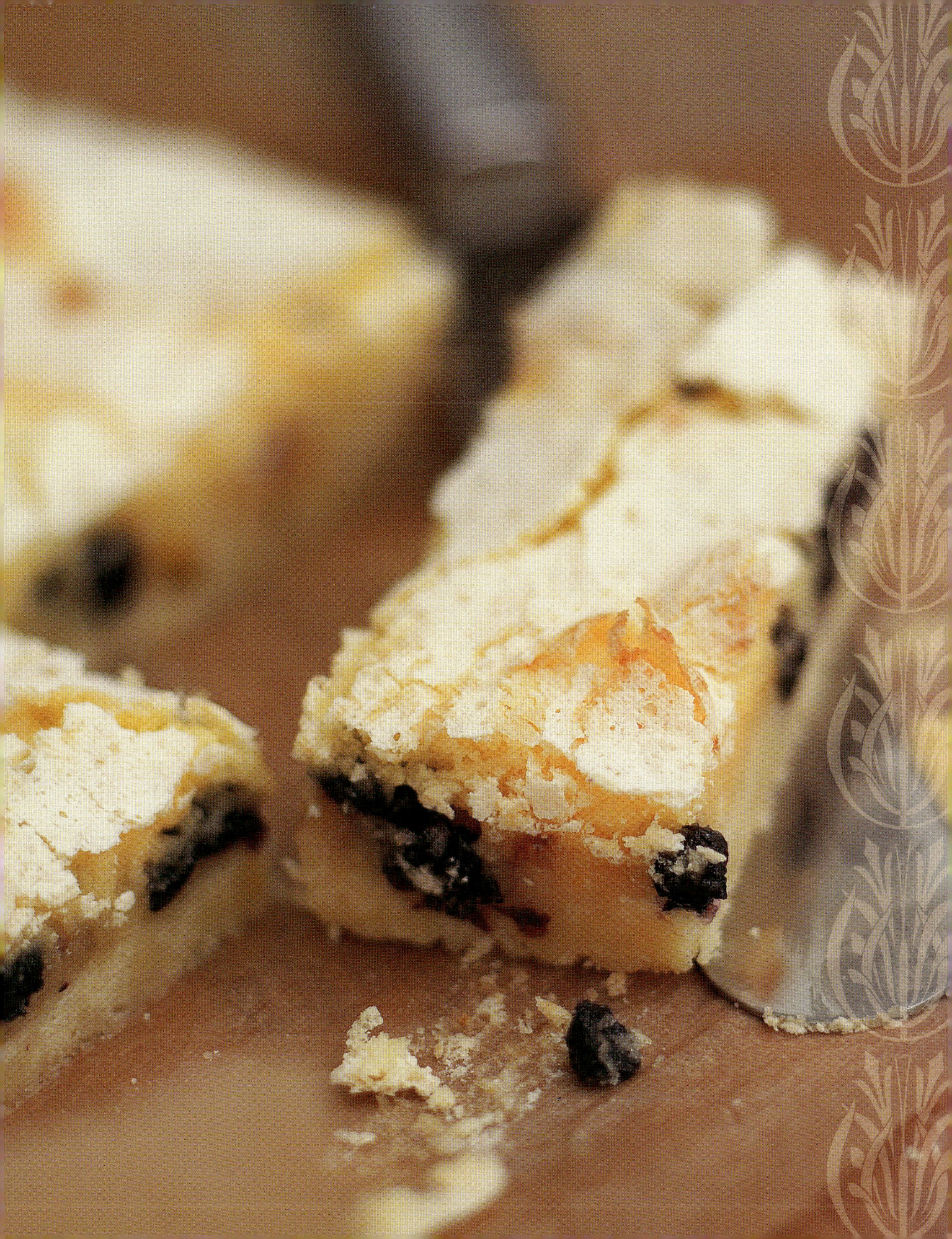

Date & Walnut Slice

INGREDIENTS:

125 g (4½ oz) butter, chopped,
at room temperature
¾ cup caster sugar
1 egg, lightly beaten
¾ cup chopped dried dates
½ cup walnuts, coarsely chopped
1 teaspoon ground ginger
1 cup self-raising (self-rising) flour

Serves 6

METHOD:

1. Preheat oven to 180°C/350°F. Grease a 20 x 20 cm (8 x 8 in) Swiss roll tin. Line base and two long sides with baking paper.
2. Place butter and sugar in a small bowl. Beat with an electric mixer until thick and creamy. Add egg, beat until just combined. Stir in remaining ingredients (except zest) until well combined. Spread mixture into prepared tin.
3. Cook for about 20 minutes or until cooked when tested. Cool slice in tin.
4. Remove slice from tin. Serve slice cut into bars.

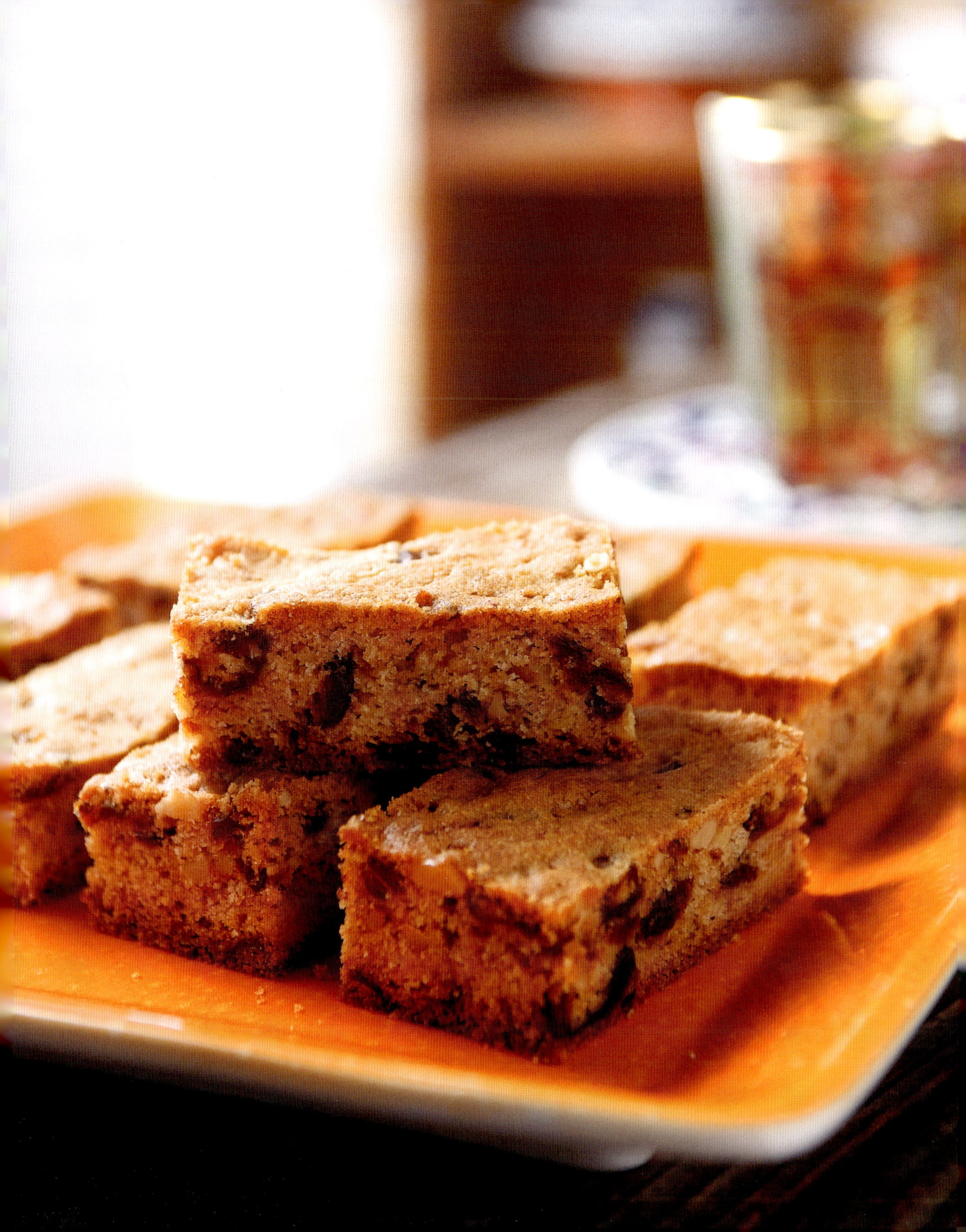

Brownies

INGREDIENTS:

150 g (5 oz) butter, softened
½ cup honey, warmed
2 eggs, lightly beaten
1¾ cups self-raising flour, sifted
⅔ cup brown sugar
125g (4 oz) dark chocolate, melted and cooled
icing sugar, sifted

Makes 25

METHOD:

1. Preheat oven to 180°C /360°F
2. Place butter, honey, eggs, flour, brown sugar, chocolate and 1 tablespoon of water in a food processor and process until ingredients are combined.
3. Spoon batter into a buttered and lined 23 cm (9 in) square cake tin and bake for 30–35 minutes or until cooked when tested with a skewer. Stand cake in tin for 5 minutes before turning onto a wire rack to cool completely.
4. Dust with icing sugar and cut into squares.

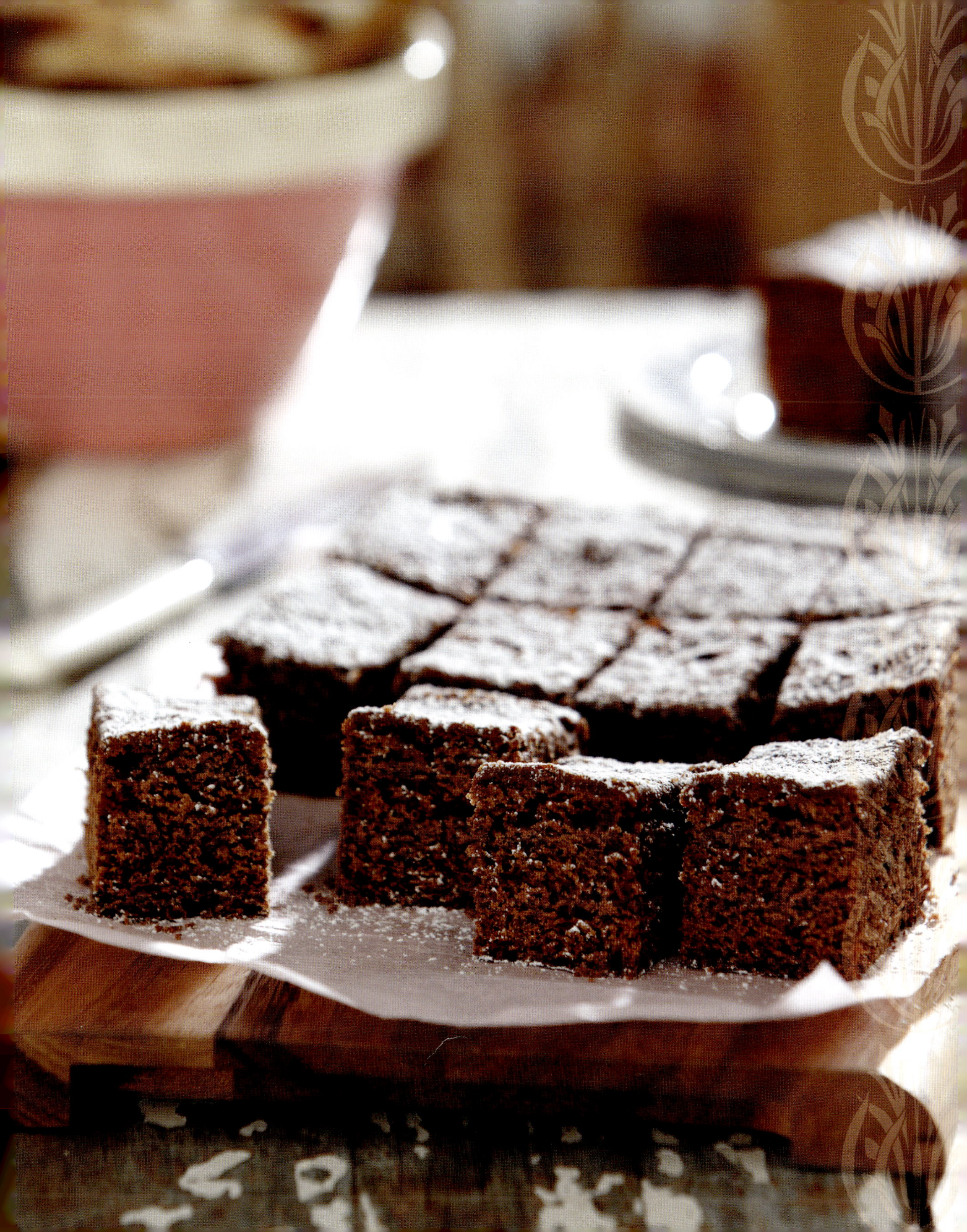

Carrot & Almond Squares

INGREDIENTS:

1 cup wholemeal self-raising flour
¼ cup wheatgerm
1 teaspoon baking soda
1 teaspoon ground cinnamon
1 teaspoon ground nutmeg
½ cup vegetable oil
⅔ cup honey
3 eggs, lightly beaten
1½ cups grated carrot, lightly packed
½ cup chopped walnuts
½ cup well drained, crushed pineapple
almonds
glacé cherries

Makes about 15

METHOD:

1. Preheat oven to 180°C /360°F.
2. Sift flour, wheatgerm, baking soda, cinnamon and nutmeg in a bowl. Beat oil, honey and eggs together until well combined, then pour into the sifted dry ingredients and beat until mixture is smooth, about 1 minute.
3. Stir in grated carrot, walnuts and pineapple and mix well. Spoon mixture into a buttered 28 x 18 cm (11 x 7 in) lamington tin, smoothing the top level with a spatula. Decorate the top with almonds and glacé cherries. Bake for 35–40 minutes or until golden brown. Cool in the tin for 5 minutes, then turn out onto a wire rack to cool. Cut into squares to serve.

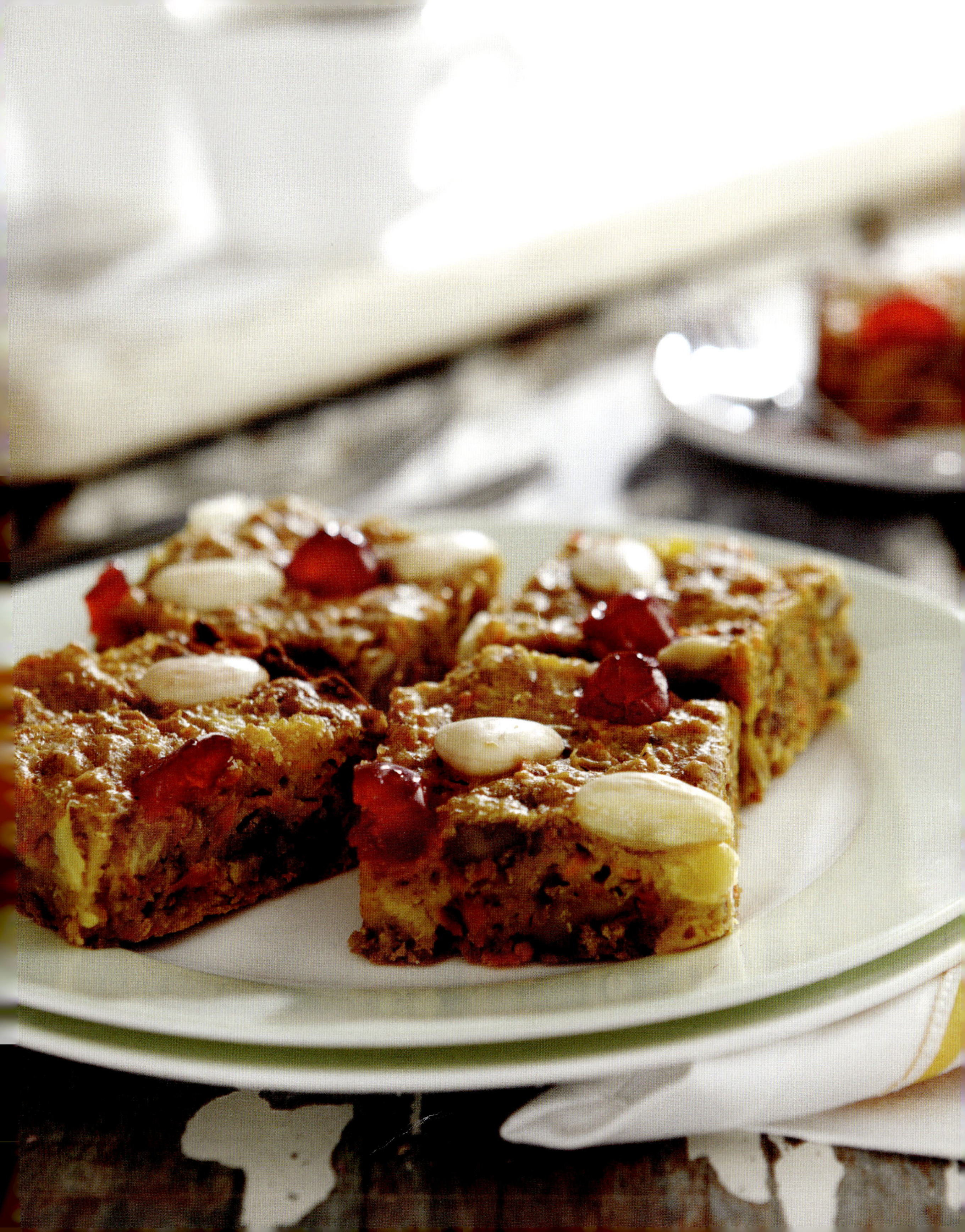

Brandy Apricot Slice

INGREDIENTS:

½ cup dried apricots, chopped
2 tablespoons brandy
100 g (3½ oz) dark chocolate
4 tablespoons butter
3 tablespoons milk
1 egg
¼ cup superfine (caster) sugar
¾ cup all-purpose (plain) flour, sifted
¼ teaspoon baking powder

CHOCOLATE FROSTING
60 g (2 oz) dark chocolate
1 tablespoon milk
1½ cups confectioners' (icing) sugar, sifted
1 tablespoon butter

Makes 16

METHOD:

1 Combine apricots and brandy, set aside for 15 minutes. Melt chocolate and butter together, stir in the milk, egg, sugar, flour and baking powder. Mix well. Stir the apricots through the chocolate mixture.

2 Spoon mixture into a lightly greased 20 cm (8 in) square sandwich pan. Bake at 180°C/360°F for 12–15 minutes or until firm. Cool in the tin. Ice with chocolate frosting.

3 To make the chocolate frosting, melt together dark chocolate and milk, blend in icing sugar and butter. Mix well. Garnish with diced apricots.

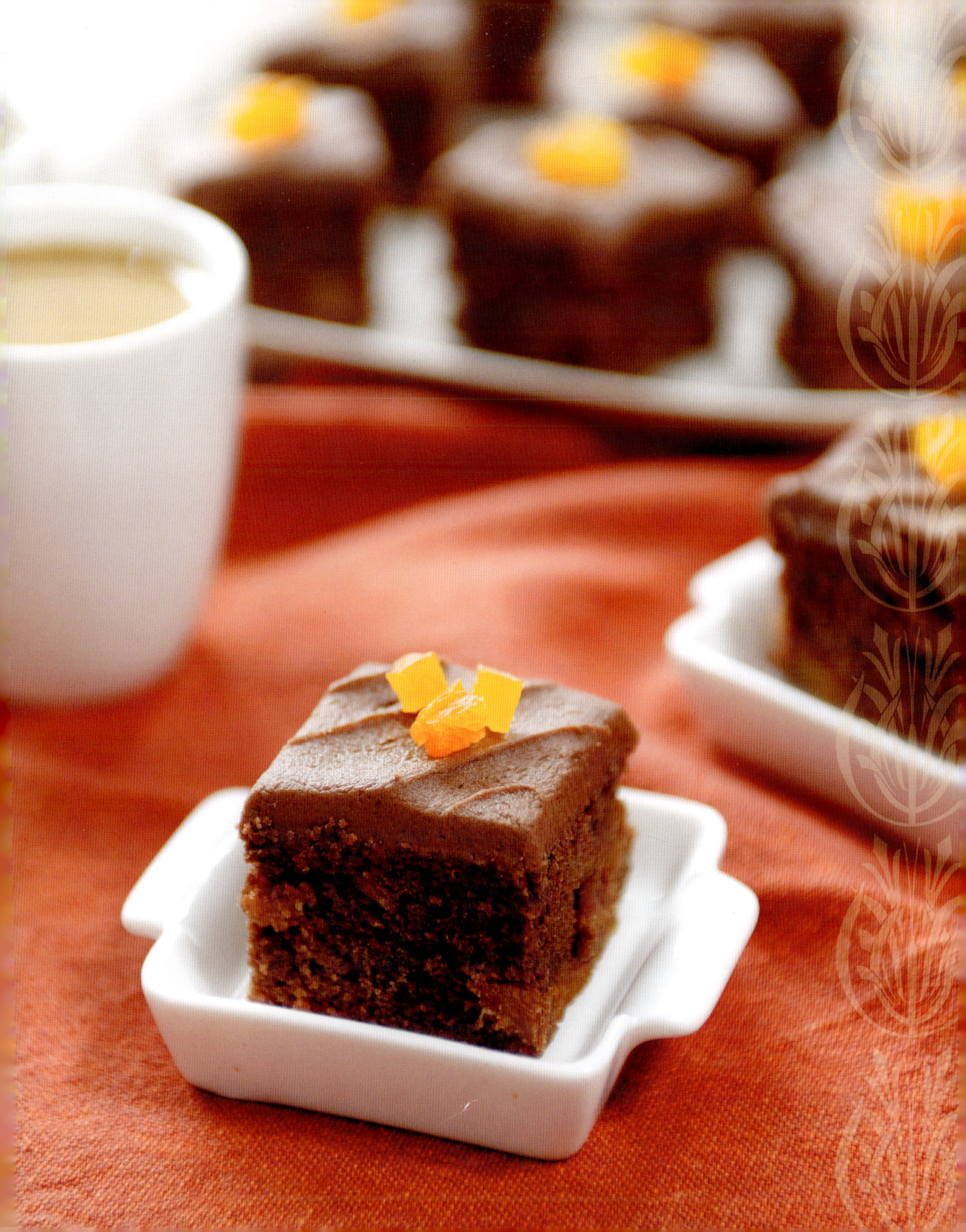

Marzipan Triangles

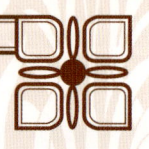

INGREDIENTS:

1 cup rolled oats
½ cup caster sugar
1 cup self-raising flour, sifted
¾ cup ground almonds
1 tablespoon golden syrup
½ cup canola oil
1 egg
 teaspoon almond extract
⅓ cup flaked almonds, to decorate

MARZIPAN

1 cup ground almonds
⅓ cup pure icing sugar
¼ cup caster sugar
3 teaspoons egg white (about half an egg white)
¼ teaspoon almond extract or ½ teaspoon amaretto liqueur
few drops orange blossom water or pure vanilla extract

Makes 42

METHOD:

1. To make the marzipan, sift almonds and sugars into a bowl. Add egg white, almond extract and orange water. Mix to a smooth stiff paste. Wrap in cling wrap. Chill until required.
2. Combine oats, sugar, flour and ground almonds in a bowl. Combine golden syrup, oil, egg and almond extract. Stir into oats mixture. Spread half the mixture evenly over base of a buttered and lined 20 x 30cm (8 x 12 in) lamington pan.
3. Preheat oven to 180°C/360°F. Roll out marzipan and cover oats mixture. Top with remaining oats mixture. Sprinkle with chopped almonds. Press into mixture.
4. Bake for 30 minutes or until golden. Stand for 10 minutes. Cut into triangles.

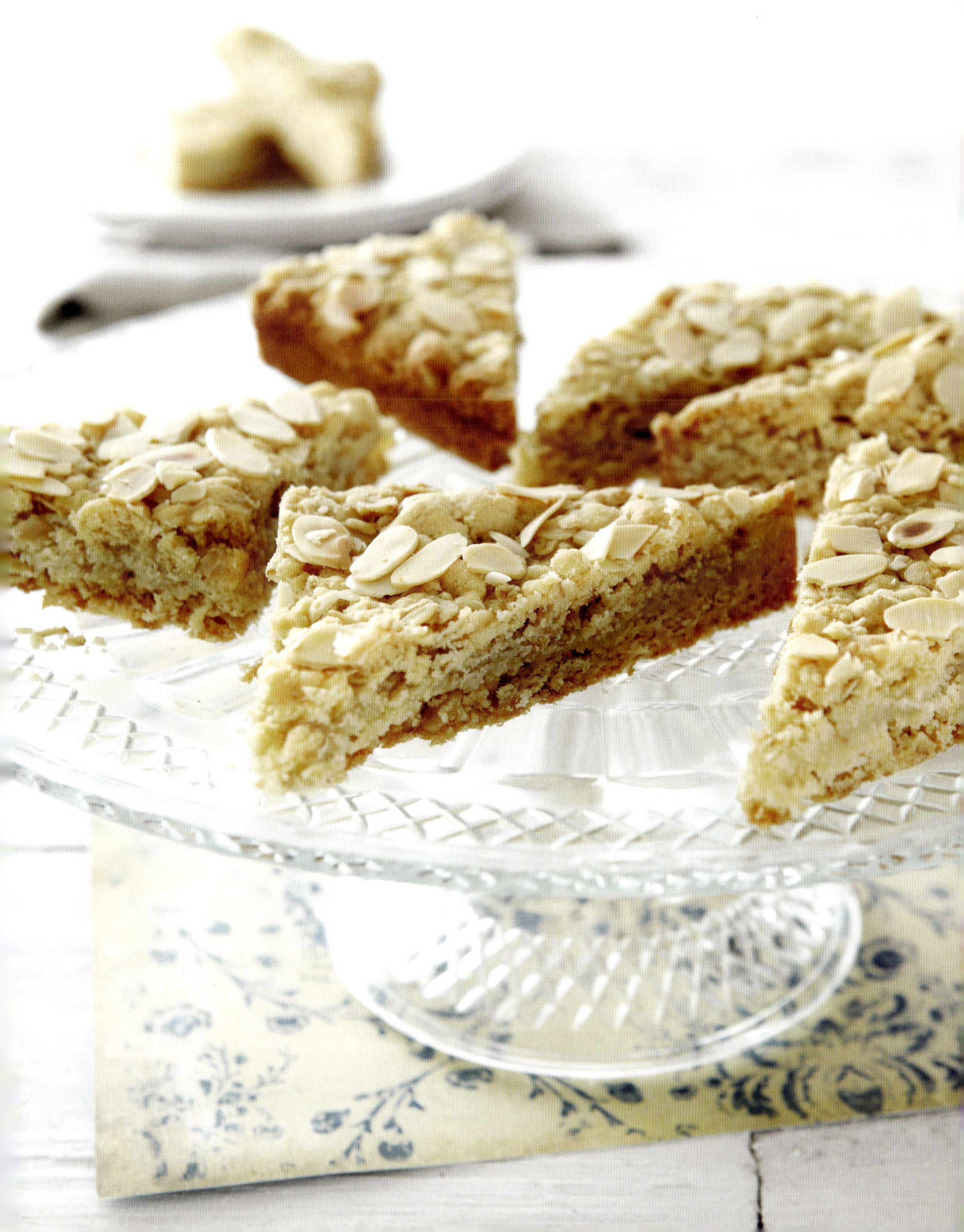

Fruit, Nut & Chocolate Nougat

INGREDIENTS:

edible rice paper

2 egg whites, at room temperature

2½ cups sugar

⅓ cup water

500 g (16 oz) jar glucose syrup

100 g (3½ oz) pistachios, shelled

100 g (3½ oz) dried cranberries

1 teaspoon vanilla extract

½ cup dark chocolate buttons

Makes 12 pieces

METHOD:

1. Line an 18 x 28 cm (7 x 11 in) slab pan with non-stick baking paper, with paper overhanging. Line the base with a sheet of rice paper. Fill the sink with 10 cm (4 in) of cold water. Place the egg whites in a large, clean, dry heatproof bowl.

2. Place the sugar, water and glucose in a medium saucepan over a low heat. Stir constantly, brushing down the sides with a pastry brush dipped in warm water, until the sugar dissolves. Place a sugar thermometer in the pan, increase heat to high and bring to the boil. Reduce heat to medium-high and boil, uncovered, without stirring. When the syrup reaches about 120°C/240°F, use a whisk to beat the egg whites until firm peaks form.

3. When the sugar syrup reaches 140°C/280°F, remove from heat and place the base in the sink until the bubbles subside. With the beater at medium speed, slowly pour syrup into the egg whites in a thin stream.

4. Once the syrup is incorporated, whisk until it is thick and glossy. With a spoon, mix in the other ingredients until well combined, working quickly. Spoon the nougat into the lined pan, smoothing the surface. Place a sheet of rice paper over the top and press down. Set aside in a cool, dry place for 6 hours or until set. To serve, cut into 2.5 cm (1 in) pieces with a sharp knife.

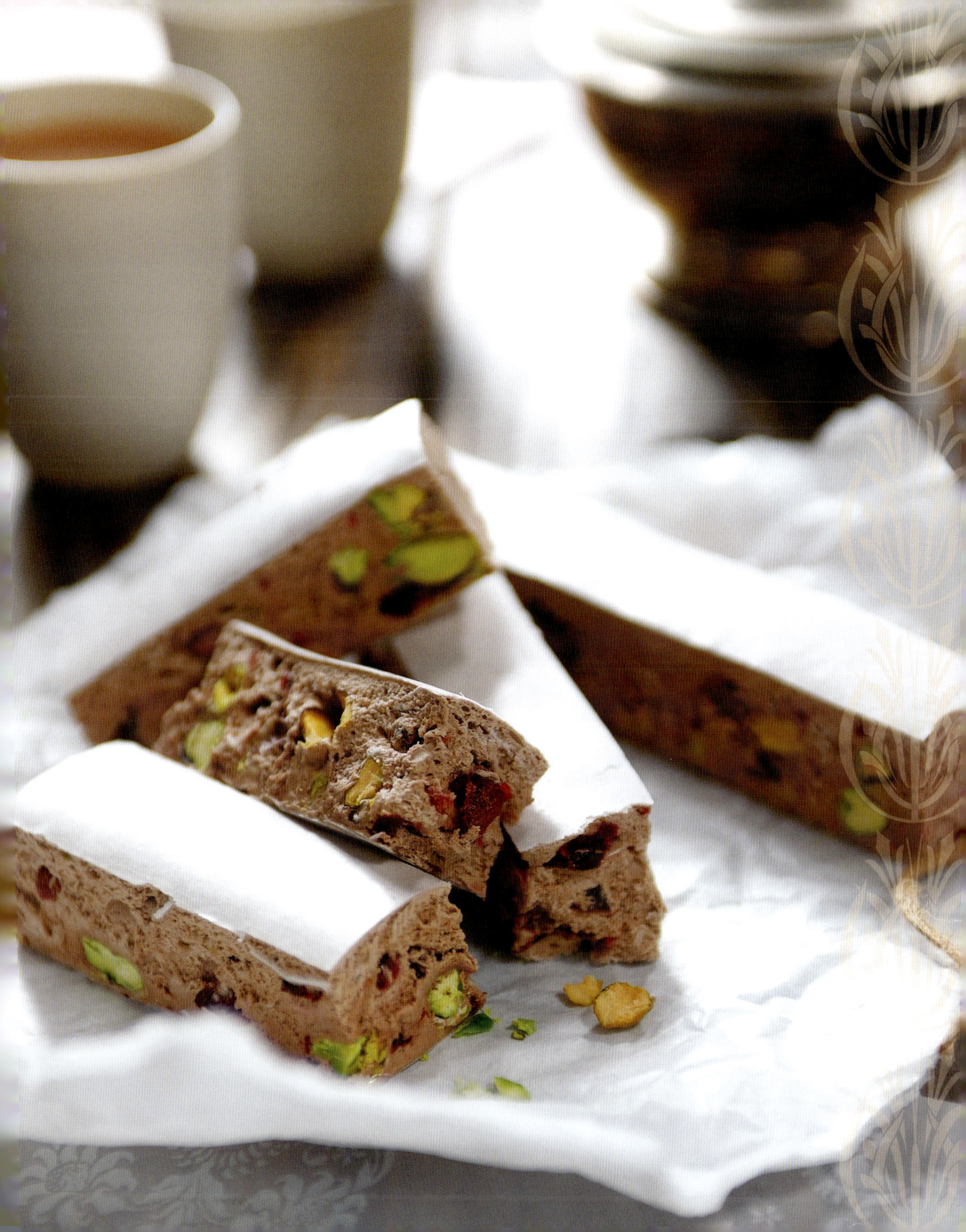

Chocolate Pecan Fingers

INGREDIENTS:

90 g (3oz) dark chocolate

125 g (4 oz) butter

2 teaspoons instant coffee powder

2 eggs

¾ cup superfine (caster) sugar

½ teaspoon vanilla

½ cup all-purpose (plain) flour

¾ cup pecans, chopped

confectioners' (icing) sugar

Makes about 15 fingers

METHOD:

1. Melt the chocolate and butter together over hot water, stir in the coffee powder and allow to cool slightly.
2. In a medium sized bowl whisk the eggs until foamy and add the sugar and vanilla. Fold the chocolate mixture through the eggs. Stir in the flour and pecans and mix until just blended.
3. Spoon the mixture into a lightly greased 20 cm (8 in) square cake pan. Bake at 180°C/ 360°F for 25 minutes or until cake springs back when touched. Cool in the tin. Dust with sifted icing sugar and cut into fingers to serve.

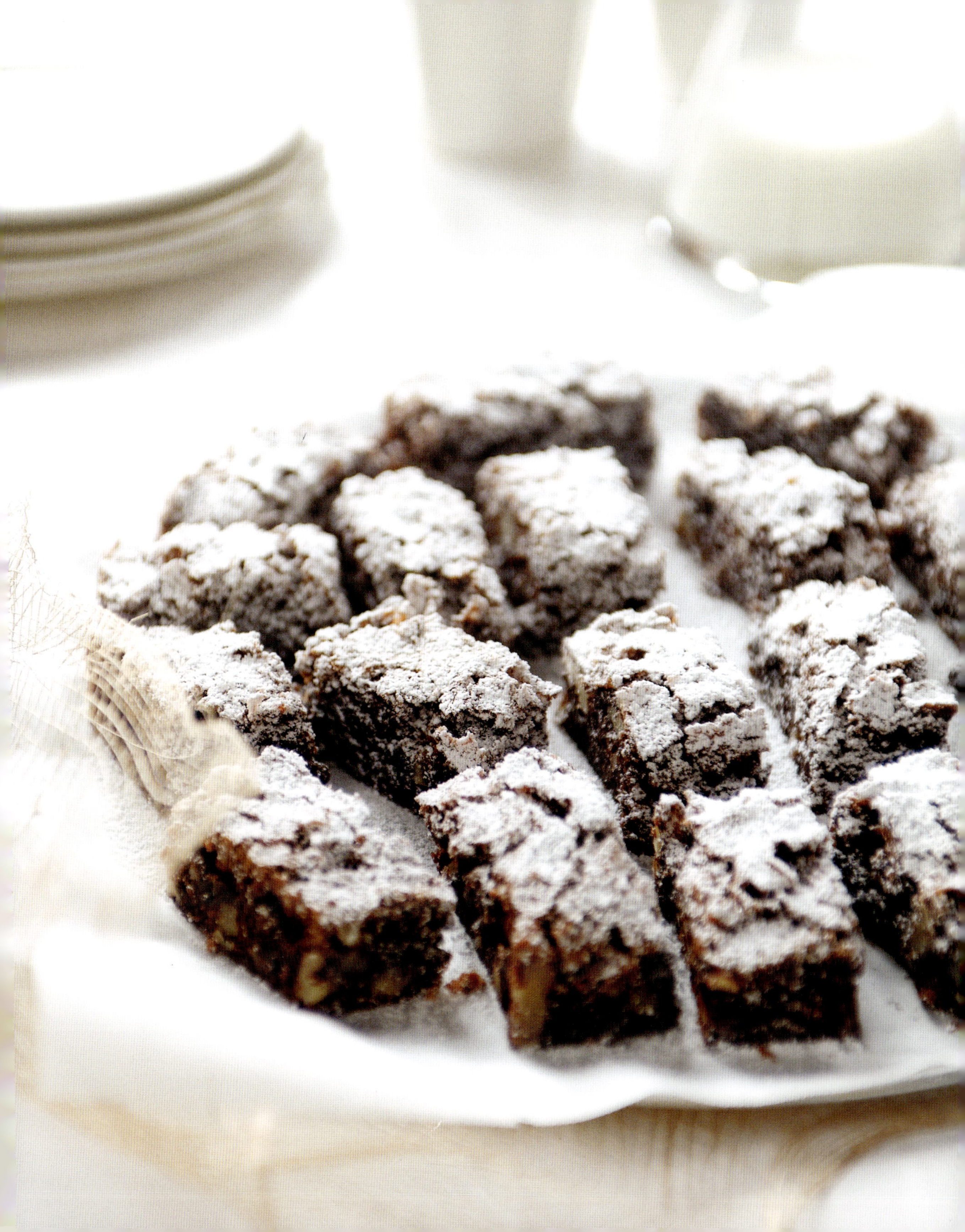

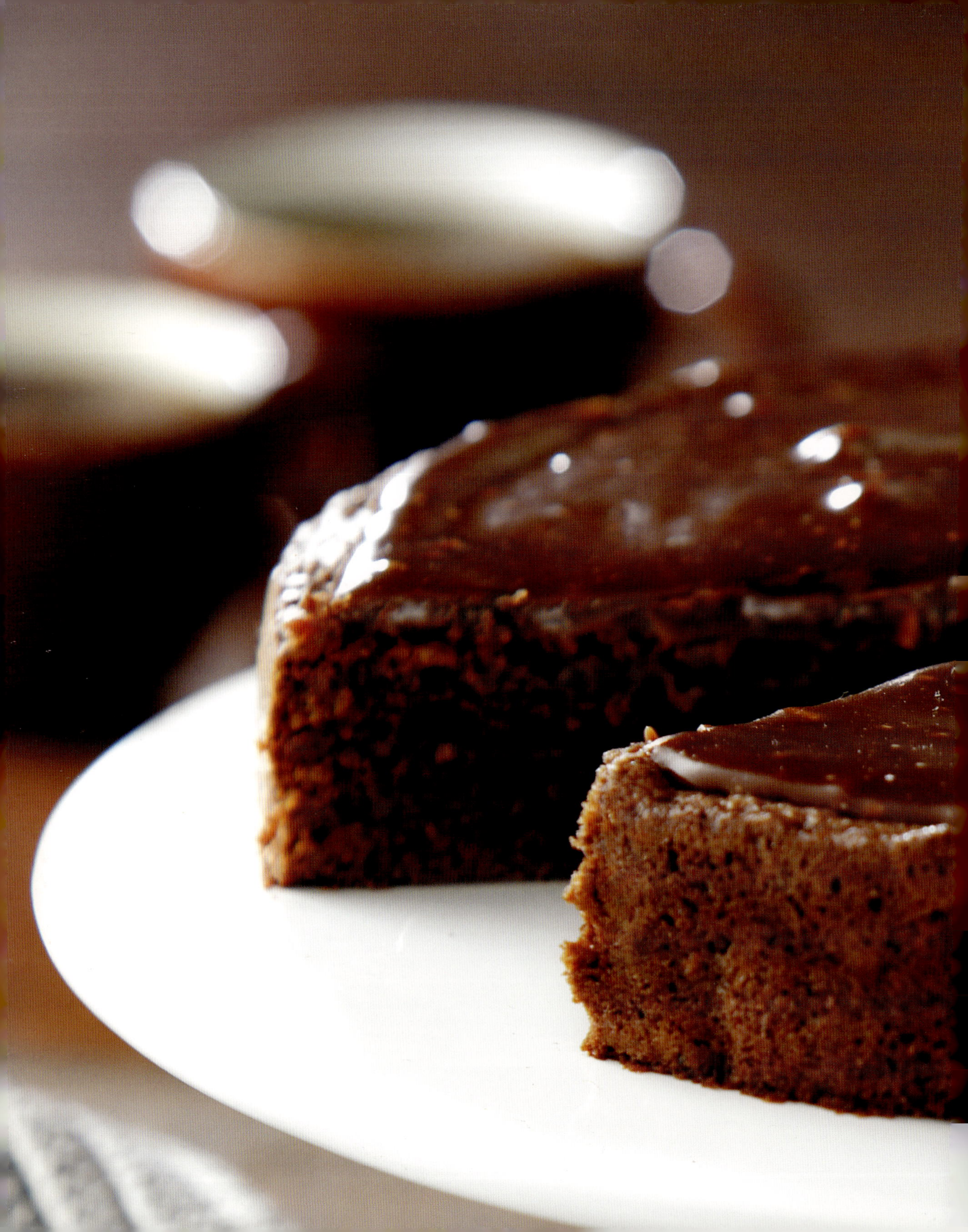

CAKES

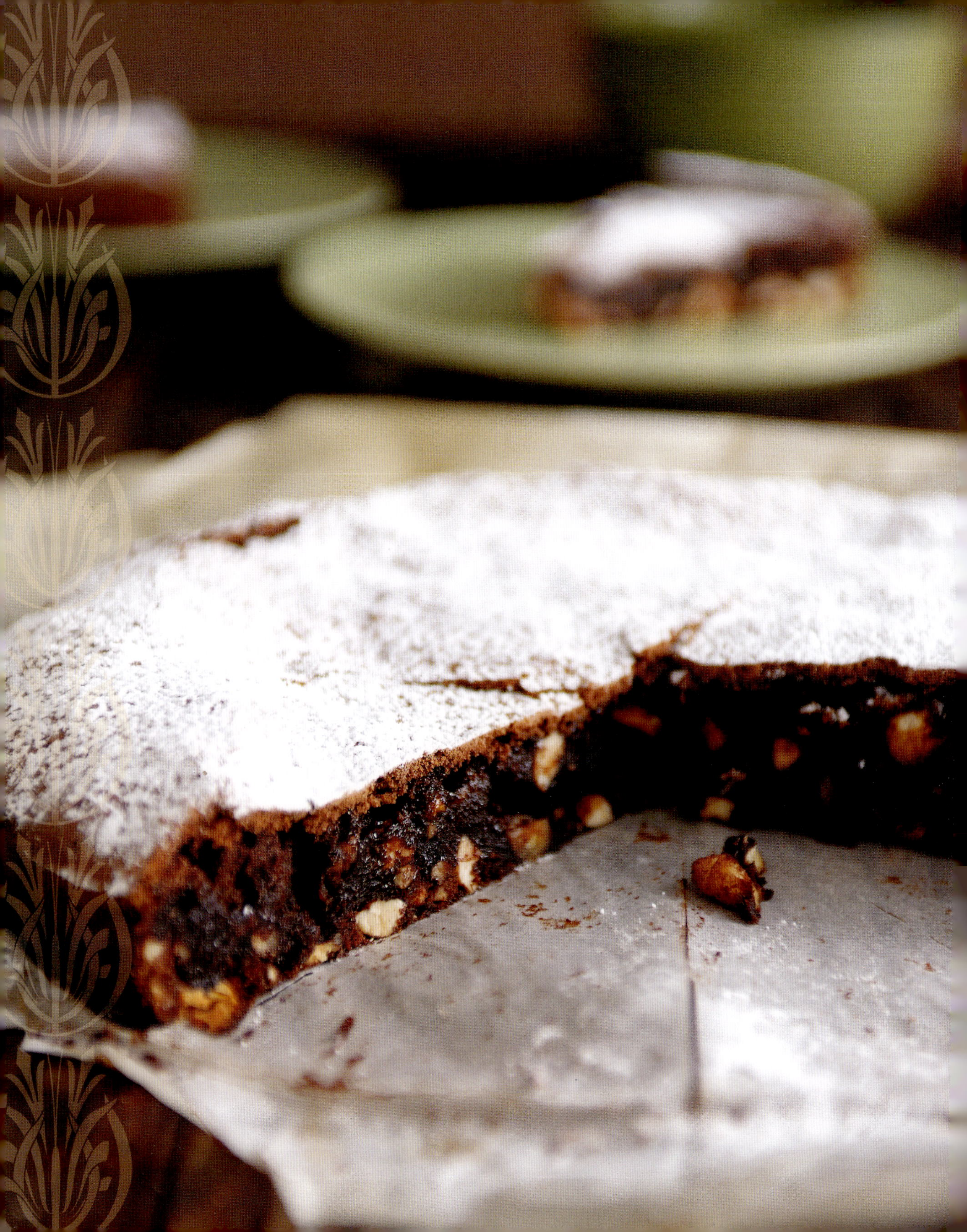

Chocolate Hazelnut Torte

To toast hazelnuts, place nuts on a baking tray and bake for 10 minutes or until skins begin to split. Place on a tea towel and rub to remove skins. Place in a food processor and process to roughly chop.

INGREDIENTS:

250 g (9 oz) dark chocolate, broken
into pieces
6 eggs, separated
1 cup sugar
325 g (11½ oz) hazelnuts, toasted
and roughly chopped
1 tablespoon rum
icing sugar, for dusting

Serves 8

METHOD:

1. Preheat the oven to 190°C/375°F. Place chocolate in a heatproof bowl set over a saucepan of simmering water and heat, stirring, until chocolate melts. Remove bowl from pan and cool slightly.
2. Place egg yolks and sugar in a bowl and beat until thick and pale. Fold chocolate, hazelnuts and rum into egg mixture.
3. Place egg whites into a clean bowl and beat until stiff peaks form. Fold egg whites into chocolate mixture. Pour mixture into a buttered d and lined 23 cm (9 in) springform tin and bake for 50 minutes or until cooked when tested with a skewer. Cool cake in tin. Just prior to serving, dust cake with icing sugar.

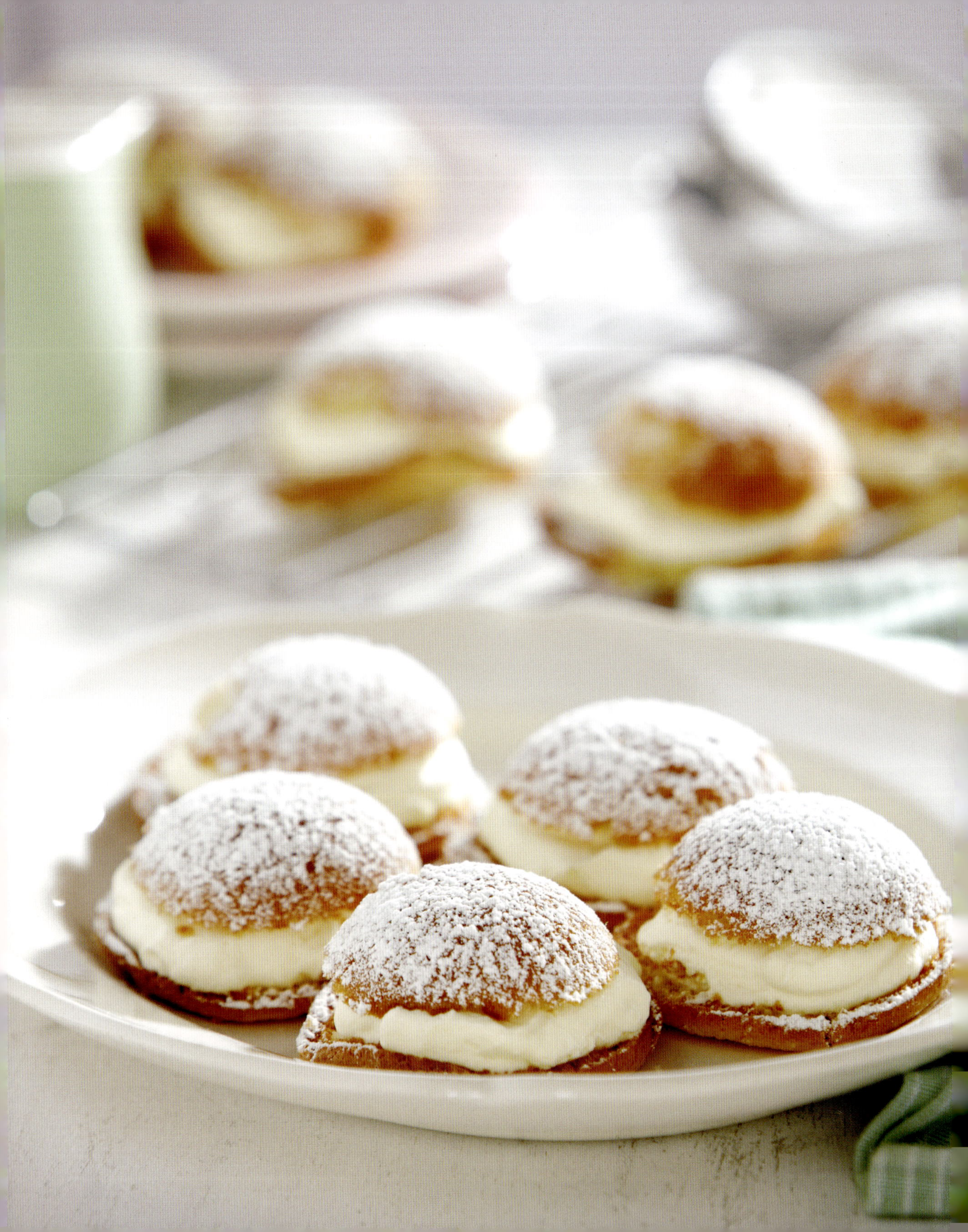

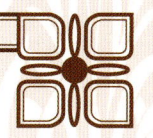

Powder Puffs

INGREDIENTS:

2 eggs, separated
pinch of salt
⅓ cup caster sugar
few drops of vanilla extract
½ cup self-raising flour, sifted with 2 tablespoons cornflour
whipped cream
icing sugar, to dust

Makes about 6-8

METHOD:

1. Preheat oven to 190°C/380°F.
2. Beat the egg whites and salt together until stiff. Add the sugar gradually and beat well between each addition until thick and glossy. Beat in the egg yolks and vanilla and fold in the sifted flours.
3. Spoon or pipe into buttered round-based patty tins and bake in the centre of the oven for 10–15 minutes. Allow to cool. Split in half, sandwich together with cream and dust with icing sugar.

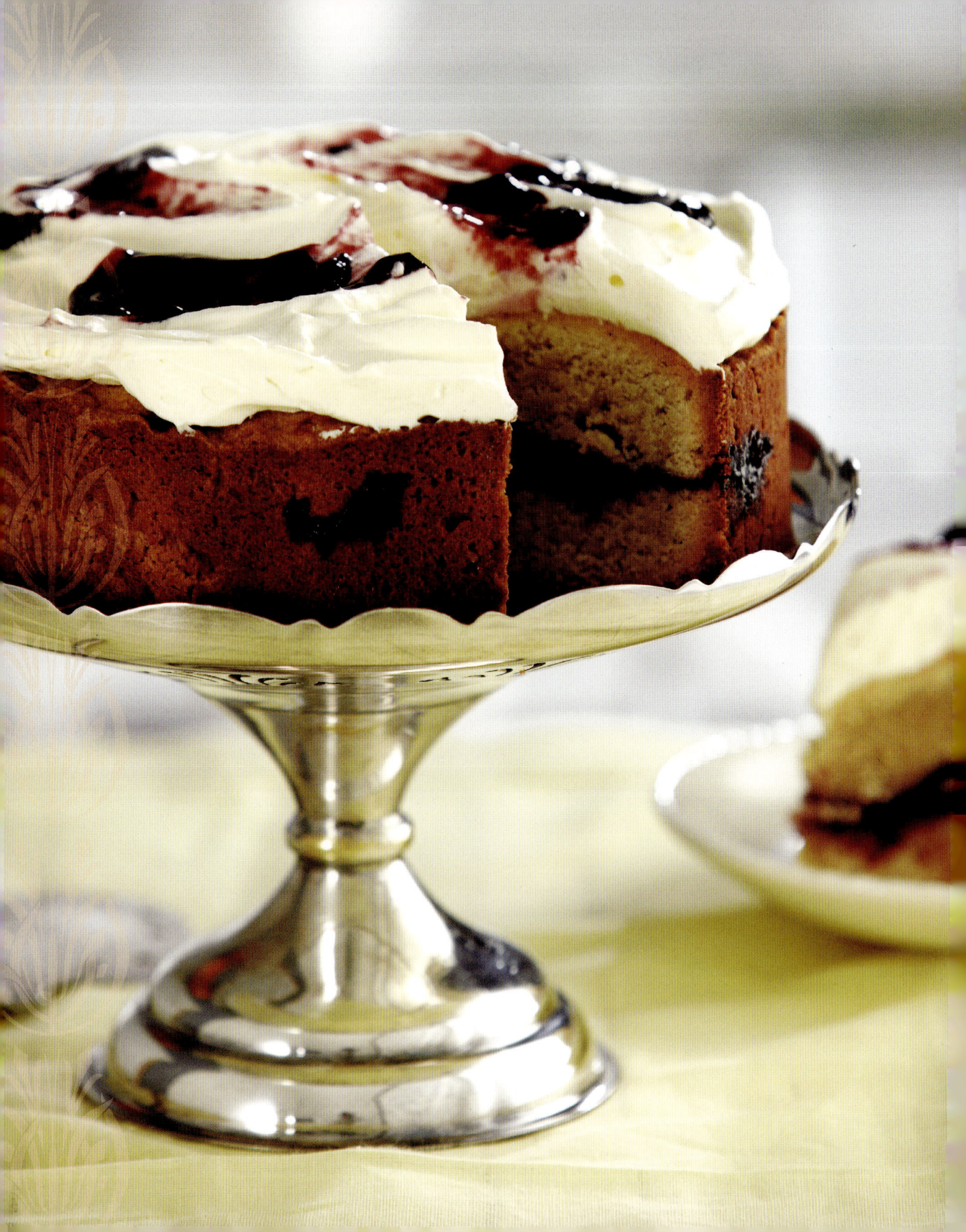

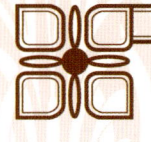

Cherry Almond Cake

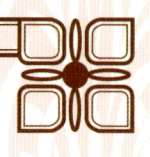

INGREDIENTS:

250 g (8 oz) butter or margarine

1 cup superfine (caster) sugar

2 eggs

2 cups plain flour

½ teaspoon ground cinnamon

½ teaspoon ground cloves

250 g (8 oz) ground almonds

1 tablespoon gin

5 tablespoons cherry jam

1 cup whipped cream

Serves 12

METHOD:

1. Preheat oven to 180°C/350°F.
2. Beat butter until soft, add sugar and continue beating until light and fluffy. Add eggs one at a time, beating well after each addition.
3. Sift flour, cinnamon, cloves and ground almonds together. Add to creamed mixture with gin, mixing with a wooden spoon until ingredients are well combined.
4. Spoon half the cake mixture into an 20 cm (8 in) round deep cake tin that has been base-lined with buttered baking paper. Spread evenly with 3 tablespoons of the jam, then spread evenly with remaining cake mixture.
5. Bake for 1 hour or until pale golden. Cool in the tin for 5 minutes, then turn out onto a wire rack to cool. Spread top of cake with cream and decorate with remaining jam.

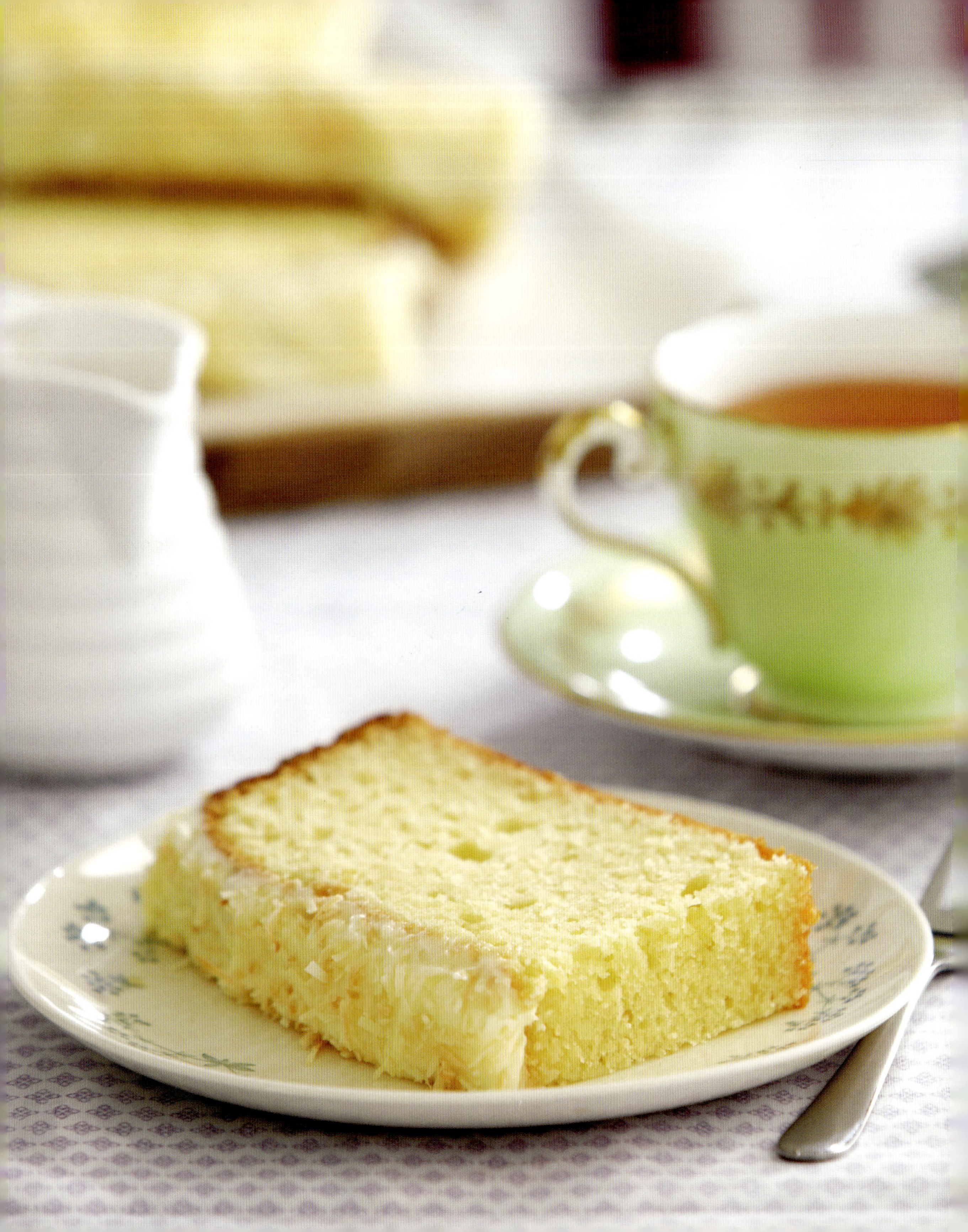

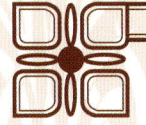

Madeira Cake

INGREDIENTS:

250 g (8 oz) butter, softened
2 teaspoons vanilla extract
1 teaspoon finely grated lemon zest
2 cups caster sugar
6 eggs
1½ cups plain flour
1 cup self-raising flour
1 cup natural yoghurt

LEMON ICING

1½ cups icing sugar, sifted
1 tablespoon lemon juice
2 tablespoons butter, softened
2 tablespoons shredded coconut, toasted

Makes 1 cake

METHOD:

1. Preheat oven to 160°C /325°F
2. Place butter, vanilla extract and lemon zest in a bowl and beat until light and fluffy. Gradually add caster sugar, beating well after each addition until mixture is creamy. Add eggs one at a time, beating well after each addition.
3. Sift together flour and self-raising flour. Fold flour mixture and yoghurt, alternately into butter mixture. Spoon batter into a buttered and lined 23 cm (9 in) square cake tin and bake for 1 hour or until cake is cooked when tested with a skewer.
4. Stand in tin for 10 minutes before turning onto a wire rack to cool completely.
5. To make icing, place icing sugar, lemon juice and butter in a bowl and mix until smooth. Add a little more lemon juice if necessary. Spread icing over cake and sprinkle with coconut.

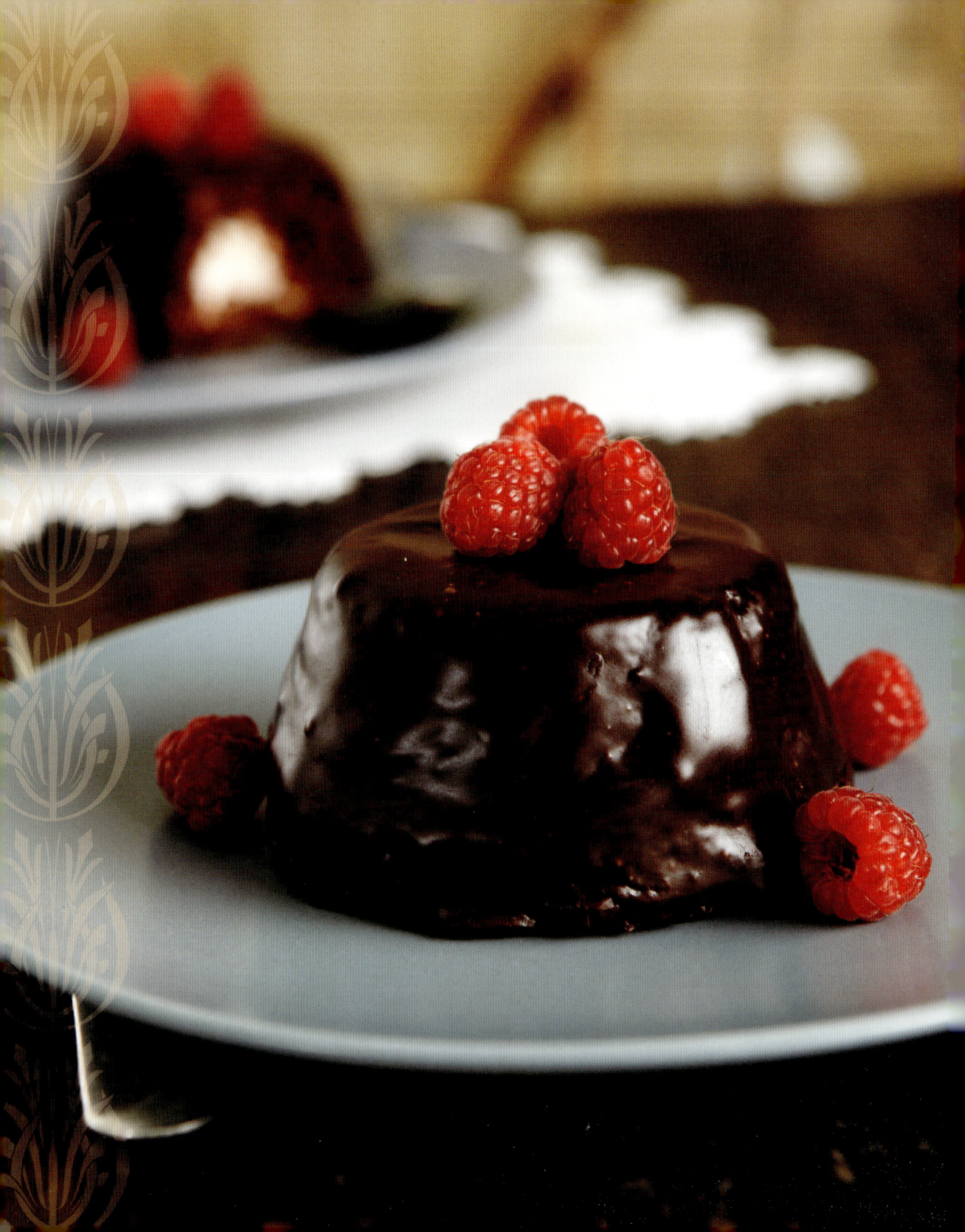

Raspberry Chocolate Truffle Cakes

INGREDIENTS:

½ cup cocoa powder, sifted
125 g (4 oz) butter
1¾ cups superfine (caster) sugar
2 eggs
1⅔ cups self-raising (self-rising) flour, sifted
400 g (14 oz) dark chocolate, melted
fresh raspberries
Raspberry cream
125 g (4 oz) raspberries, puréed and sieved
½ cup thickened cream, whipped

Makes 8

METHOD:

1. Preheat oven to 180°C/350°F.
2. Combine cocoa powder and 1 cup boiling water. Mix to dissolve and set aside to cool.
3. Place butter and sugar in a bowl and beat until light and fluffy. Beat in eggs, one at a time, adding a little flour with each egg. Fold remaining flour and cocoa mixture, alternately, into creamed butter mixture.
4. Spoon mixture into eight lightly buttered ½-cup capacity ramekins or large muffin tins. Bake for 20–25 minutes or until cakes are cooked when tested with a skewer. Cool for 5 minutes, then turn onto wire racks to cool. Turn cakes upside down and scoop out centre, leaving a 12 mm (½ in) shell. Spread each cake with chocolate to cover top and sides, then place right way up on a wire rack.
5. To make cream, fold raspberry purée into cream. Spoon cream into a piping bag fitted with a large nozzle. Carefully turn cakes upside down and pipe in cream to fill cavity. Place right way up on individual serving plates. Garnish with fresh raspberries.

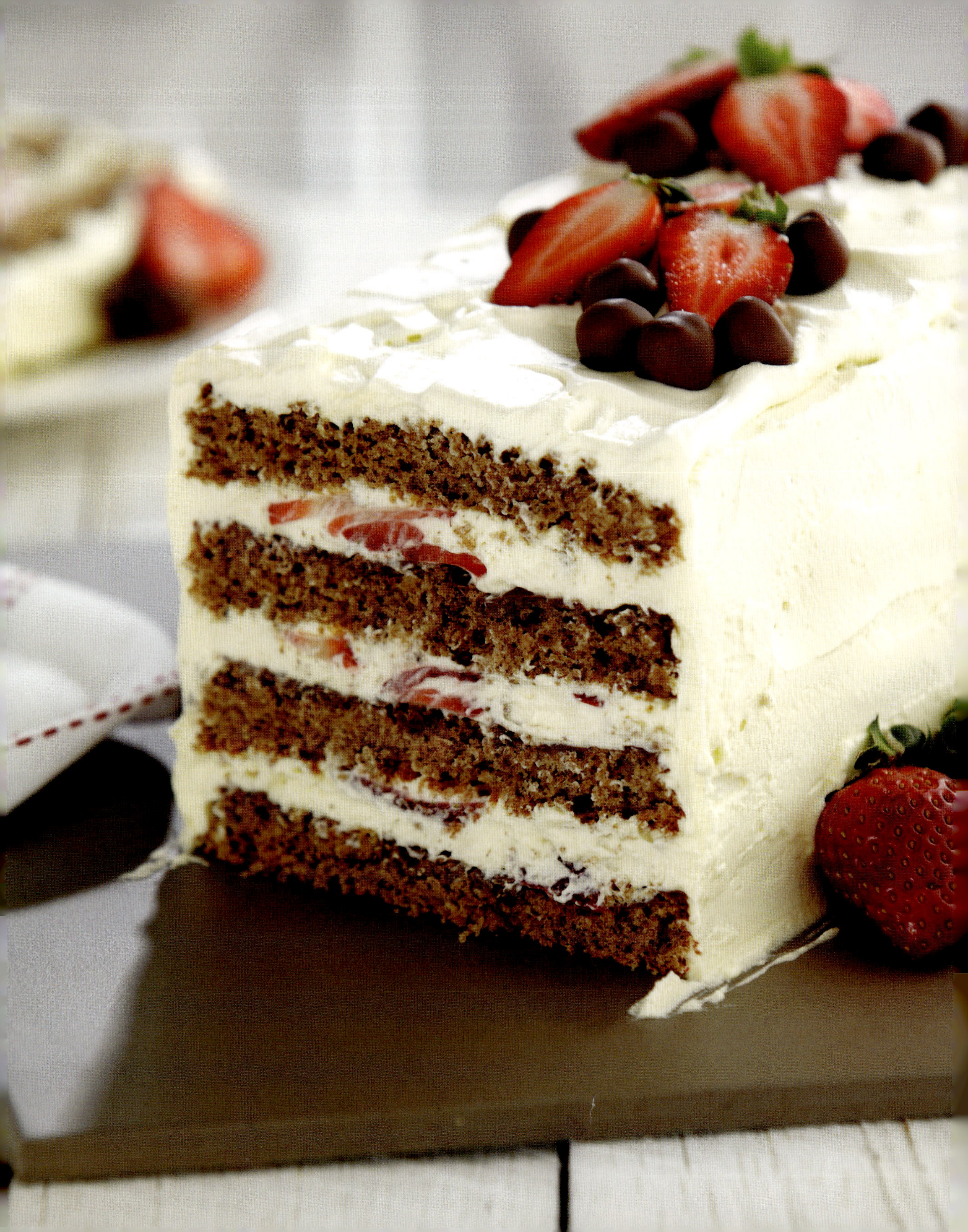

Strawberry Hazelnut Torte

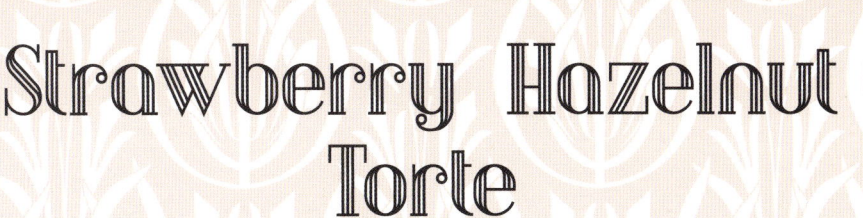

INGREDIENTS:

5 eggs
½ cup sugar
4 tablespoons plain flour
1 teaspoon coffee powder
1 teaspoon ground allspice
90 g (3 oz) ground hazelnuts
Filling and topping
20 whole hazelnuts
150 g (5 oz) chocolate, melted with 60 g (2 oz) copha
2 cups thickened cream
4 tablespoons brandy
½ cup confectioners' (icing) sugar, sifted
2 punnets strawberries, sliced

Serves 12

METHOD:

1. Preheat oven to 180°C/350°F.
2. Beat eggs until light and fluffy, gradually add sugar, beating well between each addition. Sift together the flour, coffee powder and allspice. Fold hazelnuts and sifted ingredients gently into egg mixture. Pour evenly into two square, well buttered and lined 23 cm (9 in) sandwich tins.
3. Bake in the centre of the oven for 10–15 minutes. Remove from oven, cool, then replace in oven for a further 5 minutes. Cut tortes in half to form four oblong layers.
4. To make the filling and topping, dip hazelnuts into chocolate mixture and allow to set. Spread remaining chocolate evenly over three torte layers.
5. Whip together the cream, brandy and icing sugar. Add the strawberries to half the cream mixture. Mix thoroughly and spread onto the three chocolate covered layers. Place these layers on top of each other, finishing with the uncovered layer. Spread remaining cream over the assembled torte and decorate with cream, chocolate hazelnuts and extra strawberries. Refrigerate for 2 hours before serving.

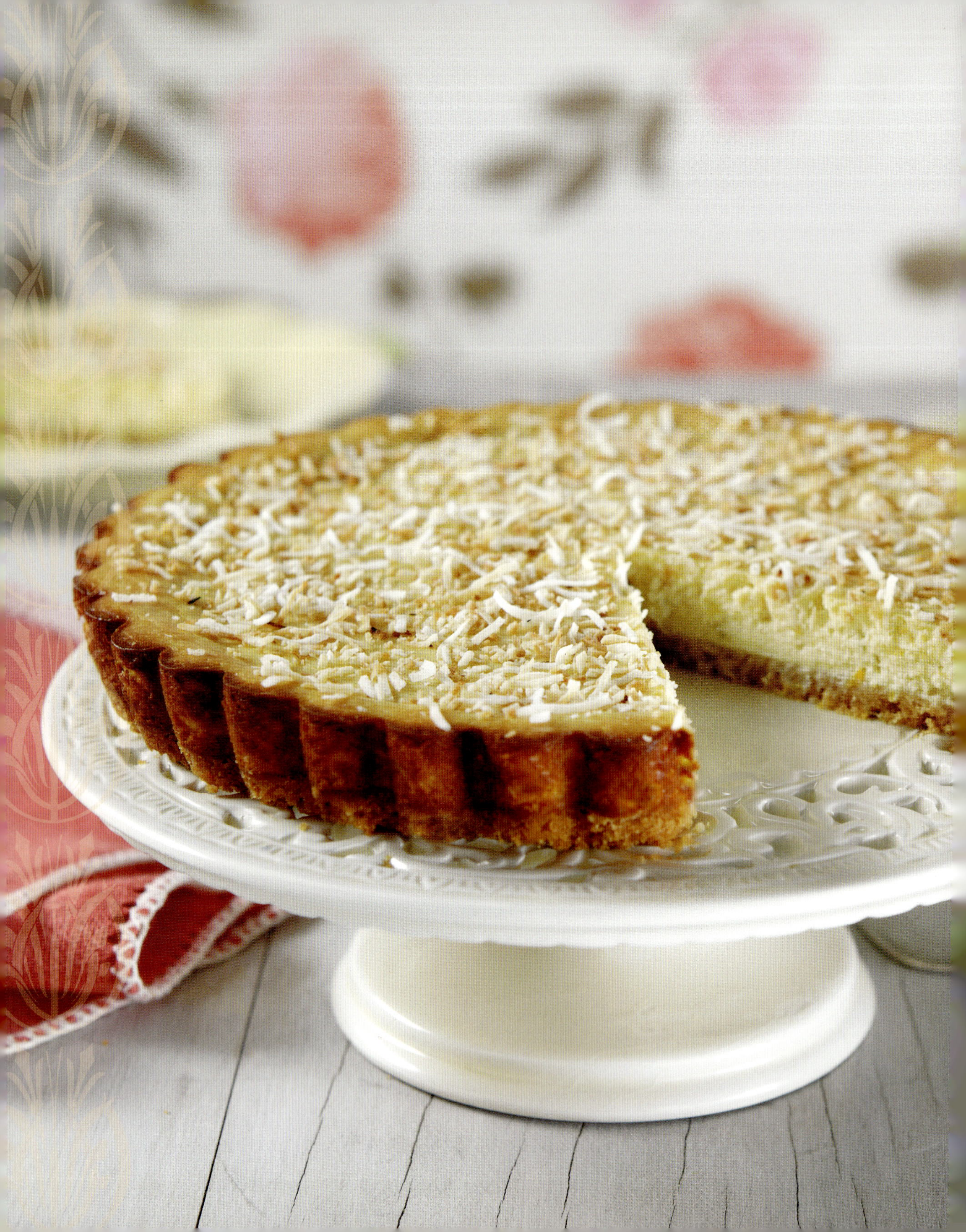

Orange & Lime Cheesecake

INGREDIENTS:

1 cup plain sweet biscuits, crushed
60 g (2 oz) butter, melted
shredded coconut, toasted
Orange and lime filling
250 g (9 oz) cream cheese, softened
2 tablespoons brown sugar
1½ teaspoons finely grated orange zest
1½ teaspoons finely grated lime zest
3 teaspoons orange juice
3 teaspoons lime juice
1 egg, lightly beaten
½ cup sweetened condensed milk
2 tablespoons double cream, whipped

Serves 8

METHOD:

1 Preheat oven to 180°C/360°F.
2 Place the biscuits and butter in a bowl and mix to combine. Press the biscuit mixture over the base and up the sides of a well-buttered 23 cm (9 in) flan tin with a removable base. Bake for 5–8 minutes, then cool.
3 To make the orange and lime filling, place the cream cheese, sugar, orange and lime zests and juices in a bowl and beat until creamy. Beat in the egg, then mix in the condensed milk and fold in the cream.
4 Spoon the filling into the prepared biscuit case and bake for 25–30 minutes or until just firm. Turn the oven off and cool the cheesecake in the oven with the door ajar. Chill before serving. Serve decorated with the toasted coconut.

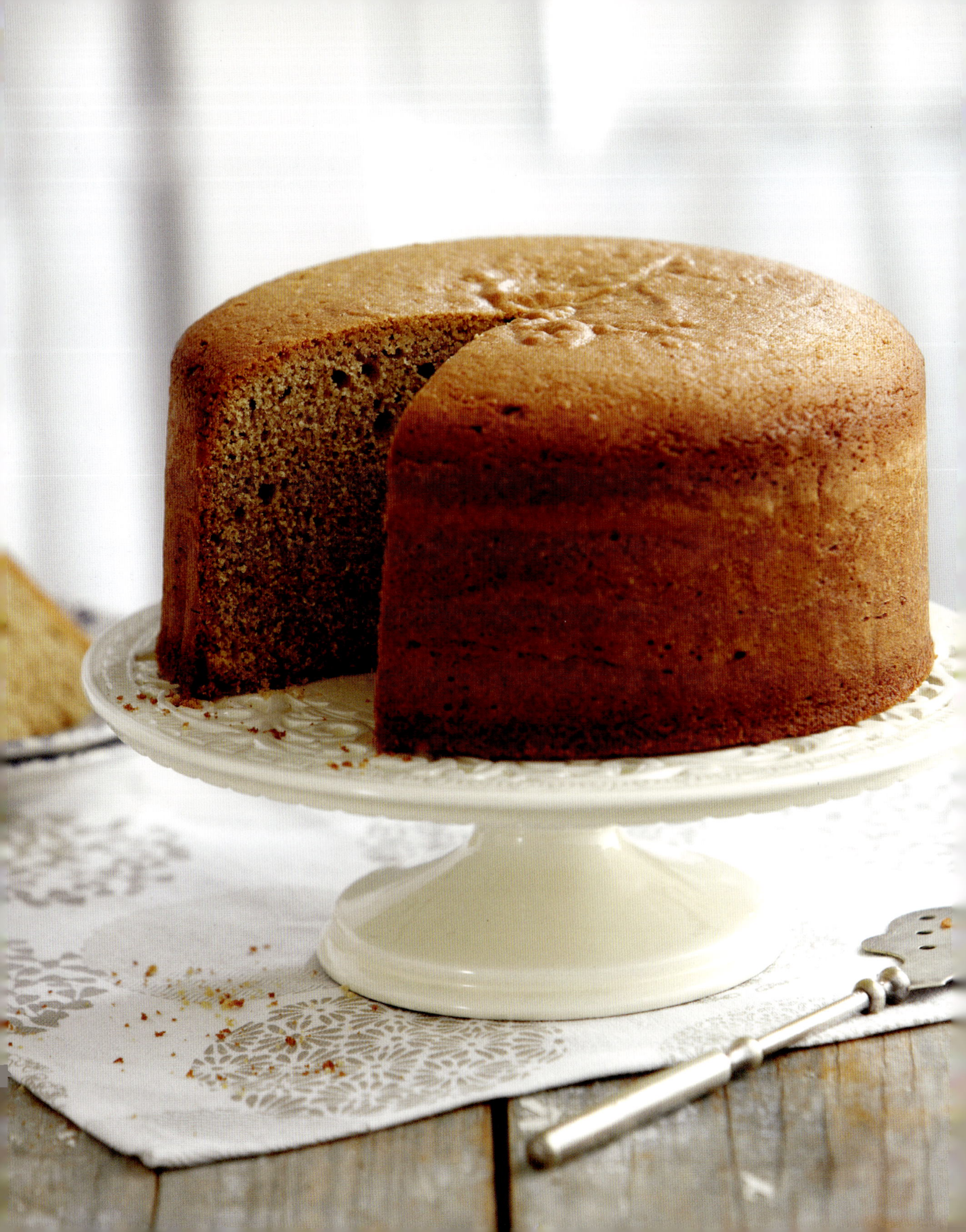

Dutch Spice Cake

INGREDIENTS:

125 g (4 oz) butter
1 1 cups brown sugar
4 eggs, beaten
½ cup milk
2½ cups plain flour
1 teaspoon salt
1½ teaspoons baking powder
2 teaspoons ground cinnamon
¼ teaspoon ground cloves
¼ teaspoon ground nutmeg

Makes 1 cake

METHOD:

1 Preheat oven to 360°F/180°C.
2 Place butter and sugar in a bowl and beat until light and fluffy. Add eggs and milk and beat well.
3 Sift flour, salt, baking powder, cinnamon, cloves and nutmeg together into butter mixture and mix well.
4 Spoon batter into a buttered and lined 20 cm (8 in) round cake tin and bake for 1 hour or until cooked when tested with skewer. Stand in tin for 5 minutes before turning onto a wire rack to cool.

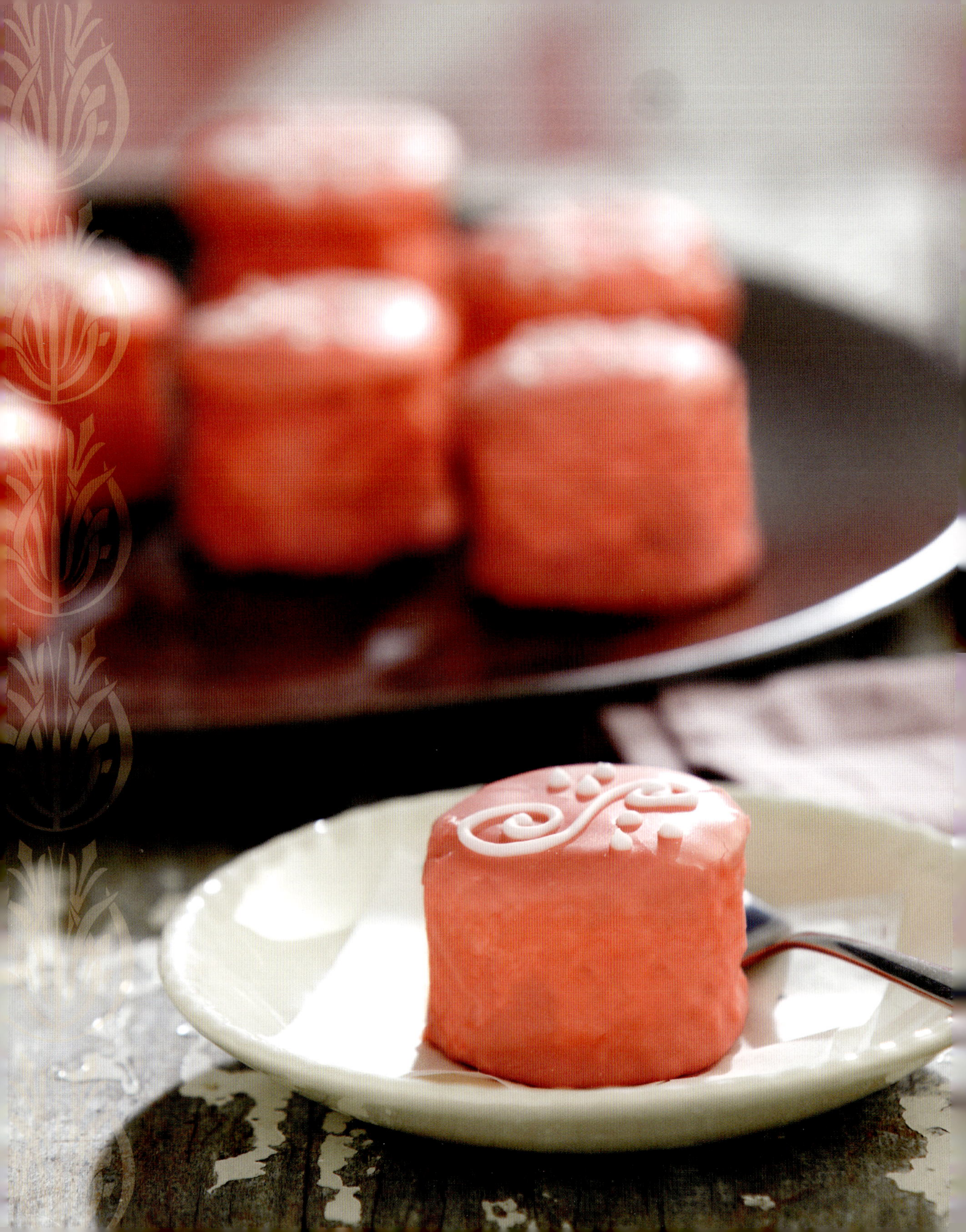

Petits Fours

INGREDIENTS:

4 eggs
¾ cup caster sugar
1¼ cups self-raising flour
pinch of salt
1 teaspoon butter or margarine, melted

GLACÉ ICING
2 cups icing sugar, sifted
2 teaspoons butter or margarine
few drops of vanilla extract
red food colouring

Makes about 15

METHOD:

1. Preheat oven to 190°C/ 375°F.
2. Beat eggs and sugar together for 8–10 minutes or until mixture is thick and creamy. Sift flour and salt together three times and lightly fold through egg mixture.
3. Mix butter and ⅓ cup boiling water together, pour around the edge of mixture and, using a metal spoon, gently fold in. Pour mixture into a 28 x 18 cm (11 x 7 in) lamington tin that has been buttered and lined with buttered baking paper. Bake for 20 minutes or until cake springs back when lightly touched. Turn out onto a wire rack to cool.
4. To make the glacé icing, place icing sugar into a heatproof bowl over a pan of simmering water. Make a well in the centre of icing sugar, add 2 tablespoons boiling water, then the butter and vanilla extract. Stir slowly until well combined, smooth and shiny. Remove 2 tablespoons icing, set aside for decorating. Colour remaining icing pink using a few drops of red food colouring.
5. Using a biscuit cutter, cut cake into 5 cm (2 in) rounds. Place rounds on a wire rack over a piece of paper or tray to catch excess icing. Spread top and sides of cakes with the pink glacé icing and allow to set. Place reserved white icing in a piping bag fitted with a writing tube. Pipe a design on each one.

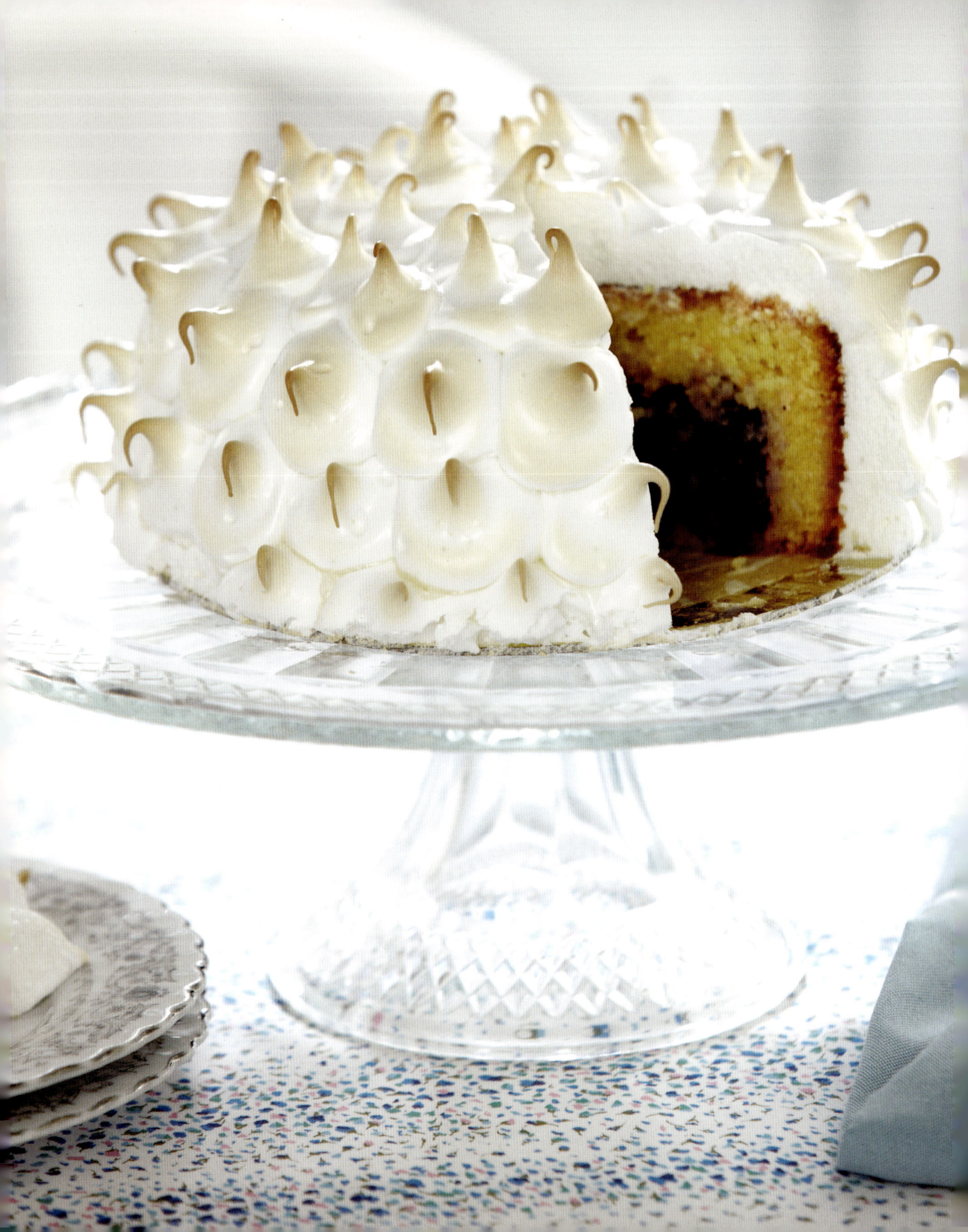

Washington Surprise

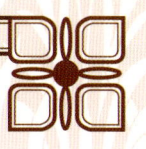

INGREDIENTS:

125 g (4 oz) butter
½ cup caster sugar
grated zest and juice of ¼ orange
2 eggs, beaten
1 cup self-raising flour, sifted with pinch of salt
300 g (10 oz) canned cranberries, drained
300 g (10 oz) canned blueberries, drained
2 tablespoons brandy
Meringue
5 egg whites
2 cups pure icing sugar, sifted

Serves 8–10

METHOD:

1 Preheat the oven to 180°C/360°F.

2 Cream butter and sugar until light and fluffy. Add orange zest and juice and mix well. Add eggs, a little at a time, and beat thoroughly. Fold in the sifted flour and pour mixture into a buttered 18 cm (7 in) round cake tin. Bake for 45–50 minutes.

3 When cooked, turn out onto an ovenproof plate and cut out a piece of cake from the base to make a hollow large enough to hold the berry mixture. Combine the fruit and brandy and fill the sponge. Replace cake piece and press down to form a flat lid.

4 To prepare the meringue, combine egg whites and icing sugar in a bowl over hot water and whisk until stiff peaks are formed. Pipe the meringue decoratively on the sponge to encase completely. Place in the upper half of the oven at 260°C/500°F or under a hot grill to brown.

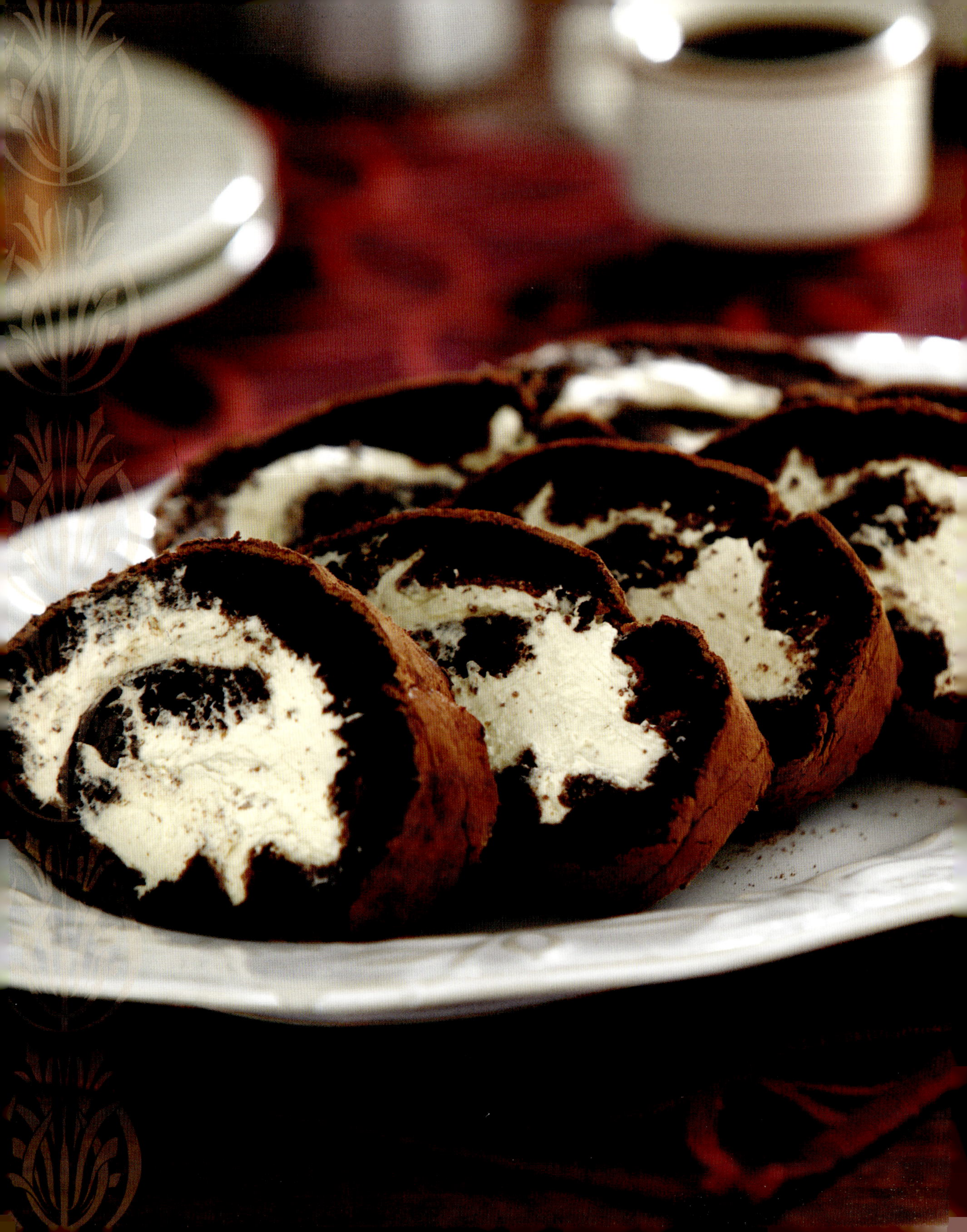

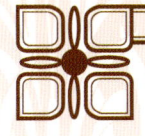

Mocha Mousse Roll

INGREDIENTS:

170 g (6 oz) dark chocolate, grated
60 g (2 oz) butter
5 eggs, separated
2 tablespoons Tia Maria
⅓ cup caster sugar
2 tablespoons cocoa powder
1 tablespoon instant coffee powder
1 cup thickened cream
1 tablespoon Tia Maria, extra

Serves 8

METHOD:

1. Preheat oven to 180°C/ 360°F.
2. Melt chocolate and butter in a bowl over a pan of simmering water. Stir until smooth. Beat in egg yolks one at a time, beating well after each addition. Stir in Tia Maria.
3. Beat egg whites in a small bowl until soft peaks form. Gradually add sugar, beating until mixture becomes thick and glossy. Fold in chocolate mixture, stir until combined.
4. Spread mixture evenly into a buttered and paper-lined Swiss roll tin. Bake for 30 minutes or until firm. Turn out onto a sheet of baking paper, sprinkle with sifted cocoa. Remove paper lining, allow to cool.
5. Combine coffee and 1 tablespoon boiling water, cool. Beat cream until soft peaks form, stir in coffee mixture and 1 tablespoon extra Tia Maria. Spread evenly over cake, roll up lengthwise, using paper to help. Refrigerate until firm, serve sliced.

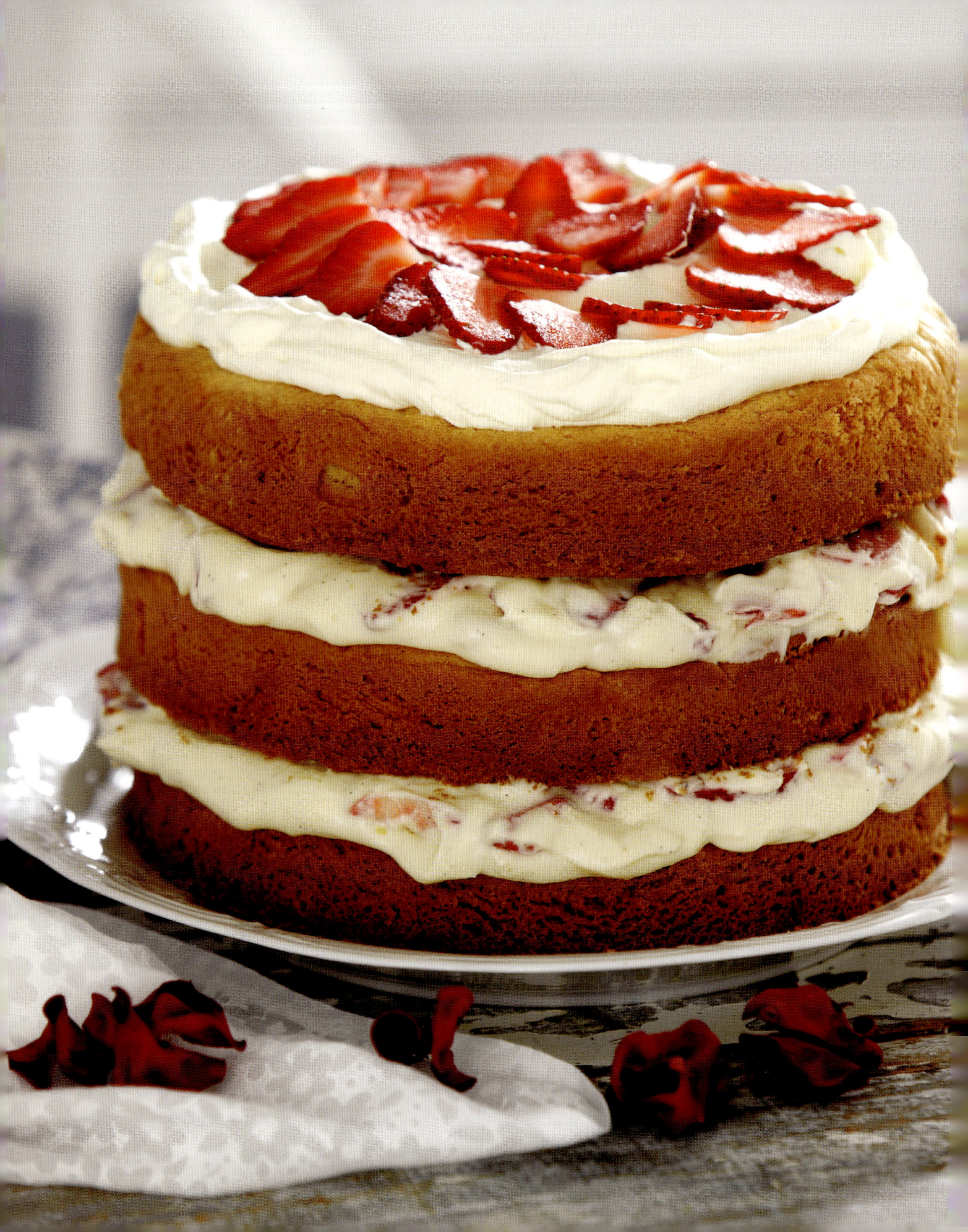

Strawberry Cake

INGREDIENTS:

250 g (8 oz) butter
½ cup caster sugar
2 eggs, lightly beaten
1 teaspoon vanilla extract
1½ cups plain flour
½ cup cornflour
1 tablespoon baking powder

STRAWBERRY CREAM
1 quantity crème pâtissière
¾ cup semi-whipped cream
1 cup sliced strawberries

Makes 1 cake

METHOD:

1 Preheat oven 180°C/360°F.
2 Cream the butter and sugar until light and fluffy, add the eggs and vanilla and beat thoroughly. Sift together the flour, cornflour and baking powder. Fold into the egg mixture and combine well. Place into three buttered 18 cm (7 in) sandwich tins and bake in the centre of the oven for 20 minutes. Allow to cool.
3 To make the strawberry cream, combine the crème pâtissière, whipped cream and strawberries.
4 Fill the cake with strawberry cream and decorate the top with extra whipped cream and sliced strawberries.

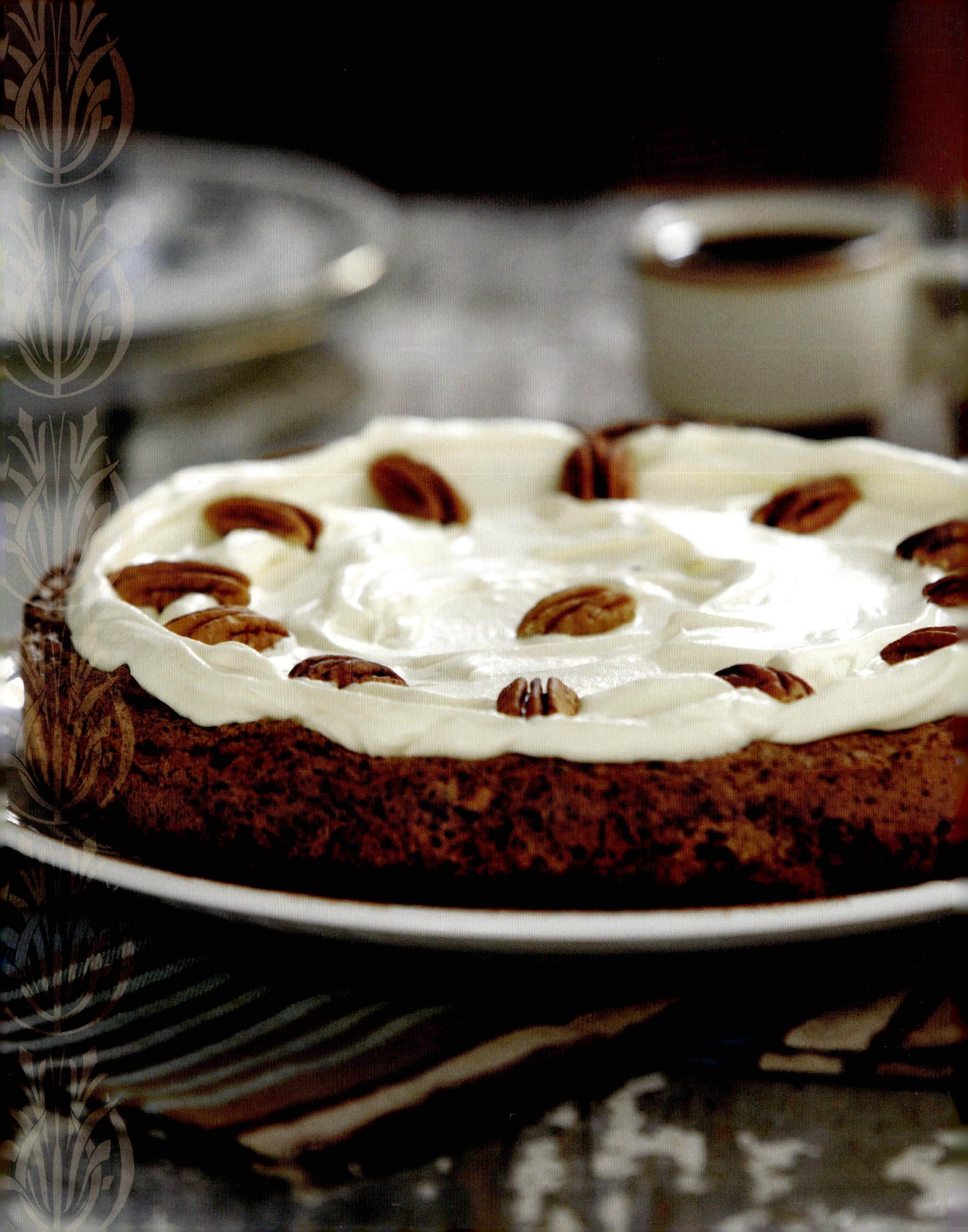

Chocolate Pecan Torte

INGREDIENTS:

4 egg whites

⅓ cup caster sugar

2 tablespoons cocoa powder, sifted

1 cup chopped pecans, extra to decorate

150 g (5 oz) dark chocolate, grated

1 cup thickened cream, whipped

Serves 6-8

METHOD:

1. Preheat oven to 160°C/325°F.
2. Beat egg whites in a large bowl until soft peaks form. Gradually add sugar, beat for a further 5 minutes until mixture is thick and glossy.
3. Fold in cocoa, pecans and grated chocolate, spread mixture into a buttered and lined 23 cm (9 in) springform tin.
4. Bake for 45 minutes. Leave to cool in tin. Decorate torte with whipped cream and extra pecan nuts.

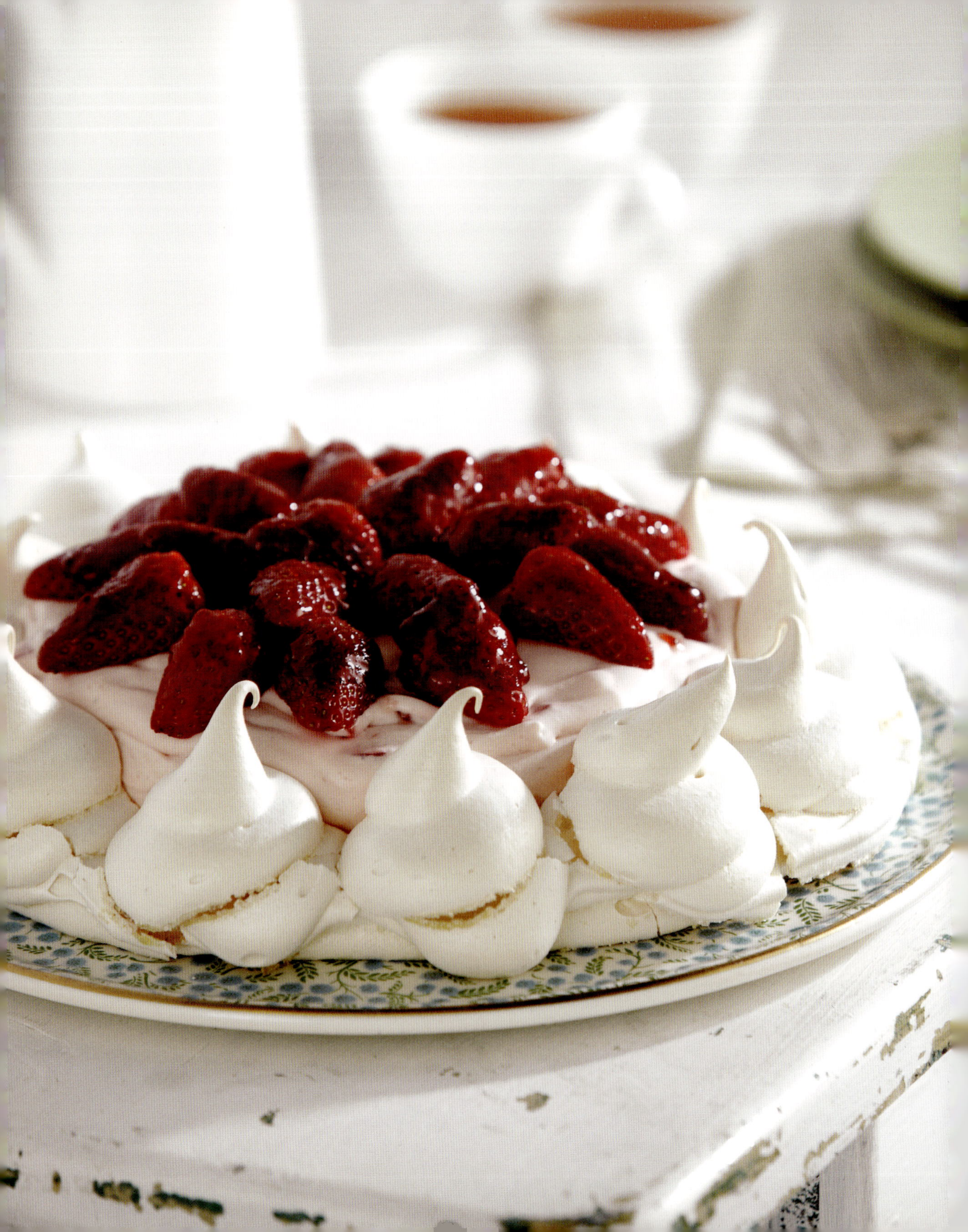

Strawberry Meringue Cake

INGREDIENTS:

6 egg whites
1¾ cups caster sugar
1 teaspoon lemon juice
¼ cup ground toasted almonds
1 punnet strawberries, halved
warm strawberry jam

FILLING
90g (3 oz) strawberry jelly crystals
1 cup thickened cream
2 tablespoons chocolate liqueur
¾ cup roughly chopped strawberries
60 g (2 oz) chocolate, melted and cooled

Makes 1 cake

METHOD:

1. Preheat oven to 140°C/280°F. Lightly butter a baking tray and dust lightly with cornflour. Trace a 20 cm (8 in) circle on a piece of baking paper.
2. Beat egg whites in a bowl until stiff peaks just form. Gradually add the sugar and continue beating until mixture is thick and glossy. Gently fold in lemon juice.
3. Fill a large piping bag fitted with a plain 12 mm (½ in) tube with meringue mixture and pipe meringue onto paper circle, starting in the centre and filling in completely. Alternatively, spread the mixture out with a spatula to form a round. Pipe large rosettes around meringue base.
4. Sprinkle almonds over base of meringue case and gently swirl into the mixture using a fork. Bake for 1¼ hours or until crisp, then turn oven off and leave in oven to dry out.
5. For the filling, place jelly crystals and 1 cup boiling water in a heatproof bowl, stir until jelly crystals dissolve. Chill until just beginning to set around the edge. Whip cream and liqueur together in a bowl until thick, and gently fold into jelly with chopped strawberries. Spread melted chocolate over base of meringue shell, and spoon cream mixture on top.
6. To decorate, top with halved strawberries. Brush strawberries with warm strawberry jam and refrigerate until ready to serve.

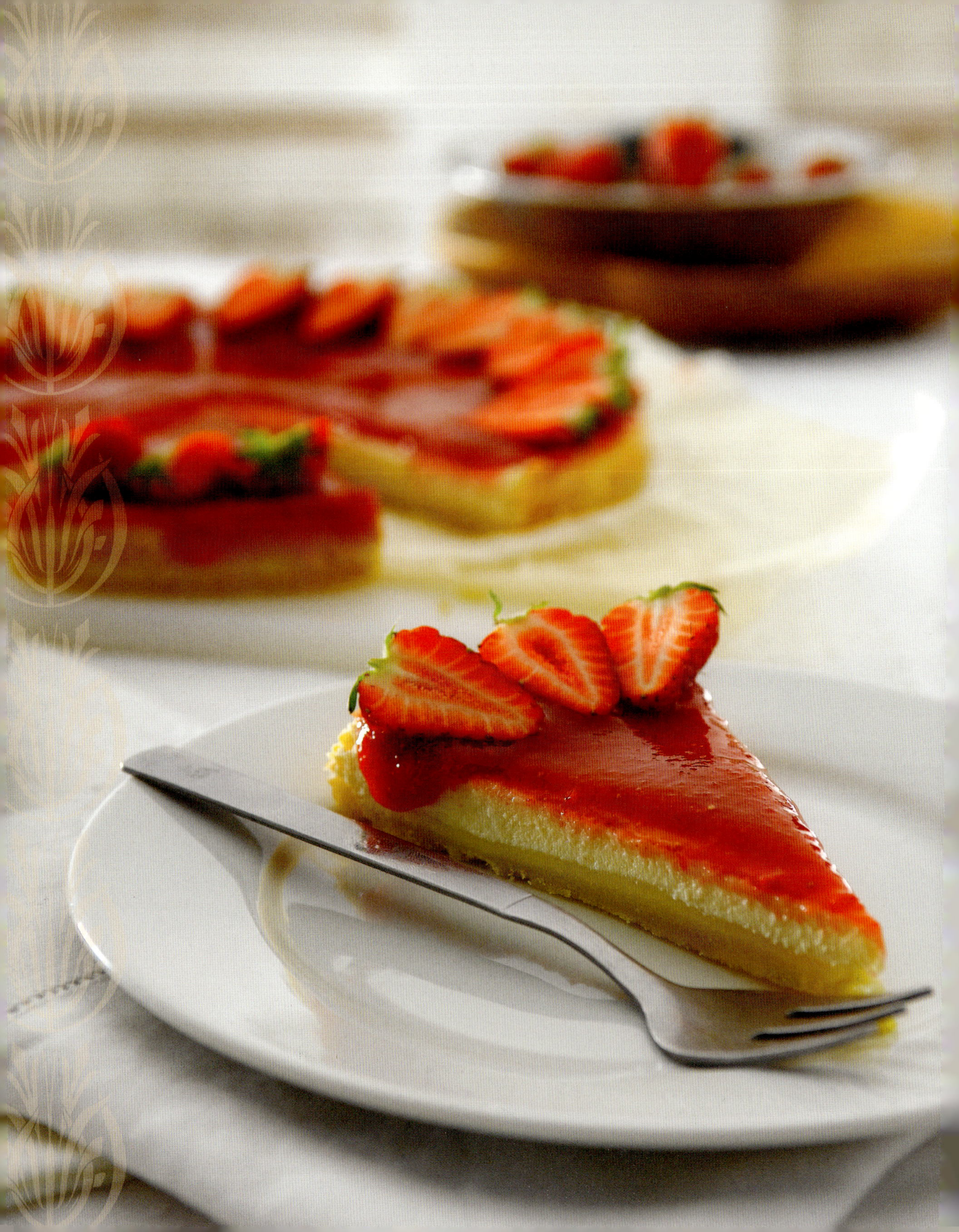

Guava Strawberry Cheesecake

INGREDIENTS:

BASE
125 g (4oz) plain flour
60 g (2oz) butter
1 egg yolk
3 tablespoons lemon juice

FILLING
250 g (9oz) ricotta
½ cup natural yoghurt
2 eggs
2 tablespoons lemon juice
60 g (2oz) sugar
250 g (9oz) strawberries, sliced
100 g (3½oz) guava jam

Serves 12

METHOD:

1 To make base, sift the flour into a bowl. Rub in the butter. Add the egg yolk and lemon juice, with a little cold water if required, to make a soft dough. Knead on a lightly floured surface until smooth, then press the dough evenly over the bottom of a 23 cm (9 in) springform tin. Rest in the refrigerator for 30 minutes.

2 Preheat oven to 190°C/375°F. Cover loosely with baking paper and dried beans. Bake blind for 10 minutes, remove the paper and beans and return to the oven for 5 minutes more. Cool.

3 To make filling, reduce the oven temperature to 180°C/350°F. Beat the ricotta, yoghurt, eggs, lemon juice and sugar in a bowl until smooth. Pour over the pastry base. Bake for 30 minutes or until set, then cool.

4 Purée 100 g (3½ oz) of the strawberries in a blender or food processor with the guava jam. Spread over the cheesecake. Place in the refrigerator for 1 hour. Decorate with the remaining strawberries to serve.

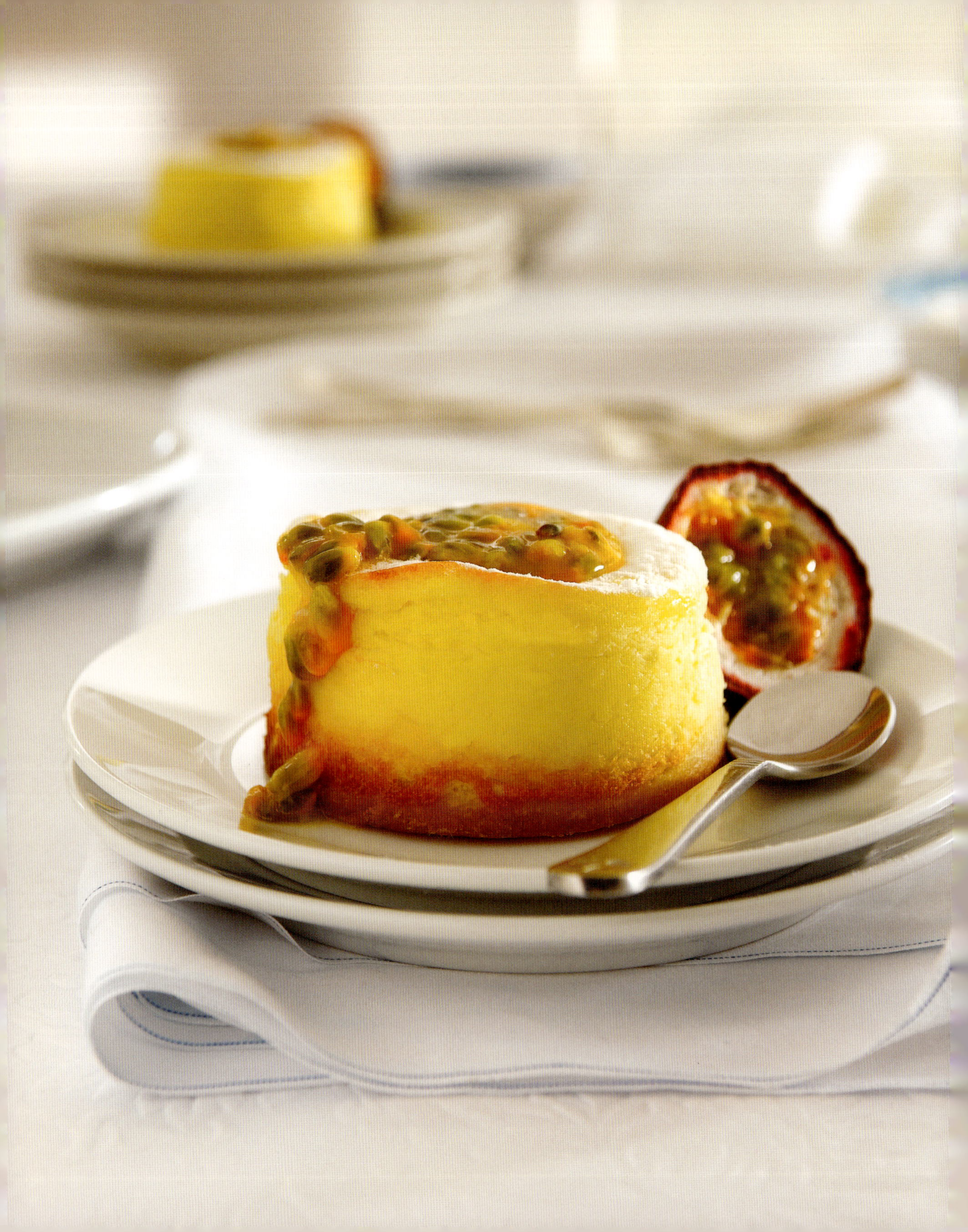

Mini Passionfruit Cheesecake

INGREDIENTS:

BASE

60 g (2 oz) digestive biscuits, finely crushed

30 g (1 oz) butter, melted

¼ cup sugar

FILLING

500 g (1 lb) cream cheese, softened

¼ cup passionfruit pulp, strained

1 teaspoon vanilla extract

¼ cup sugar

2 large eggs

4 fresh passionfruit

Serves 4

METHOD:

1. Preheat oven to 165°C/330°F.
2. To make the base, combine crumbs, butter and sugar. Line four 10 cm (4 in) springform tins with baking paper, then press mixture evenly onto bottoms of tins. Bake for 5 minutes.
3. To make the filling, combine cream cheese, passionfruit pulp, vanilla and sugar in an electric mixer, mix on medium speed until well combined. Add the eggs one at a time, mixing well after each addition. Divide filling evenly between the bases.
4. Bake for 25 minutes. Cool before removing from tins.
5. Decorate with fresh passionfruit and serve.

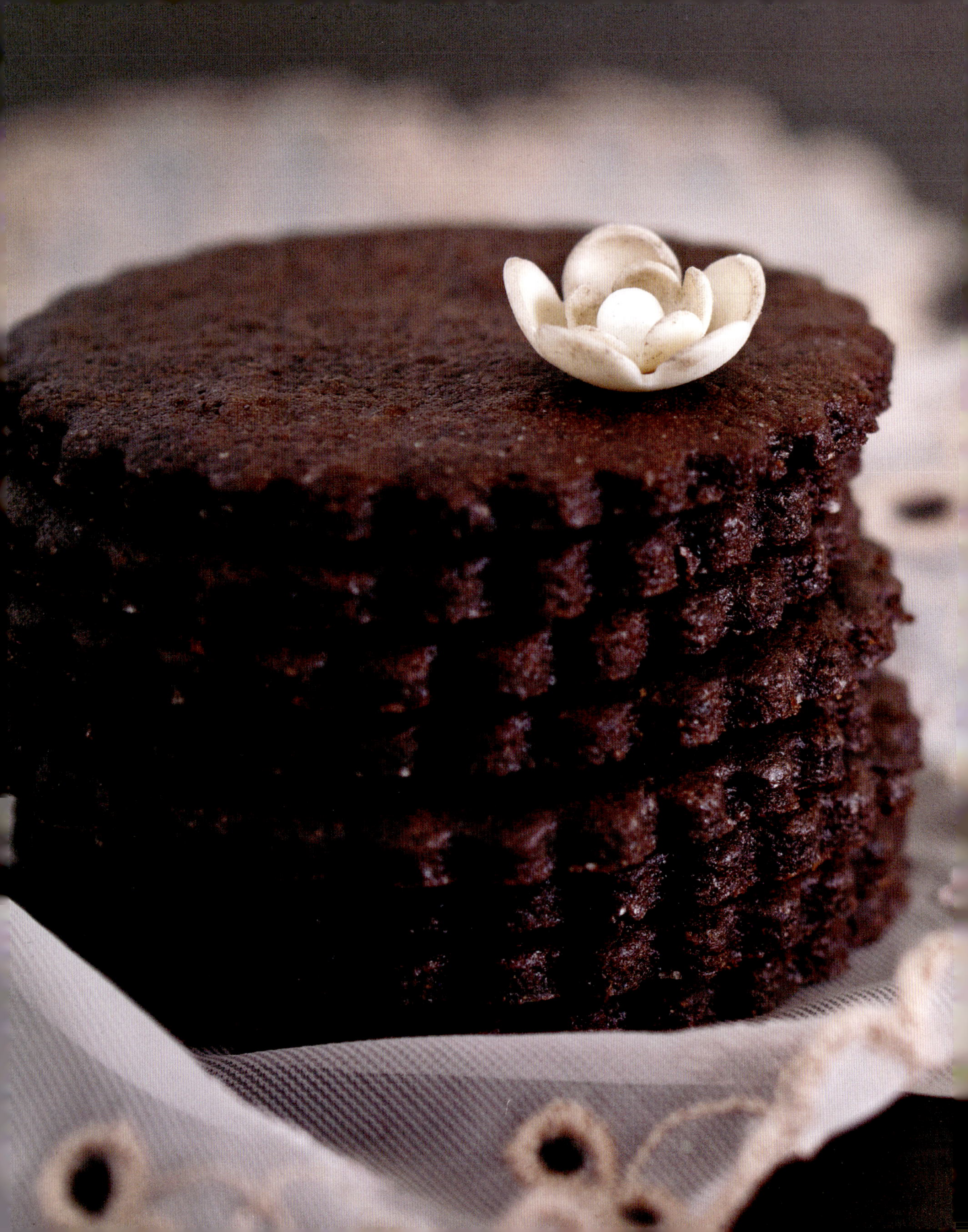

BISCUITS

Coffee Kisses

Note: These coffee-flavoured biscuits have a similar texture to shortbread, making the dough perfect for piping. For something different, pipe 5 cm (2 in) lengths instead of rounds. Rather than sandwiching the biscuits together with chocolate, you may prefer to leave them plain and simply dust with icing sugar.

INGREDIENTS:

250g (9 oz) butter, at room temperature
½ cup icing sugar, sifted
2 teaspoons instant coffee powder, dissolved in 1 tablespoon hot water, then cooled
2 cups flour, sifted
3 tablespoons bittersweet chocolate, melted

Makes 25

METHOD:

1. Preheat oven to 180°C/ 355°F..
2. Place the butter and icing sugar in a bowl and beat until light and fluffy. Stir in the coffee mixture and flour.
3. Spoon the mixture into a piping bag fitted with a medium star nozzle and pipe 2 cm (½ in) rounds of mixture 2 cm (½ in) apart on greased baking trays. Bake for 10–12 minutes or until lightly browned. Stand on trays for 5 minutes before removing to wire racks to cool completely.
4. Join the biscuits with a little melted chocolate, then dust with icing sugar.

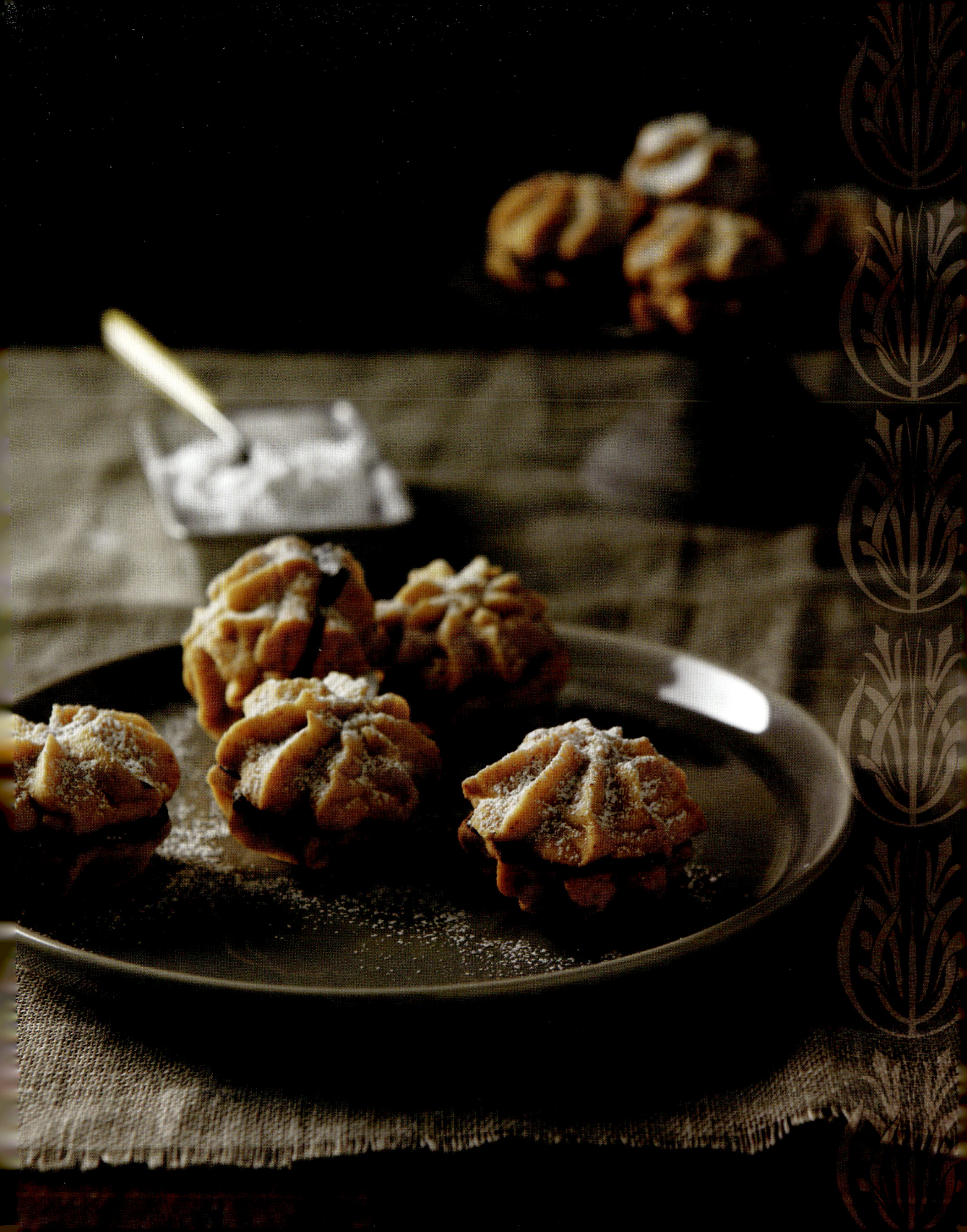

Hazelnut Shortbreads

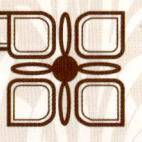

INGREDIENTS:

250 g (9 oz) butter, chopped
1½ cups plain flour, sifted
45 g (1½ oz) hazelnuts, ground
¼ cup ground rice
¼ cup superfine (caster) sugar
100 g (3½ oz) chocolate, melted

Makes 40

METHOD:

1 Preheat oven to 160°C/325°F.

Place butter, flour, hazelnuts and ground rice in a food processor and process until mixture resembles coarse breadcrumbs. Add sugar and process to combine.

2 Turn mixture onto a floured surface and knead lightly to make a pliable dough. Place dough between sheets of baking paper and roll out to 5 mm (¼ in) thick. Using a 5 cm (2 in) fluted cutter, cut out rounds of dough and place 25 mm (1 in) apart on buttered baking trays. Bake for 10—15 minutes or until lightly browned. Stand on baking trays for 2–3 minutes before transferring to wire racks to cool.

3 Place melted chocolate in a plastic food bag, snip off one corner and pipe lines across each biscuit before serving.

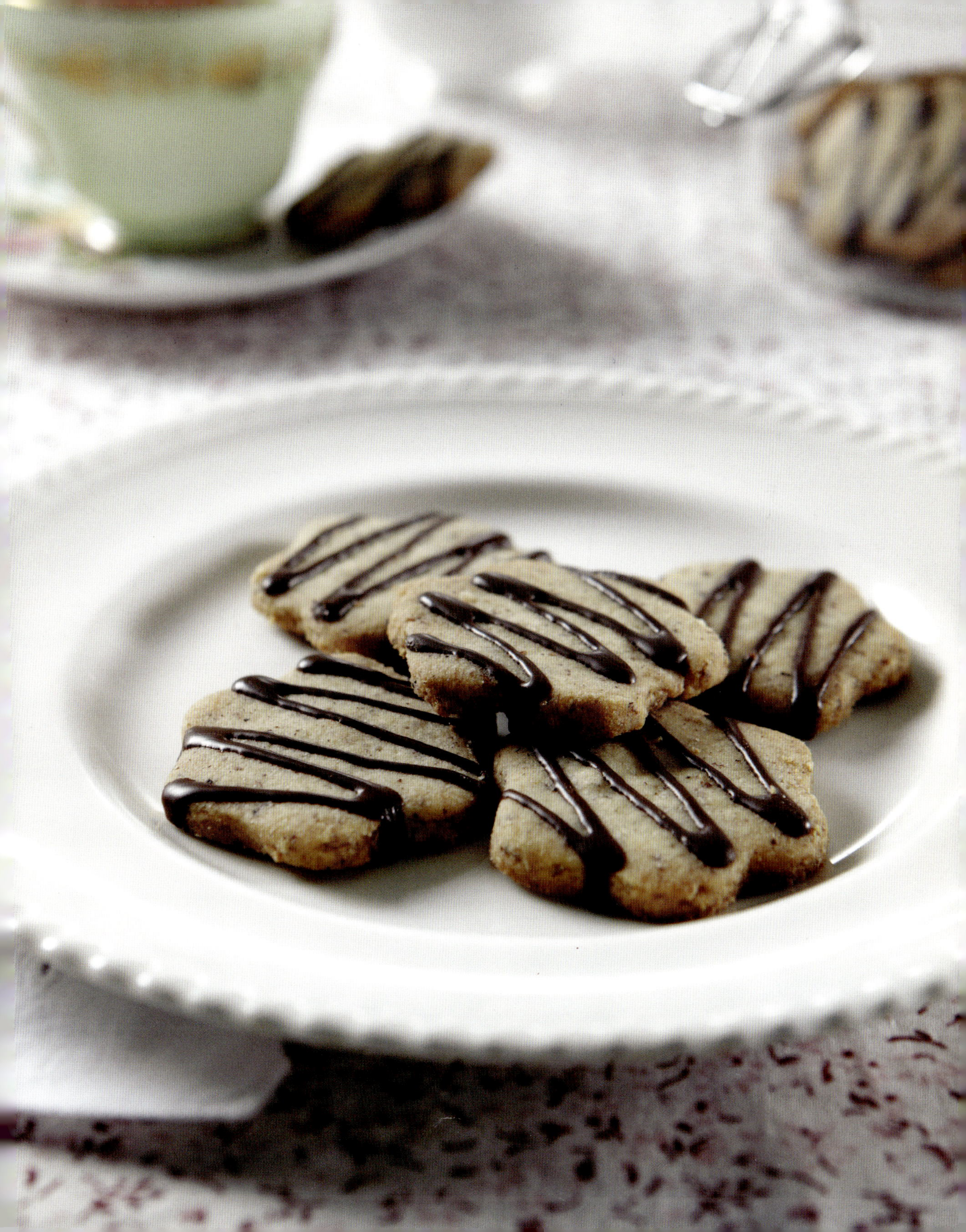

Coffee Pecan Biscuits

INGREDIENTS:

125 g (4½ oz) butter, at room temperature
½ cup caster sugar
½ teaspoon vanilla extract
1 egg, at room temperature
2 teaspoons instant coffee powder
2 cups plain flour
1 teaspoon baking powder
1 tablespoon milk
250 g (9 oz) pecans, finely chopped

ICING

¾ cup icing sugar
1 tablespoon boiling water
1 tablespoon butter, at room temperature
2 teaspoons instant coffee powder

Makes 30

METHOD:

1 Using an electric mixer, beat butter, sugar and vanilla in a small bowl until pale and creamy. Add egg and coffee and mix until well combined. Sift flour and baking powder over butter mixture. Add milk and stir until just combined. Divide dough in half.

2 Roll each piece of dough into a 4.5 cm (2 in) diameter log. Roll the logs in the chopped pecans until well coated. Wrap each log in cling wrap. Refrigerate for at least 30 minutes or until firm.

3 Preheat oven to 180°C/360°F. Line 2 baking trays with baking paper.

4 Using a sharp knife, carefully cut logs into 1.5 cm (½ in) slices. Place on the lined baking trays. Bake for 15–18 minutes or until light golden colour. Allow to cool for about 5 minutes, then transfer to wire racks to cool completely.

5 Make coffee icing. Sift icing sugar into a bowl. Combine the boiling water, butter and coffee in a separate bowl and stir until coffee is dissolved. Add to icing sugar and stir until mixture is smooth.

6 Drop 1 teaspoon of icing onto the centre of each biscuit. Top with a pecan. Allow icing to set before serving.

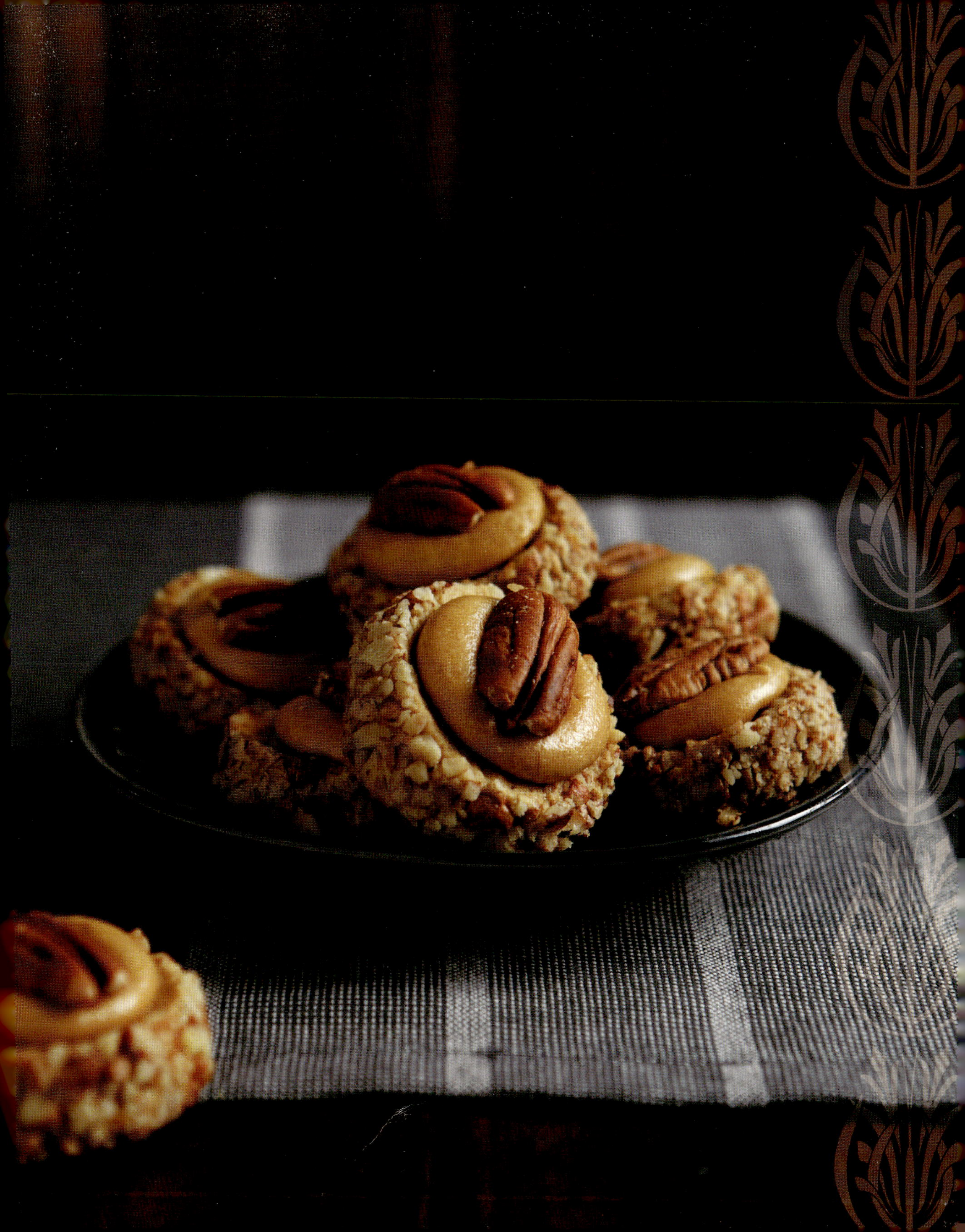

Truffle Cookies

This is the biscuit version of the traditional rich truffle confection and tastes delicious as an afternoon treat with coffee or tea.

INGREDIENTS:

250 g (9 oz) butter, chopped
90 g (3 oz) dark chocolate, broken into pieces
2 ½ cups plain flour
½ cup cocoa powder
1 teaspoon baking powder
3 eggs, lightly beaten
1 cup sugar
1 cup brown sugar
2 teaspoons vanilla extract
125 g (4 ½ oz) pecans, chopped

Makes 40

METHOD:

1. Preheat oven to 180°C/ 355°F. Place butter and chocolate in a heatproof bowl set over a saucepan of simmering water and heat, stirring, until mixture is smooth. Remove bowl from pan and set aside to cool slightly.
2. Sift together flour, cocoa powder and baking powder into a bowl. Add eggs, sugar, brown sugar, vanilla and chocolate mixture and mix well to combine. Stir in pecans.
3. Drop tablespoonfuls of mixture onto buttered baking trays and bake for 12 minutes or until puffed. Stand on trays for 2 minutes before transferring to wire racks to cool.

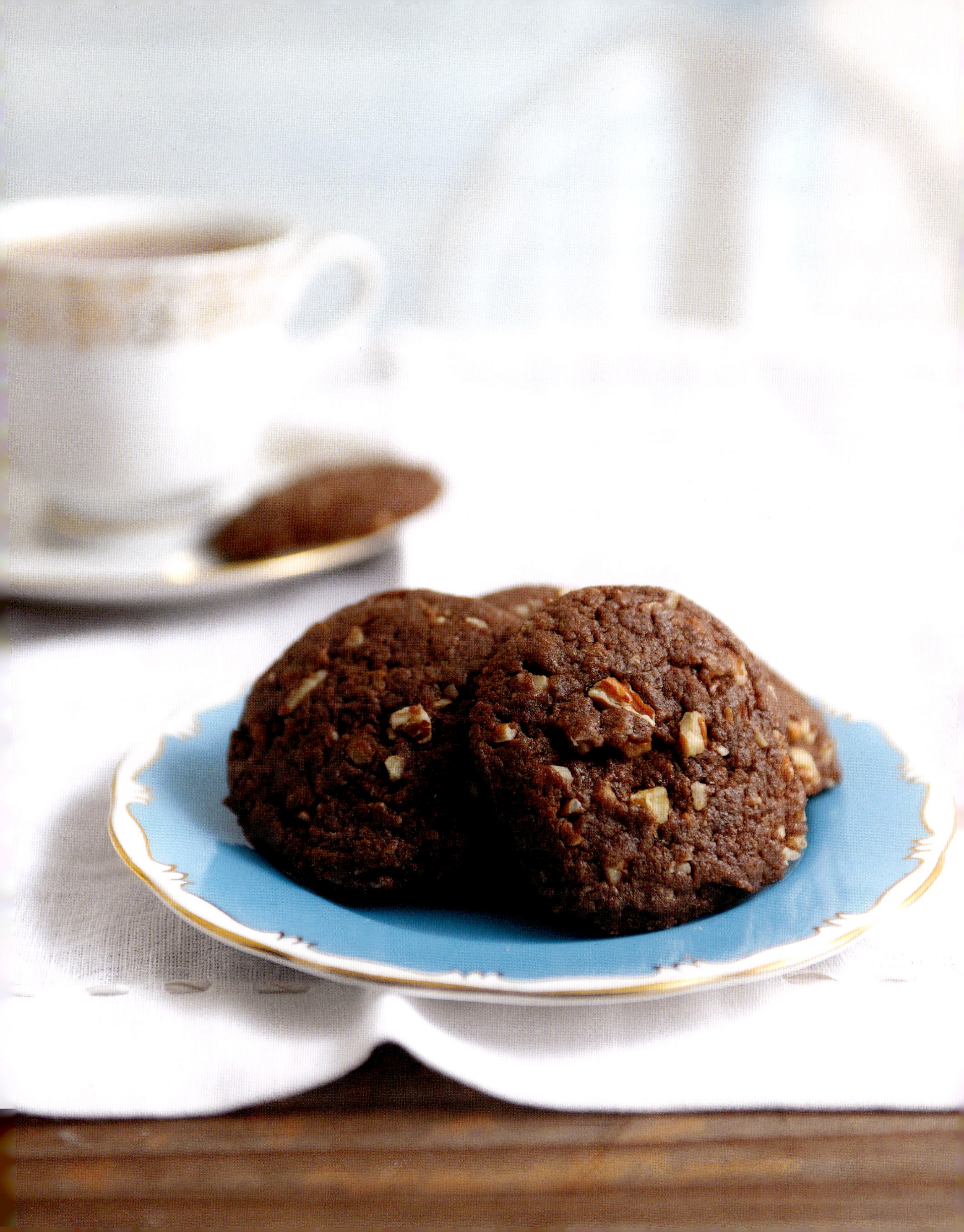

Bourbon Biscuits

INGREDIENTS:

60 g (2 oz) butter
¼ cup caster sugar
1 tablespoon golden syrup
1 cup plain flour
15 g (½ oz) cocoa powder
½ teaspoon baking soda

FILLING
50 g (1½ oz) butter
⅔ cup icing sugar, sifted
1 tablespoon cocoa powder
1 teaspoon instant coffee powder

Makes 14–16

METHOD:

1. Preheat the oven to 160°C/320°F. Cream the butter and sugar together very thoroughly, then beat in the syrup.
2. Sift the flour, cocoa and baking soda together, then work into the creamed mixture to make a stiff paste.
3. Knead well, and roll out on a lightly floured surface into an oblong strip about 5mm thick. If the rolled dough is too long for your baking tray, cut it in half. Place on a lightly buttered baking tray covered with baking paper. Bake for 15–20 minutes.
4. Cut into fingers of equal width while still warm. Cool on a wire rack while you prepare the filling.

Filling

1. Beat the butter until soft, then add the sugar, cocoa and coffee. Beat until smooth. Sandwich the cooled fingers with a layer of filling.

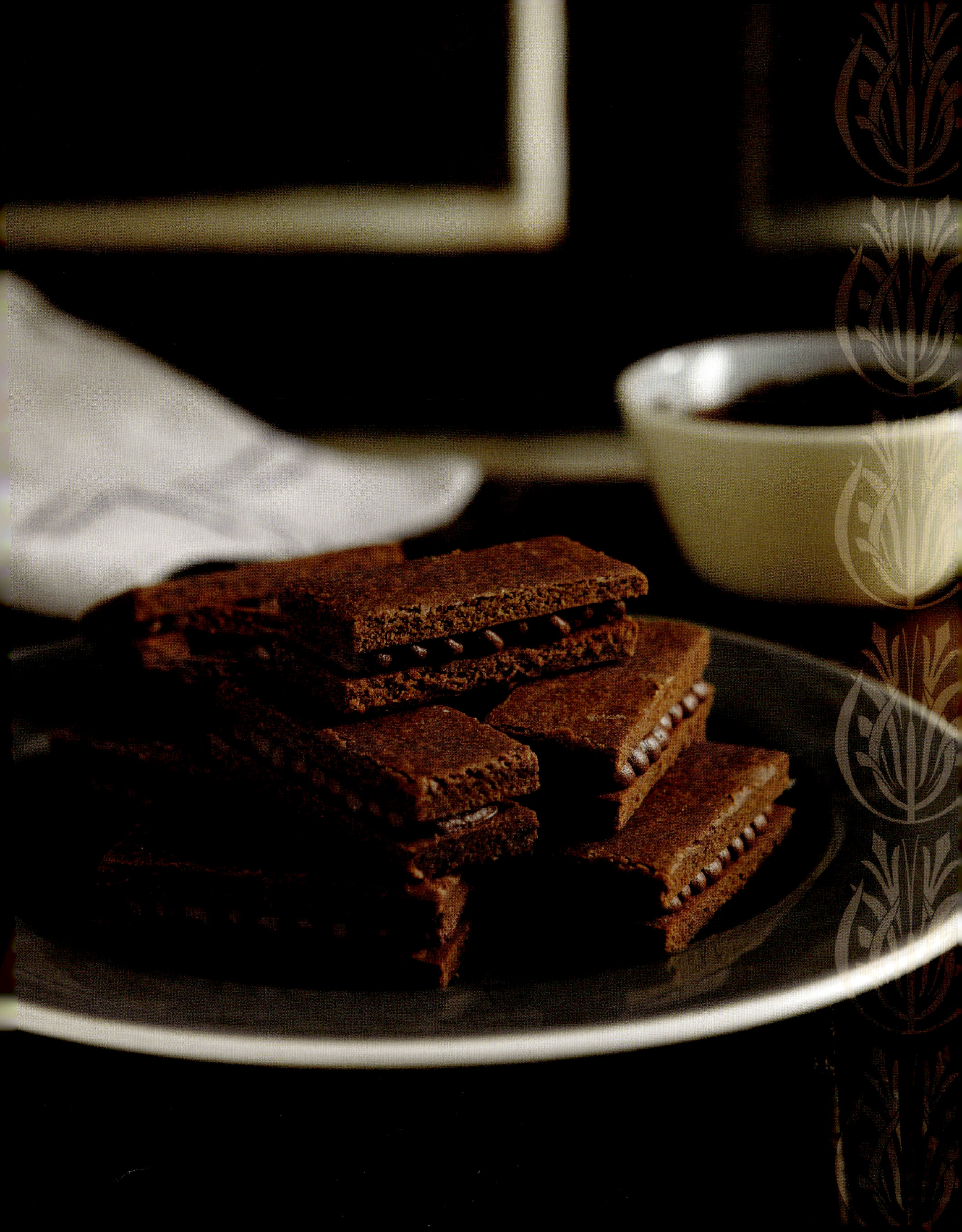

Monte Carlo Biscuits

INGREDIENTS:

250 g (9 oz) butter, at room temperature

1 cup brown sugar

3 teaspoons vanilla extract

1 egg, lightly beaten

1 cup plain flour, sifted

½ cup self-raising flour, sifted

1 cup desiccated coconut

¾ cup rolled oats

1 cup icing sugar

½ cup raspberry jam

Makes 20

METHOD:

1. Preheat oven to 180°C/355°F. Lightly butter a baking tray.
2. Place half the butter, the brown sugar and 2 teaspoons of the vanilla in a bowl and beat until light and fluffy. Add the egg, plain flour, self-raising flour, coconut and rolled oats, and mix well to combine.
3. Roll heaped tablespoonfuls of the mixture into oval balls, place on the baking tray and flatten slightly with a fork. Bake for 12 minutes or until golden. Transfer to a wire rack to cool.
4. Place the remaining butter, the icing sugar and remaining vanilla in a bowl and beat until light and fluffy.
5. Spread half the biscuits with raspberry jam and top with the icing sugar mixture. Top with the remaining biscuits.

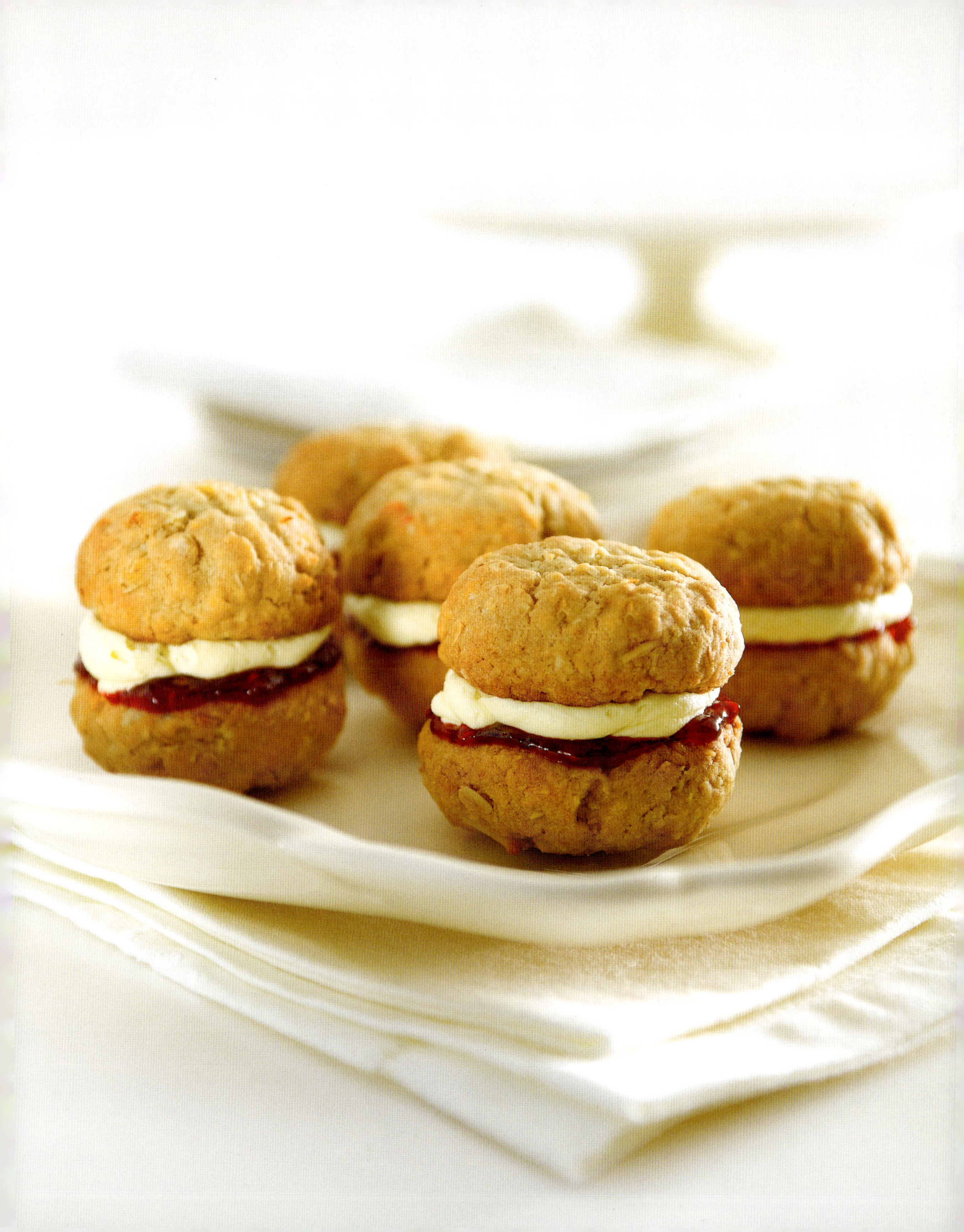

Chocolate Coffee Tuiles

INGREDIENTS:

2 egg whites
½ cup caster sugar
½ teaspoon instant coffee powder, dissolved in
½ teaspoon water
1 teaspoon vanilla extract
1 tablespoon cocoa powder, sifted
1¼ tablespoons milk
60 g (2 oz) butter, melted and cooled

Makes 25

METHOD:

1. Preheat oven to 170°C/340°F.
2. Place egg whites in a bowl and beat until soft peaks form. Gradually add sugar, beating well after each addition, until mixture is glossy and sugar dissolved. Fold coffee mixture, vanilla, cocoa powder, milk and butter into egg white mixture.
3. Drop spoonfuls of mixture 10 cm (4 in) apart onto greased baking tray and bake for 5 minutes or until edges are set. Remove from tray and wrap each biscuit around the handle of a wooden spoon. Allow to cool for 2 minutes or until set. Repeat with remaining mixture.

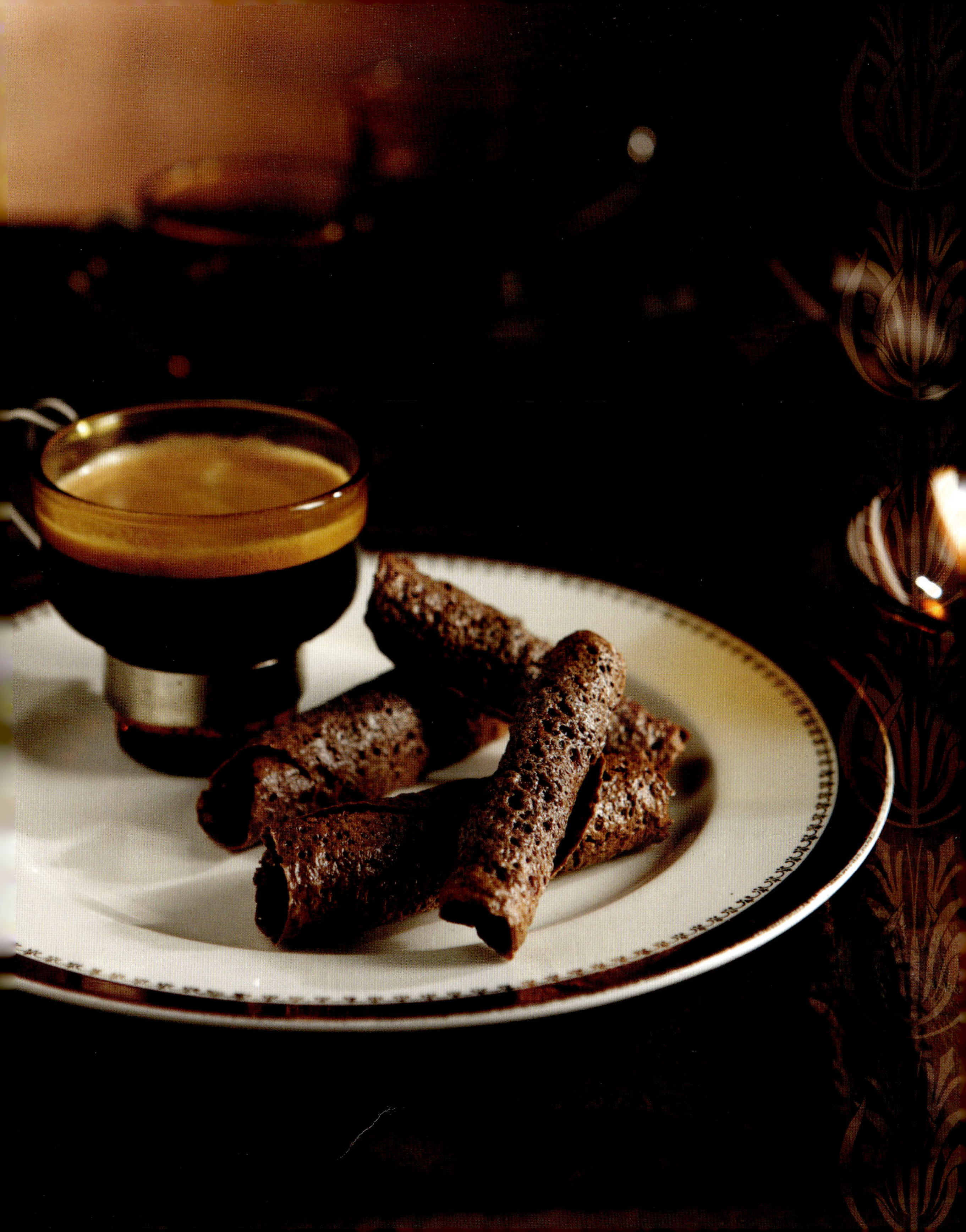

Pecan Chocolate Drizzles

INGREDIENTS:

100 g (3½ oz) unsalted butter, at room temperature
100 g (3½ oz) brown sugar
1 egg, lightly beaten
100 g (10½ oz) plain flour
1 teaspoon baking powder
75 g (2½ oz) pecans, roughly chopped
80g (3 oz) milk chocolate, melted
2 tablespoons icing sugar

Makes 20

METHOD:

1. Beat together the butter and sugar in a bowl until light and creamy, add the egg and beat well. Add the flour and baking powder, then work together with your hands until the dough is smooth. Refrigerate for 10 minutes.
2. Preheat oven to 180°C/350°F. Lightly butter a baking tray.
3. Roll out half of the mixture between two sheets of baking paper – the dough should be about 5mm thick. Cut into rounds using a 6cm cookie cutter. Repeat with the remaining dough.
4. Place the cookies on the baking tray and bake for 10 minutes. Remove the cookies to a wire rack and sprinkle with nuts.
5. Melt the chocolate the icing sugar and stir to combine. Drizzle the melted chocolate mixture over the cooled cookies. Leave to set.

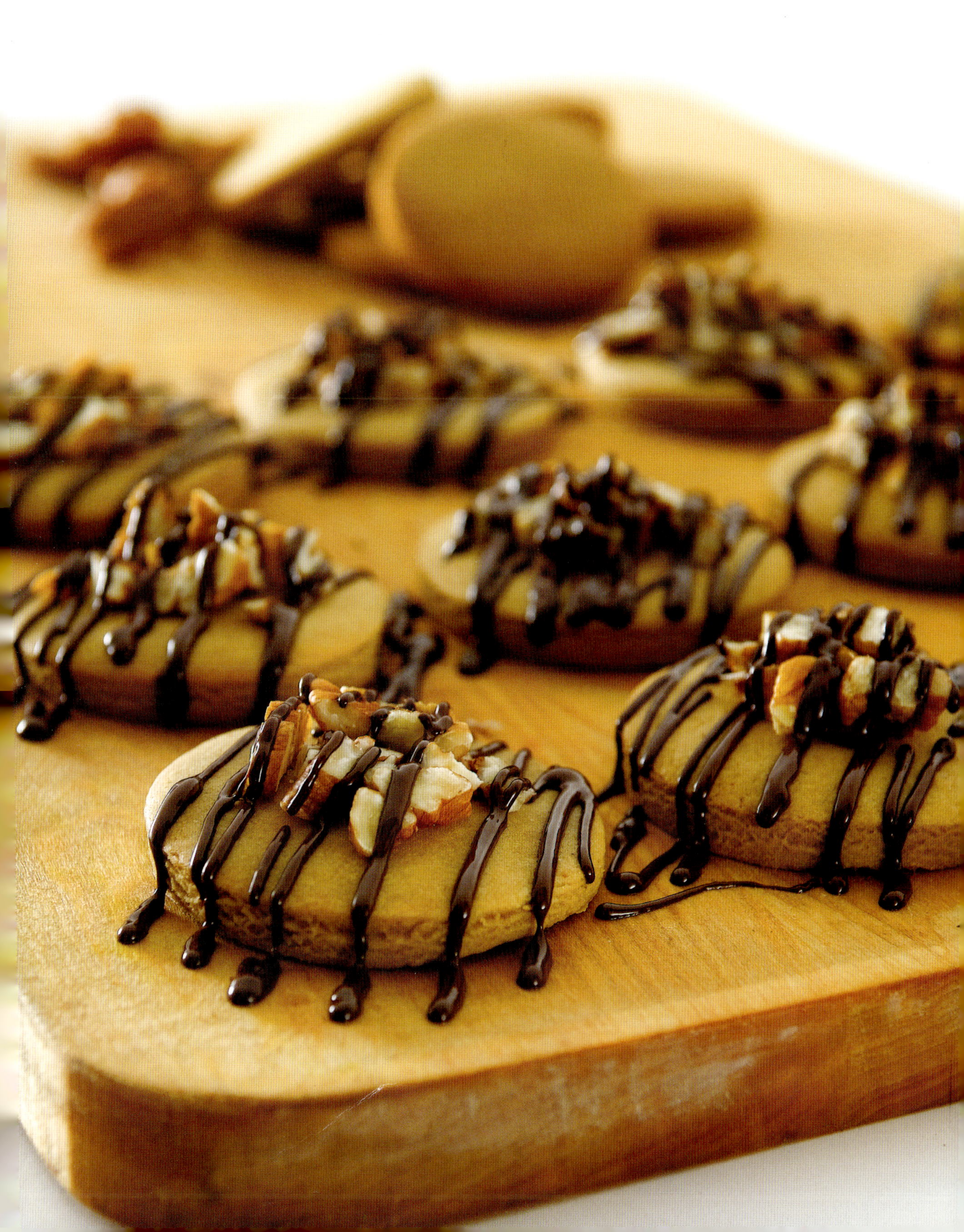

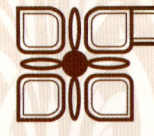

Coffee & Ginger Almond Crisps

Note: This recipe is only limited by your imagination. You can use any nuts, dried fruit or spices you fancy. For something festive, try cherries, mixed peel and brazil nuts, or for an exotic Eastern feel use pistachios, glacé pears and ground cardamom.

INGREDIENTS:

1 cup plain flour
2 teaspoons good quality ground coffee
3 egg whites
½ cup caster sugar
¾ cup unsalted almonds or hazelnuts
½ cup glacé ginger, finely diced

Makes 40 pieces

METHOD:

1. Preheat oven to 170°C/ 340°F. Lightly spray or brush a 7 x 24cm (2¾ x 9½ in) bar tin with unsaturated oil.

2. Sift together flour and coffee into a bowl. Place egg whites in a separate bowl and beat until soft peaks form. Gradually beat in sugar. Continue beating until sugar dissolves. Fold in flour mixture. Fold in nuts and ginger.

3. Spoon batter into prepared tin. Bake for 35 minutes. Stand tin on a wire rack and cool completely. When cold, remove bread from tin. Wrap in aluminium foil. Store in a cool place for 1–3 days – the finished bread will be crisper if you can leave it for 2–3 days.

4. Preheat oven to 120°C/250°F. Using a very sharp serrated or electric knife, cut cooked loaf into wafer thin slices. Place slices on ungreased baking trays. Bake for 45–60 minutes or until dry and crisp. Cool on wire racks. Store in an airtight container.

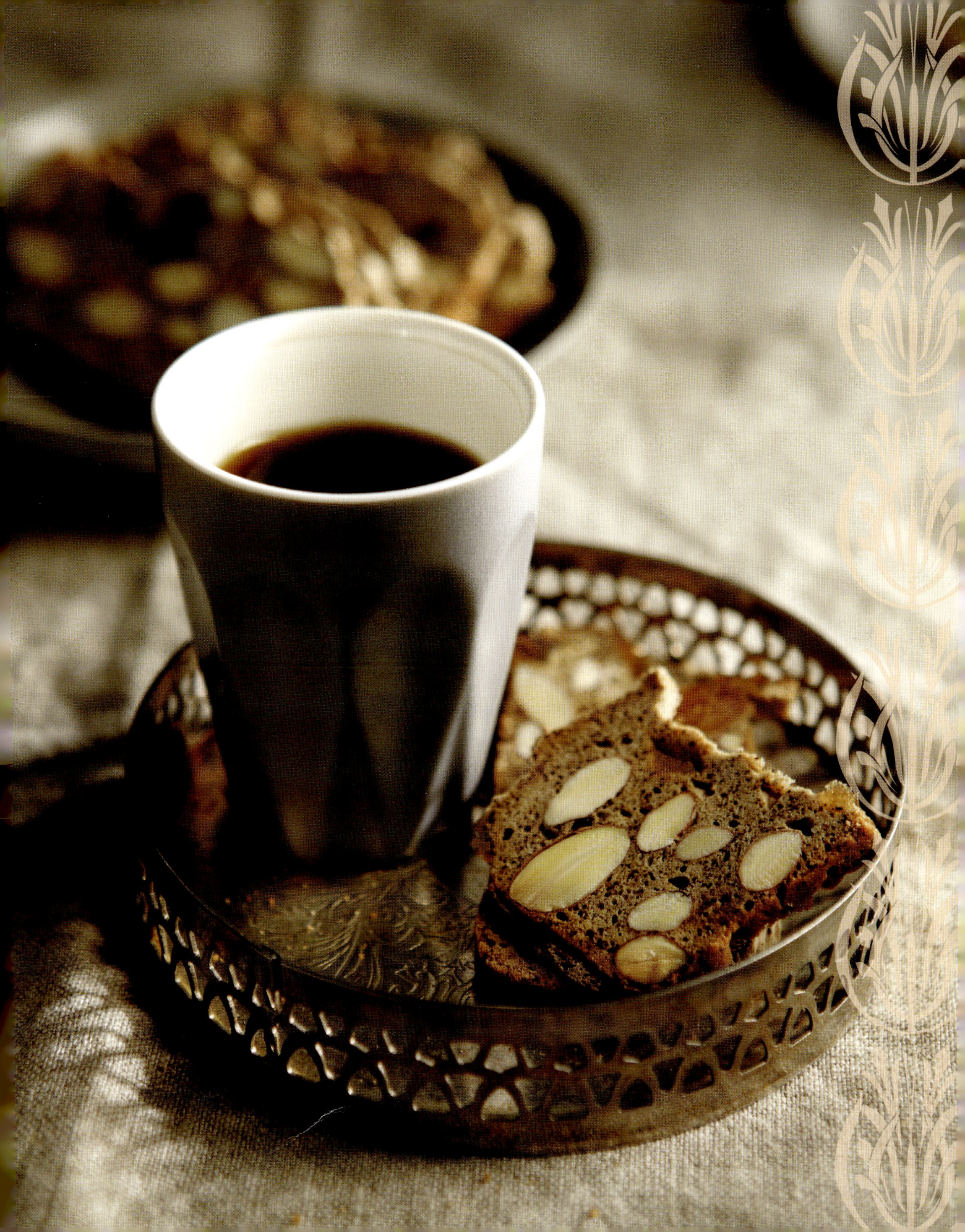

Chewy Coffee Cookies

INGREDIENTS:

125 g (4½ oz) butter, at room temperature

½ cup brown sugar

1 large egg, plus 1 yolk

2 tablespoons coffee liqueur

⅓ cup molasses

3 tablespoons instant coffee

2½ cups plain flour

1 teaspoon ground cinnamon

½ teaspoon ground cardamom

2 teaspoons baking soda

½ cup icing sugar

Makes 25

METHOD:

1. Preheat oven to 180°C/ 350°F. Lightly butter 2 cookie sheets.
2. Cream the butter and brown sugar. Add egg, egg yolk, liqueur and molasses, and fold together thoroughly.
3. Combine instant coffee, flour, spices and baking soda in a medium bowl. Add dry ingredients to wet and work them in.
4. Roll mixture into balls, 2 tablespoonfuls at a time, then roll the balls in the icing sugar. Place on the cookie sheets and bake for 12–14 minutes.

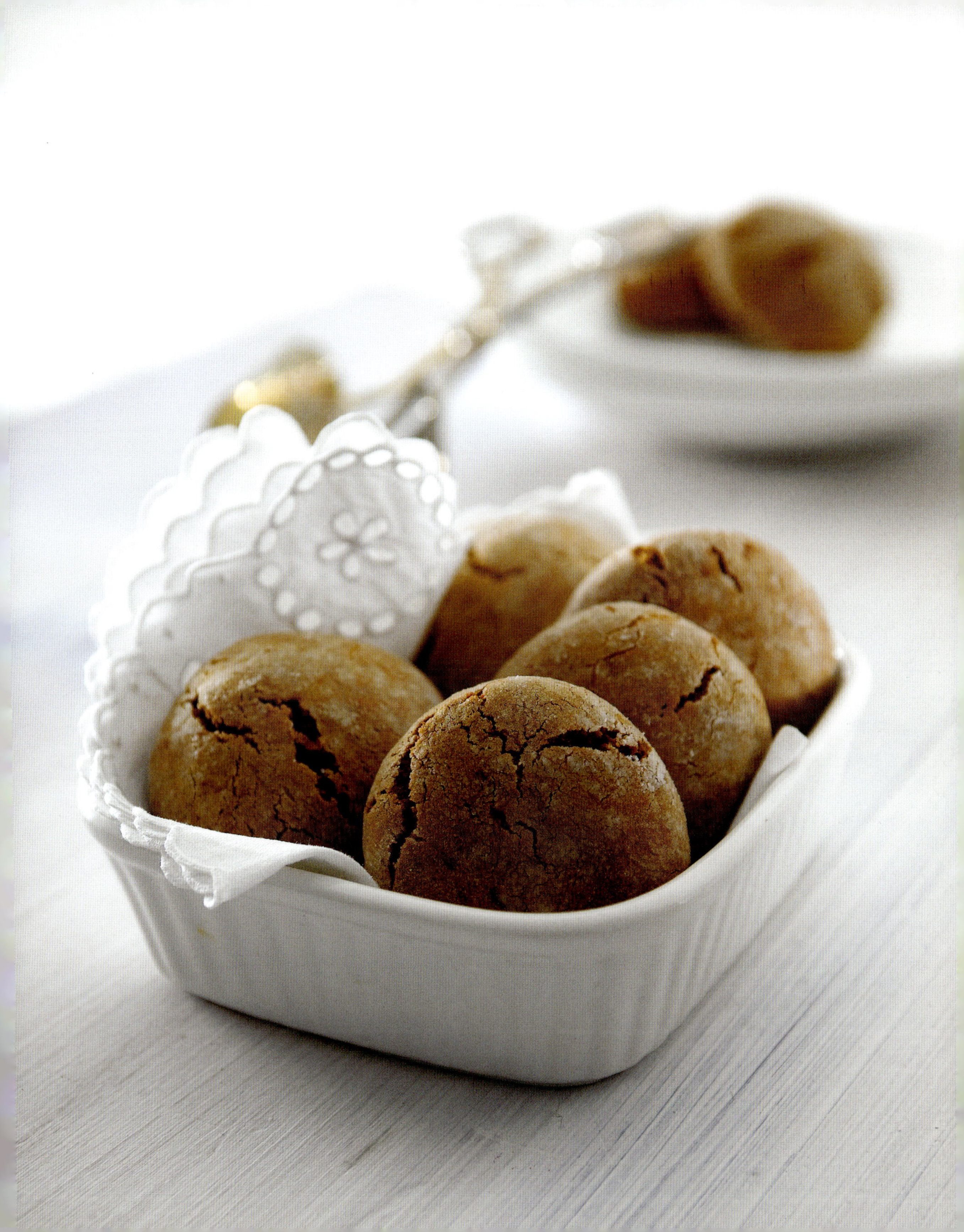

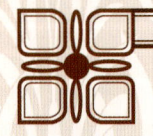

Chocolate Viennese Shortbreads

INGREDIENTS:

250 g (8oz) butter
¼ cup superfine (caster) sugar
½ teaspoon vanilla extract
2 tablespoons cocoa powder
1½ cups plain flour
⅓ cup cornflour
150 g (5 oz) milk chocolate melts, melted
confectioners' (icing) sugar, to dust

Makes 24

METHOD:

1. Preheat oven to 180°C/350°F.
2. Beat butter and sugar together until light and creamy, add vanilla and cocoa and beat until well combined. Fold in sifted flours and spoon mixture into a large piping bag fitted with a large fluted pipe.
3. Pipe mixture into shapes onto lightly buttered baking trays. Bake for 12–15 minutes then cool on trays.
4. Dip ends of each biscuit into melted chocolate and set aside to cool until chocolate is set. Dust with icing sugar.

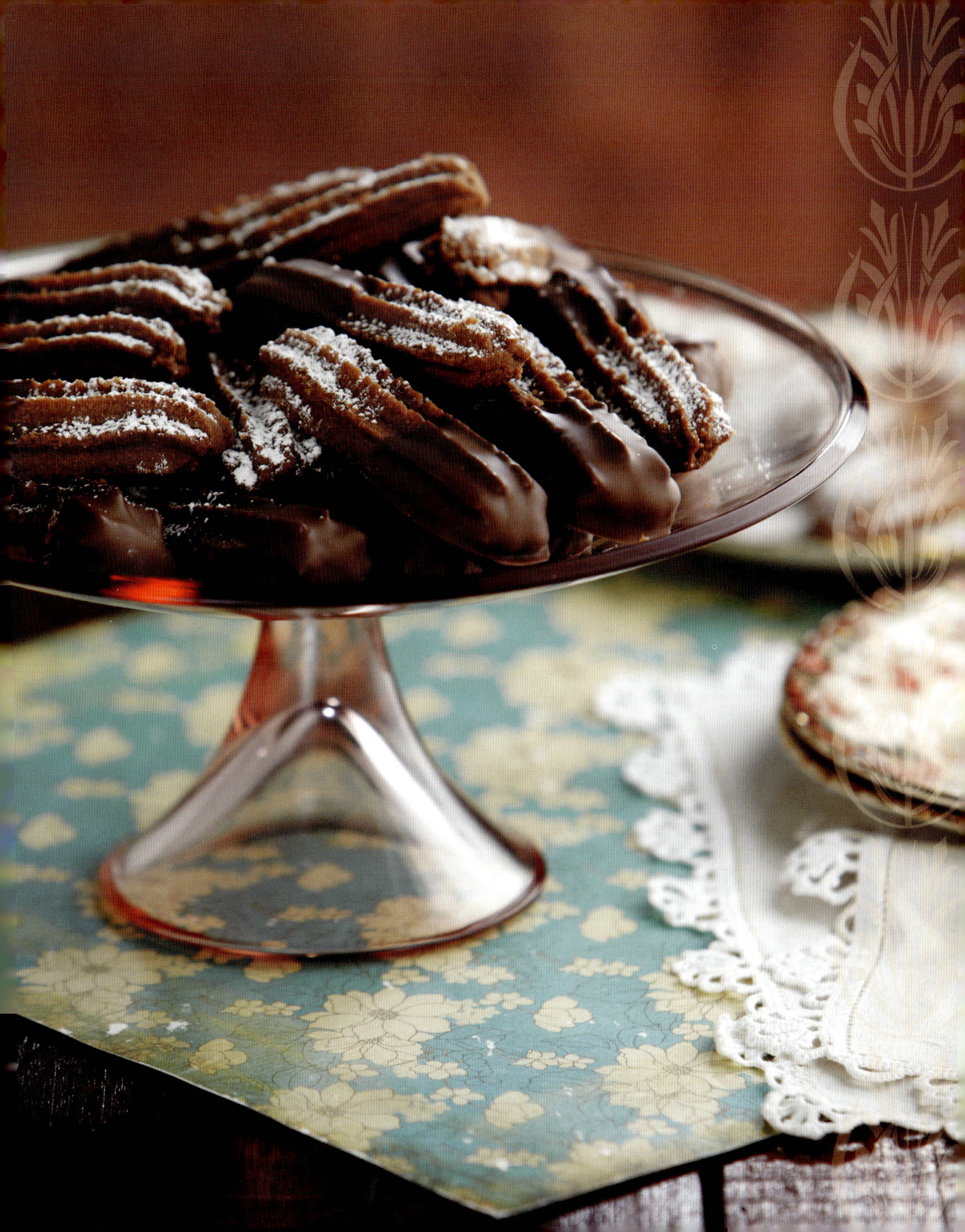

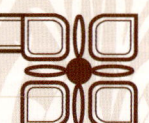

Almond & Walnut Petits Fours

INGREDIENTS

125g (4½ oz) whole skinned almonds
125g (4½ oz) walnuts
250g (9 oz) caster sugar
finely grated zest of ½ orange
2 medium egg whites
10 large glacé cherries, halved
1 tablespoon icing sugar

Makes 20

METHOD

1. Preheat the oven to 180°C/ 350°F and line a baking sheet with rice paper.
2. Put the almonds and walnuts in a food processor and grind briefly. Add half the caster sugar and grind again until it becomes a powder.
3. Mix in the remaining caster sugar and the grated orange zest. Transfer the mixture to a bowl.
4. In another bowl, whisk the egg whites lightly with an electric whisk, then stir the egg whites into the almond and walnut mixture to bind it. Take heaped teaspoonfuls of the mixture and roll it into balls on a work surface dusted with icing sugar.
5. Flatten the balls with a palette knife and press half a cherry into the centre of each. Place them well apart on the baking sheet.
6. Bake for 15 minutes or until just firm but pale golden brown. Cool on the baking sheet then trim the rice paper around the biscuits.
7. Serve the petits fours on the day of baking, dusted with icing sugar.

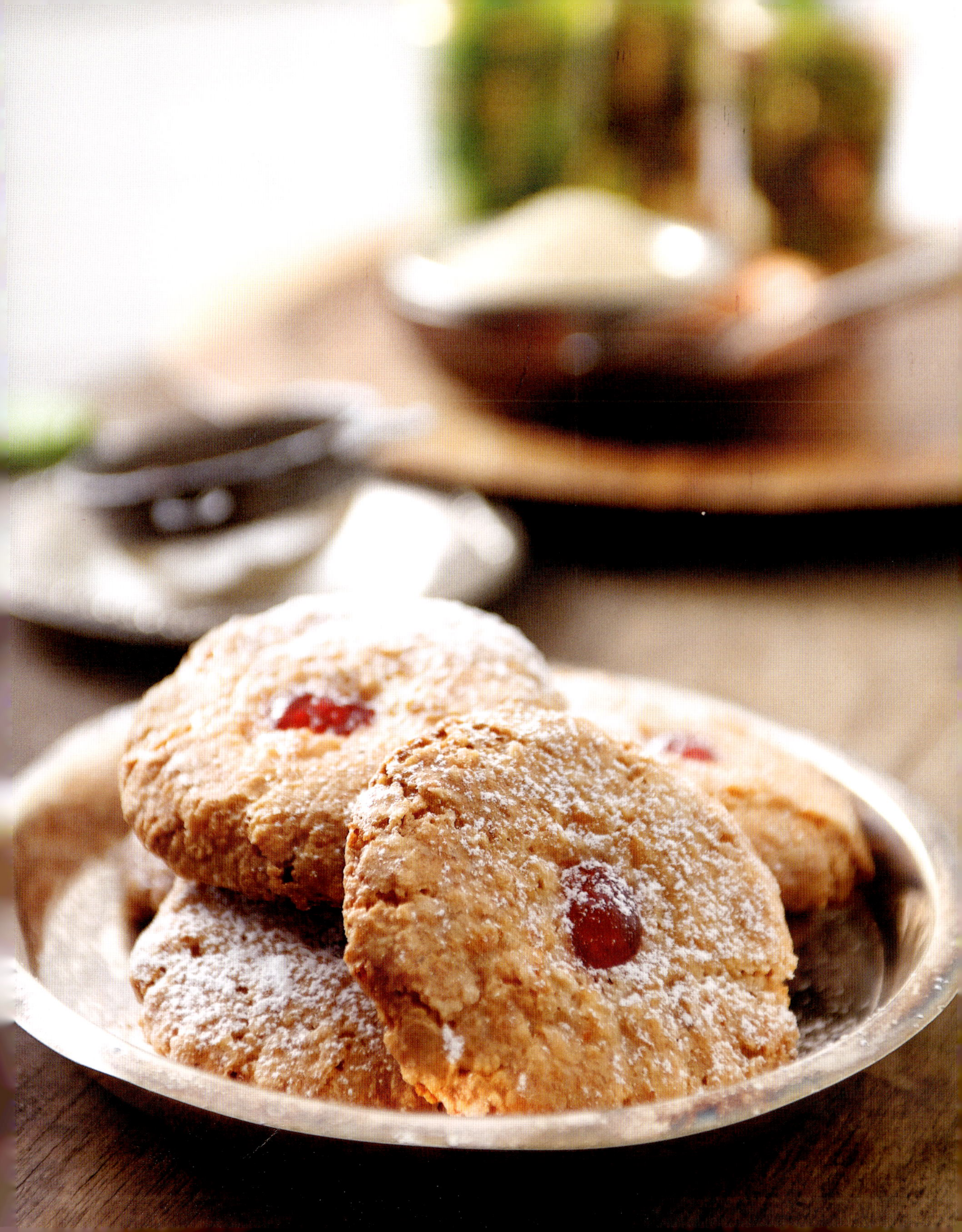

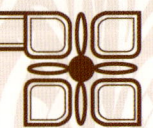

Almond Biscuits

INGREDIENTS

1 cup plain flour
1 cup ground almonds
¼ teaspoon baking powder
⅛ teaspoon salt
90g (1 oz) butter, softened
¾ cup sugar
1 large egg white
½ teaspoon almond extract
48 whole blanched almonds

Makes 48

METHOD

1. Preheat oven to 180°C/350°F. Stir together flour, ground almonds, baking powder, and salt and set aside.
2. In a mixing bowl, cream butter and sugar with an electric mixer on medium. Beat in egg white and almond extract.
3. Stir flour and ground almond mixture into the creamed mixture. Cover with cling wrap and chill for about 2 hours.
4. Shape dough into small balls, about 4 cm in (1½ in). Place balls 5cm apart and flatten slightly with the bottom of a glass. Press an almond into the centre of each biscuit. Bake for about 12 minutes, or until set but not browned.

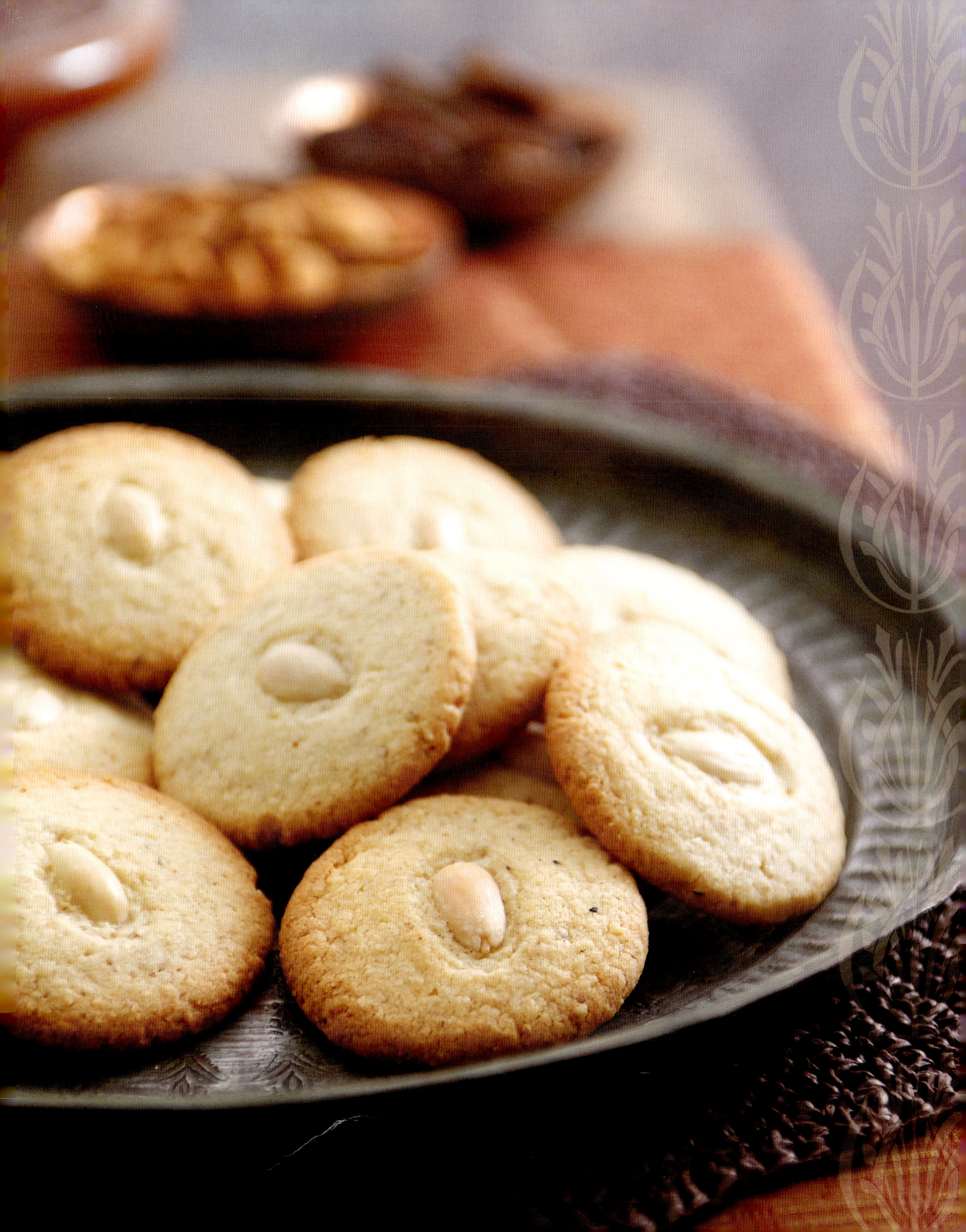

Madeleines

INGREDIENTS:

2 eggs

1 cup caster sugar

1¼ cups plain flour

2 teaspoons baking powder

60 g (2 oz) butter or margarine, melted

1 teaspoon vanilla extract

warm jam, sieved

desiccated coconut

10 glacé cherries, halved

Makes about 20

METHOD:

1. Preheat oven to 375°F/190°C.
2. Beat eggs and sugar together in a bowl until thick and creamy. Sift flour and baking powder, add to egg mixture with melted butter, vanilla extract and 1 tablespoon hot water. Gently fold into the mixture.
3. Spoon small amounts of mixture into well-buttered madeleine moulds. Bake in the oven for 12–15 minutes or until golden brown. Remove from moulds and cool on a wire rack.
4. To decorate, brush each madeleine with the sieved jam. Coat well in coconut and top with a glacé cherry half. If liked, madeleines can be coated in coloured coconut.

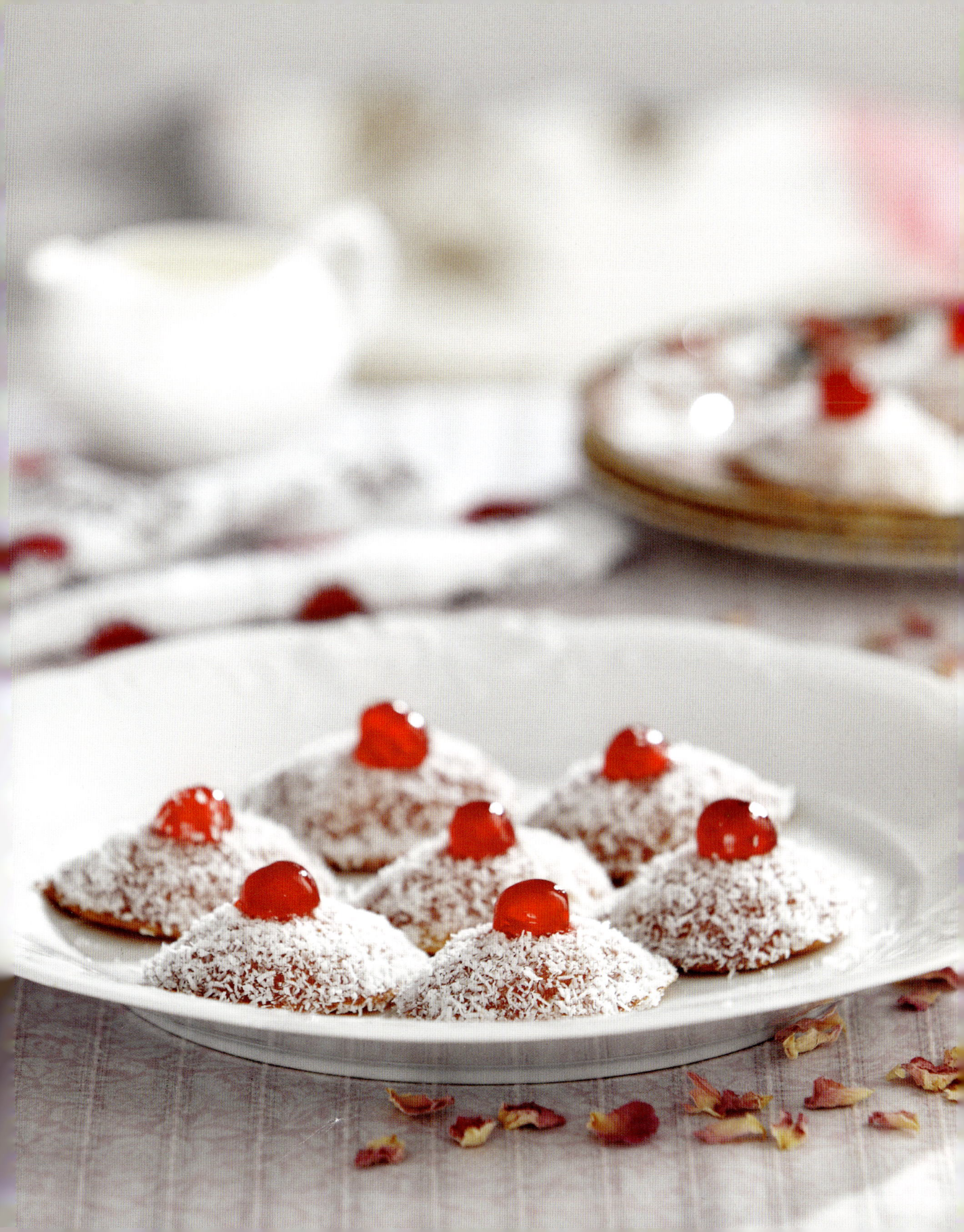

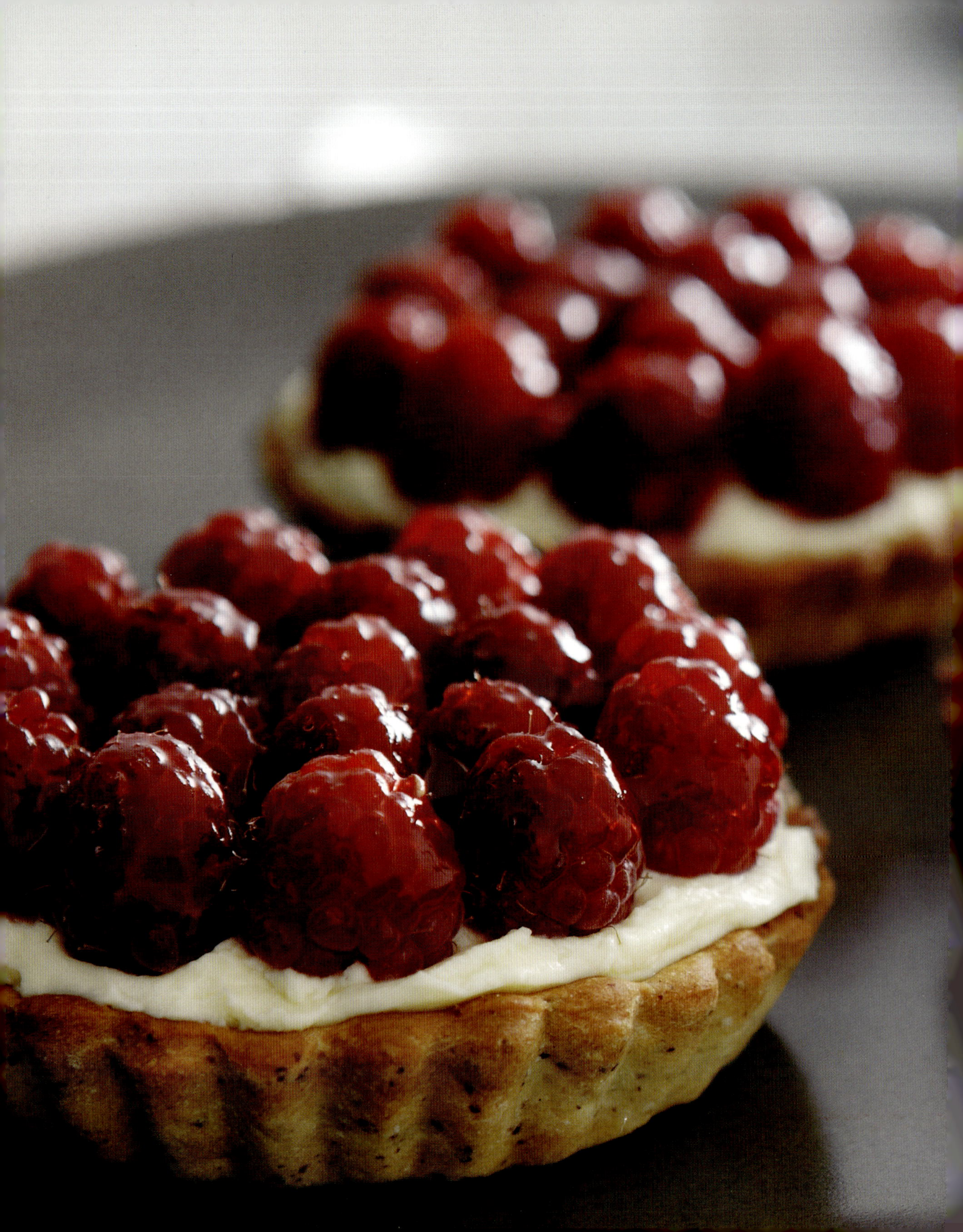

TARTS

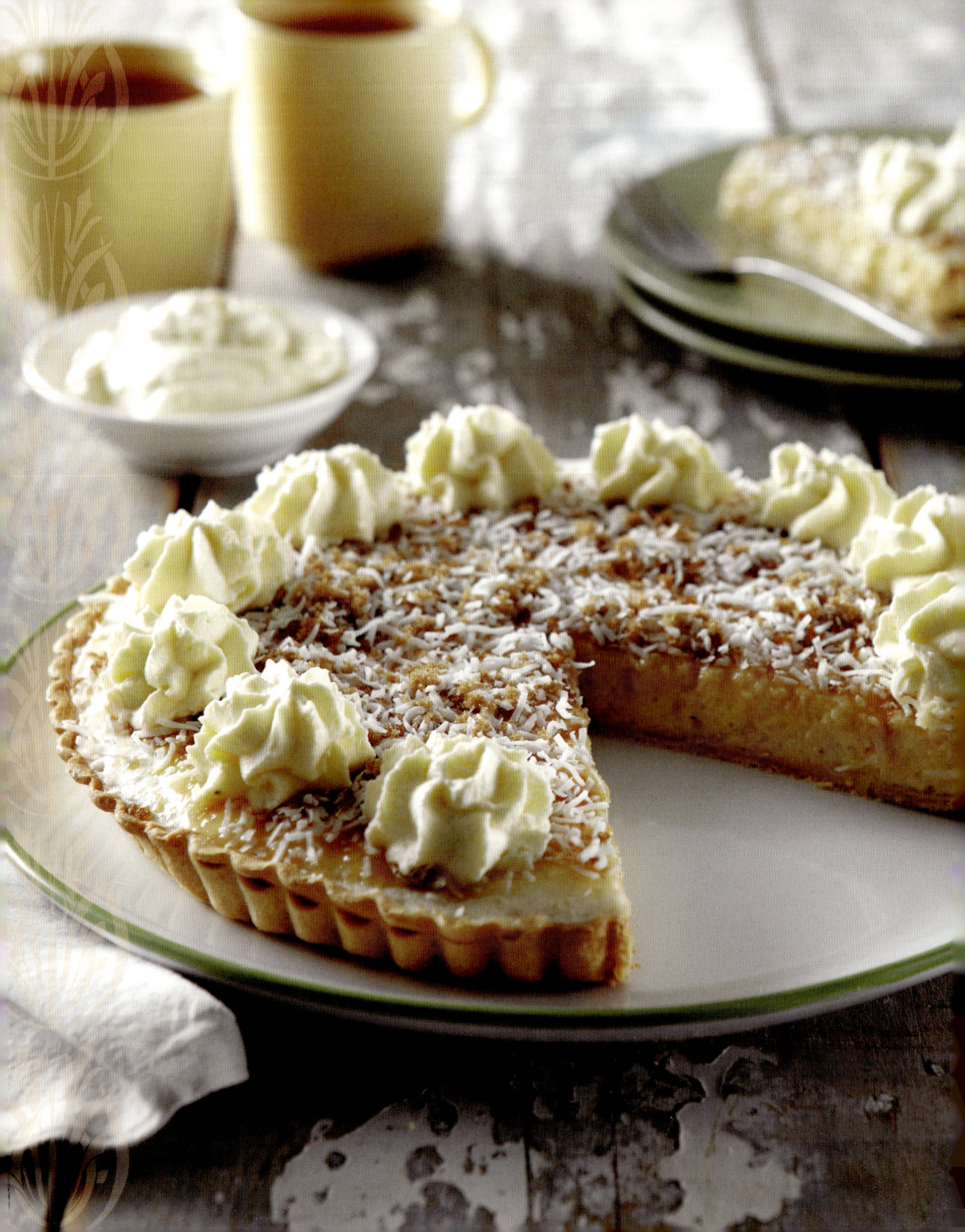

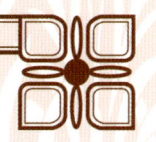

Apple Chiffon Tart

INGREDIENTS:

1 23cm (9 in) shortcrust pastry case

FILLING

4 teaspoons gelatin
1 cup canned apple purée
1 tablespoon caster sugar
½ cup cream
2 egg whites

TOPPING

¼ cup apple purée
½ cup coconut
¼ cup brown sugar
½ cup cream

Serves 12

METHOD:

1. Add the gelatin to ¼ cup hot water and stir briskly with a fork until dissolved. Add to the apple purée.
2. Whisk the egg whites until stiff, continue whisking and gradually add the caster sugar to form a meringue. Fold the cream and meringue into the gelatin/apple mixture. Pour into the pastry shell. Refrigerate until set.
3. To make the topping, spread the apple purée over the top of the tart. Sprinkle the combined coconut and brown sugar over the apple. Whip cream and pipe around the edge.

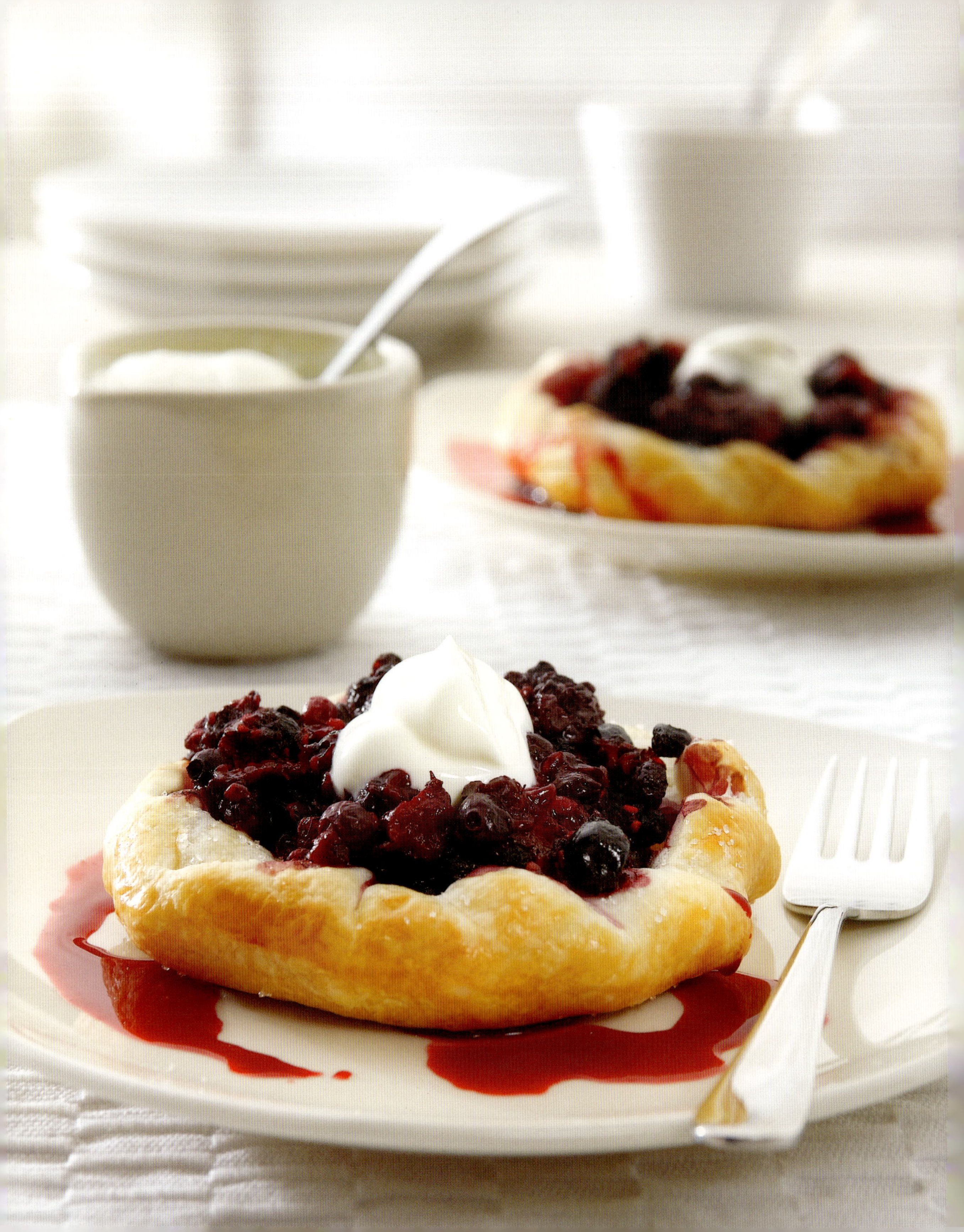

Berry Tarts

INGREDIENTS:

- 1 sheet puff pastry, thawed
- 3 cups fresh berries
- 1½ tablespoons caster or brown sugar
- 1 tablespoon milk

Makes 4

METHOD:

1. Preheat oven to 200°C/400°F and line an oven tray with baking paper. Cut pastry into quarters and place on the prepared oven tray. In a small saucepan over a medium-low heat, cook the berries with the sugar for 2 minutes until soft. Strain through a sieve and reserve the liquid. Divide mixture evenly between pastry squares, then roll edges of pastry in to form a 10cm round shape. Brush pastry edges with milk and scatter with a little extra sugar.
2. Bake for 15 minutes or until crisp and golden brown. Use reserved liquid to decorate the serving plate by pouring a thin circle around the edge of each plate.
3. Serve with vanilla yoghurt or vanilla ice cream.

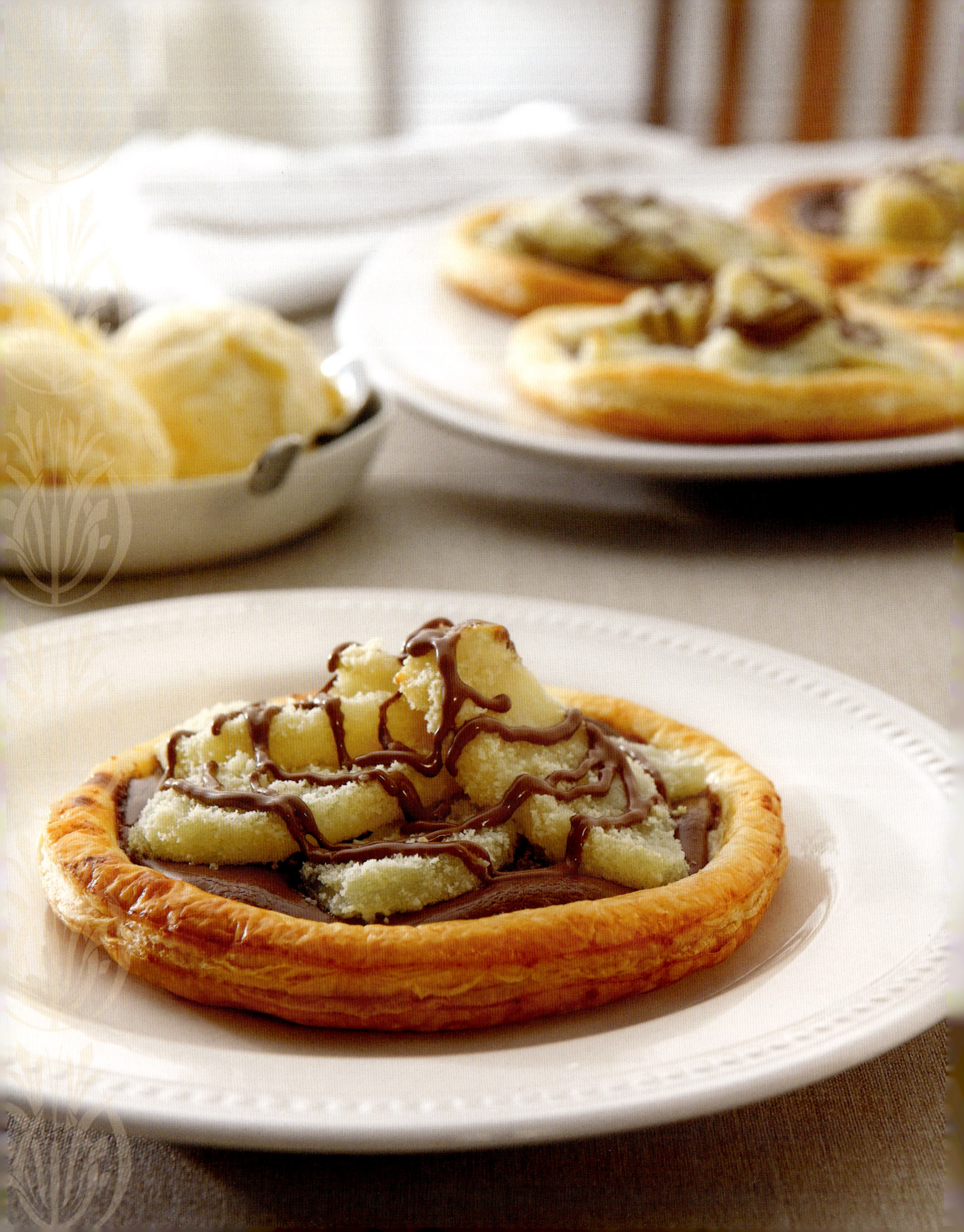

Chocolate Pear Delights

INGREDIENTS:

3 sheets puff pastry, thawed

1 cup milk chocolate buttons, melted

825 g (32 oz) canned pear halves, drained and sliced thickly

⅓ cup almond meal

Makes 6

METHOD:

1. Preheat oven to 200°C/400°F and line 2 oven trays with baking paper. Using a 14 cm (6 in) plate as a stencil, cut out 2 rounds from each pastry sheet, making a total of 6 rounds. Pierce each pastry round all over with a fork, leaving a 1 cm (½ in) border, then place on the prepared oven trays.

2. Spread each round with 1–2 tablespoons of melted chocolate, leaving a 1 cm (½ in) border. Add the sliced pear halves and almond meal to a bowl and gently mix to combine. Divide the pear slices evenly between the pastry rounds and arrange decoratively. Bake for 12–15 minutes.

3. Serve with ice cream, and if you prefer, drizzle with melted chocolate.

4. One of the easiest ways to melt chocolate is to place chopped chocolate in a microwave-safe container and cook on high in 30-second bursts, stirring a little each time until melted.

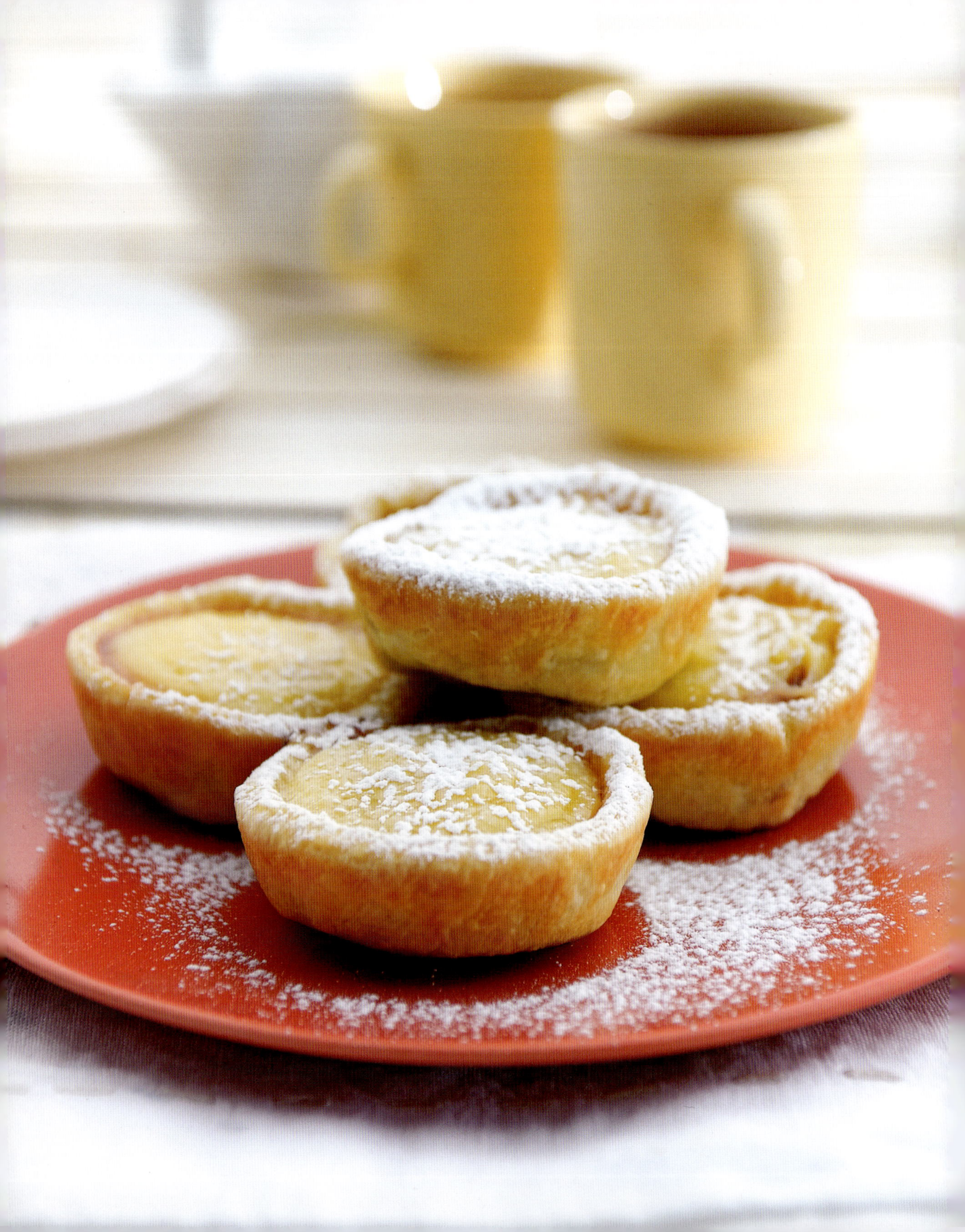

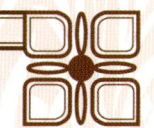

Apple Jam Tarts

INGREDIENTS:

250 g (9 oz) shortcrust pastry
500 g (1 lb) apples, peeled and cored
juice and zest of 1 lemon
60 g (2 oz) sugar
30 g (1 oz) butter
2 eggs, lightly beaten
⅓ cup blackberry jam

Makes 8

METHOD:

1. Preheat oven to 200°C/400°F. Line 8 patty tins with the pastry, prick with a fork and cook for about 10–15 minutes, until browned. Cook the apples with water for 15 minutes.
2. When cooked, rub through a sieve, return to the saucepan and add lemon zest, juice, sugar, butter and eggs. Allow to cook over a low heat until the mixture thickens slightly.
3. Place a teaspoon or two of the jam in the bottom of each pastry case and then fill the cases with the apple mixture and return to oven to set. Serve sprinkled with sifted icing sugar.

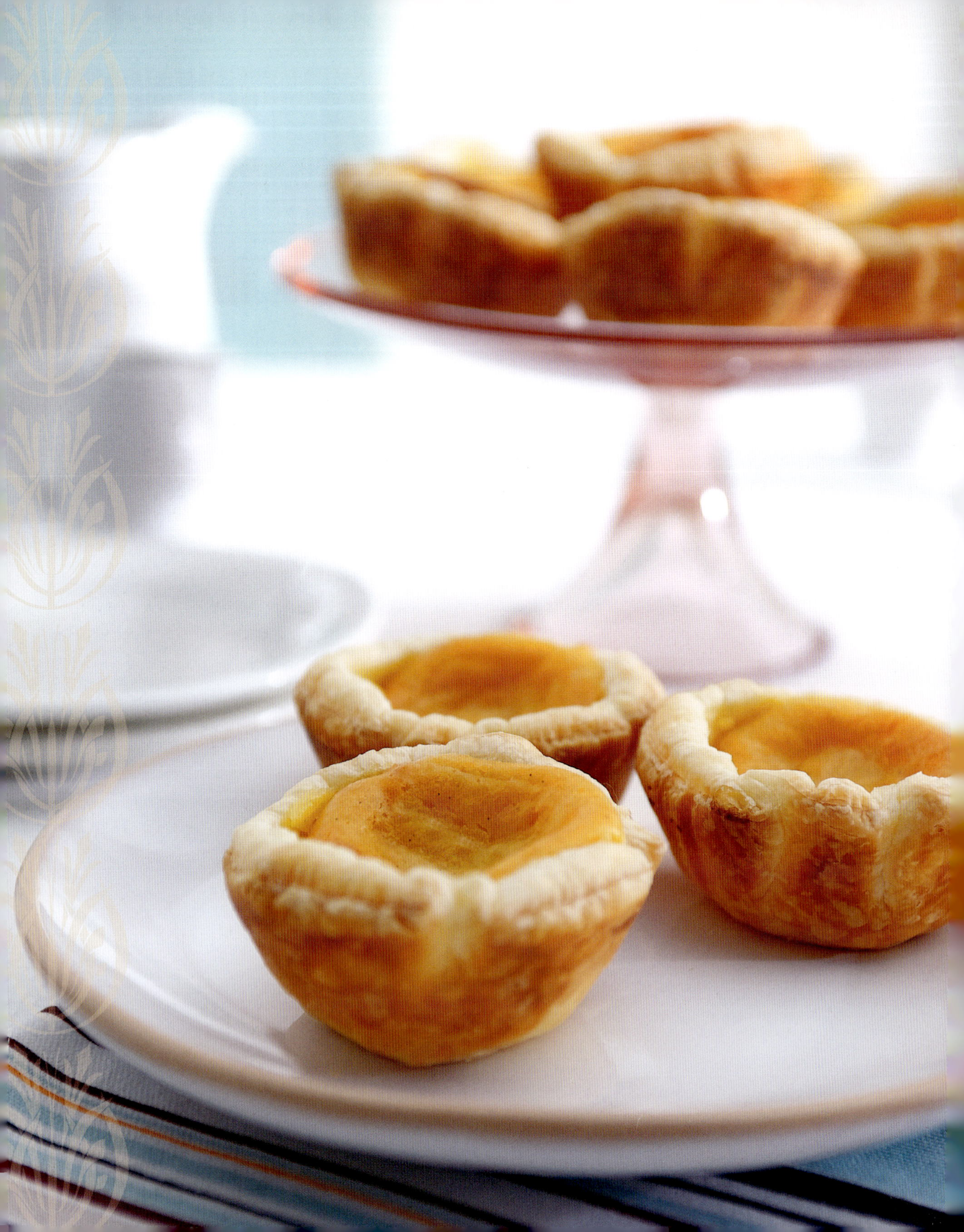

Portuguese Custard Tarts

INGREDIENTS:

3 sheets frozen puff pastry, thawed

1½ cups milk

5 tablespoons cornflour

300 g (10½ oz) superfine (caster) sugar

½ vanilla bean

9 egg yolks

Makes 12

METHOD:

Preheat oven to 190°C/375°F. Lightly grease a 12-cup muffin tin and line bottom and sides of cups with puff pastry.

In a saucepan, combine milk, cornflour, sugar and vanilla bean. Cook, stirring constantly, until mixture thickens.

Place egg yolks in a medium bowl. Slowly whisk half of the hot milk mixture into the egg yolks. Gradually add egg yolk mixture back to remaining milk mixture, whisking constantly.

Cook, stirring constantly, for 5 minutes or until thickened. Remove vanilla bean.

Fill pastry-lined muffin cups with egg mixture and bake for 25 minutes, or until pastry is golden brown and filling is lightly browned on top.

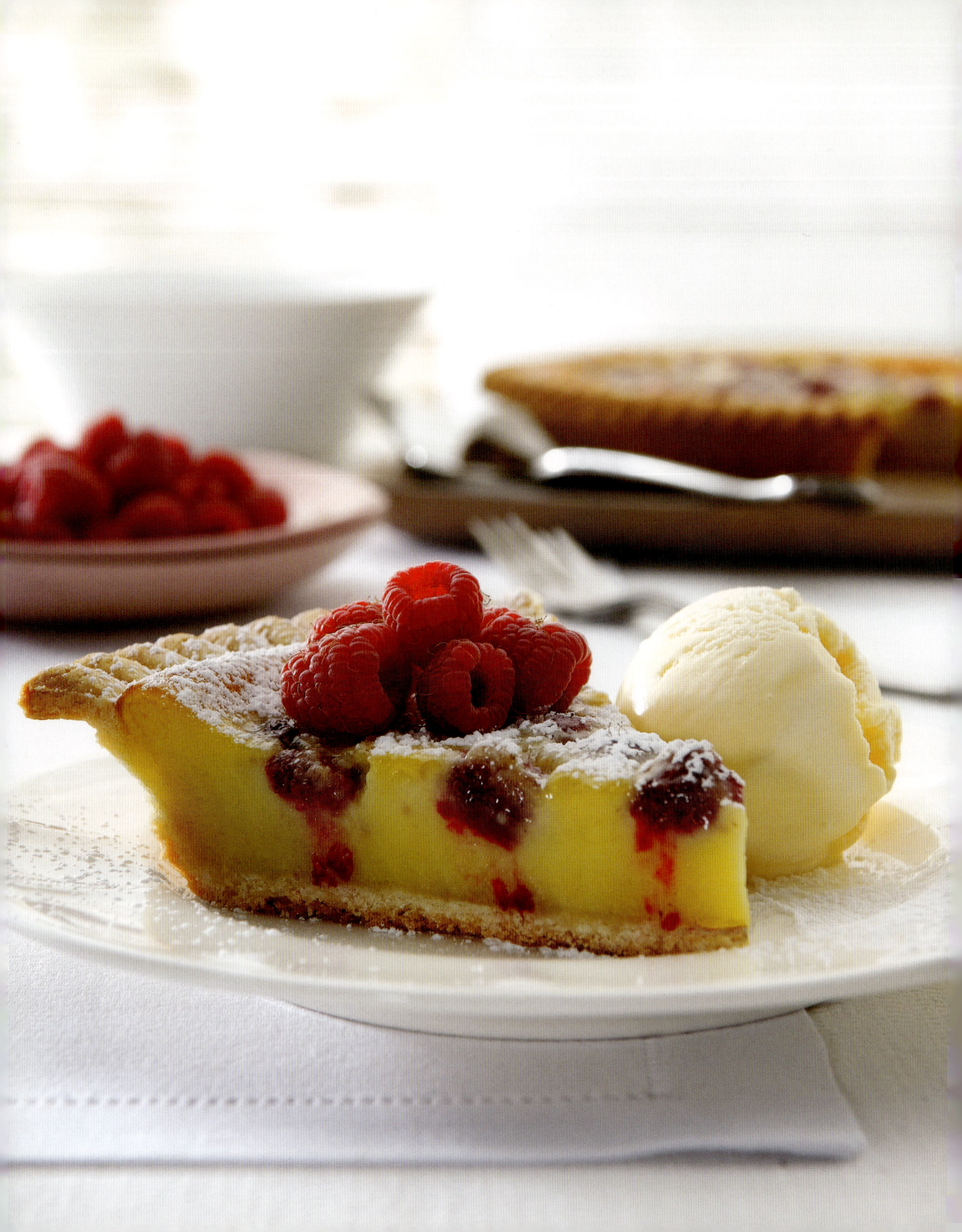

Lemon & Raspberry Tart

INGREDIENTS:

23 cm (9 in) sweet flan case, frozen
150 g (5 oz) fresh raspberries
4 eggs
⅔ cup superfine (caster) sugar
zest of 2 lemons
½ cup thickened cream
1 tablespoon confectioners' (icing) sugar

Serves 6

METHOD:

1. Preheat oven to 180°C/350°F. Place frozen pastry case on an oven tray – do not remove from the foil tin provided. Scatter the raspberries in the base of the flan case.
2. Beat together the eggs, caster sugar, lemon zest and cream. Strain mixture through a fine sieve and pour over the raspberries. Bake for 30 minutes or until just set.
3. Allow to cool to room temperature, then dust with the icing sugar. Serve with ice cream and raspberries.
4. If using frozen berries, make sure they are thawed – this is important as frozen berries retain excess water which, if it goes into the custard, will increase the volume of liquid and the recipe will not work.

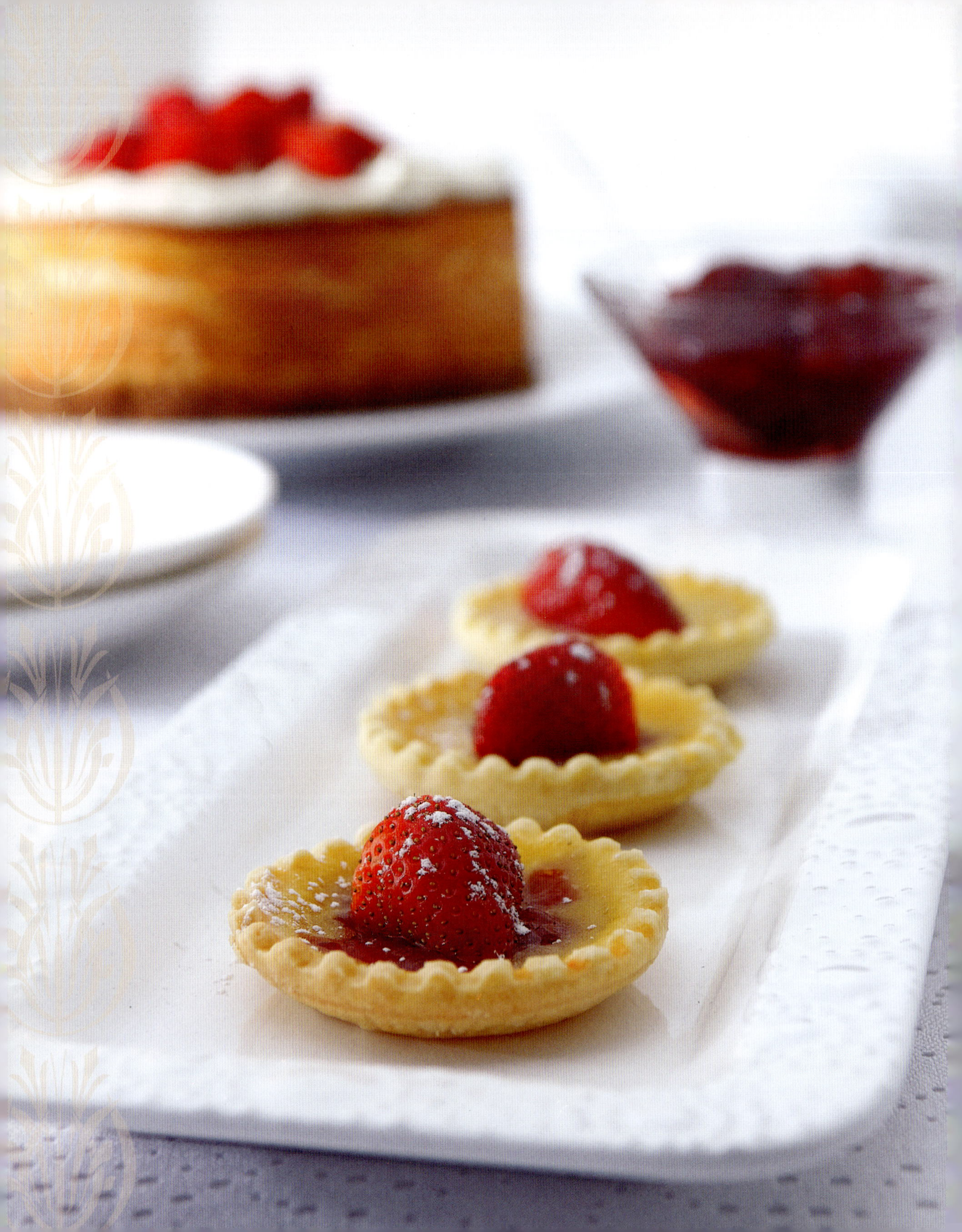

Mini Strawberry Custard Tarts

INGREDIENTS:

12 frozen mini shortcrust pastry cases
2 egg yolks
2 tablespoons superfine (caster) sugar
⅓ cup thickened cream
1½ tablespoons strawberry jam
6 small strawberries, hulled and halved
1 tablespoon confectioners' (icing) sugar

Makes 12

METHOD:

1. Preheat the oven to 160°C/325°F. Place the frozen tart cases on an oven tray and bake for 10 minutes. Remove from the oven and set aside to cool slightly.
2. Meanwhile, whisk the egg yolks and sugar by hand until the sugar dissolves, then stir in the cream.
3. Spread the base of each tart case with ½ teaspoon of strawberry jam. Spoon the egg mixture evenly into each tart case, then bake for 10–12 minutes until the custard is set. When set, take from the oven and place a strawberry half, cut-side down, onto each tart.
4. Leave to cool for 15 minutes, then remove tarts from the foil cases. Place on a platter and dust with icing sugar to serve.

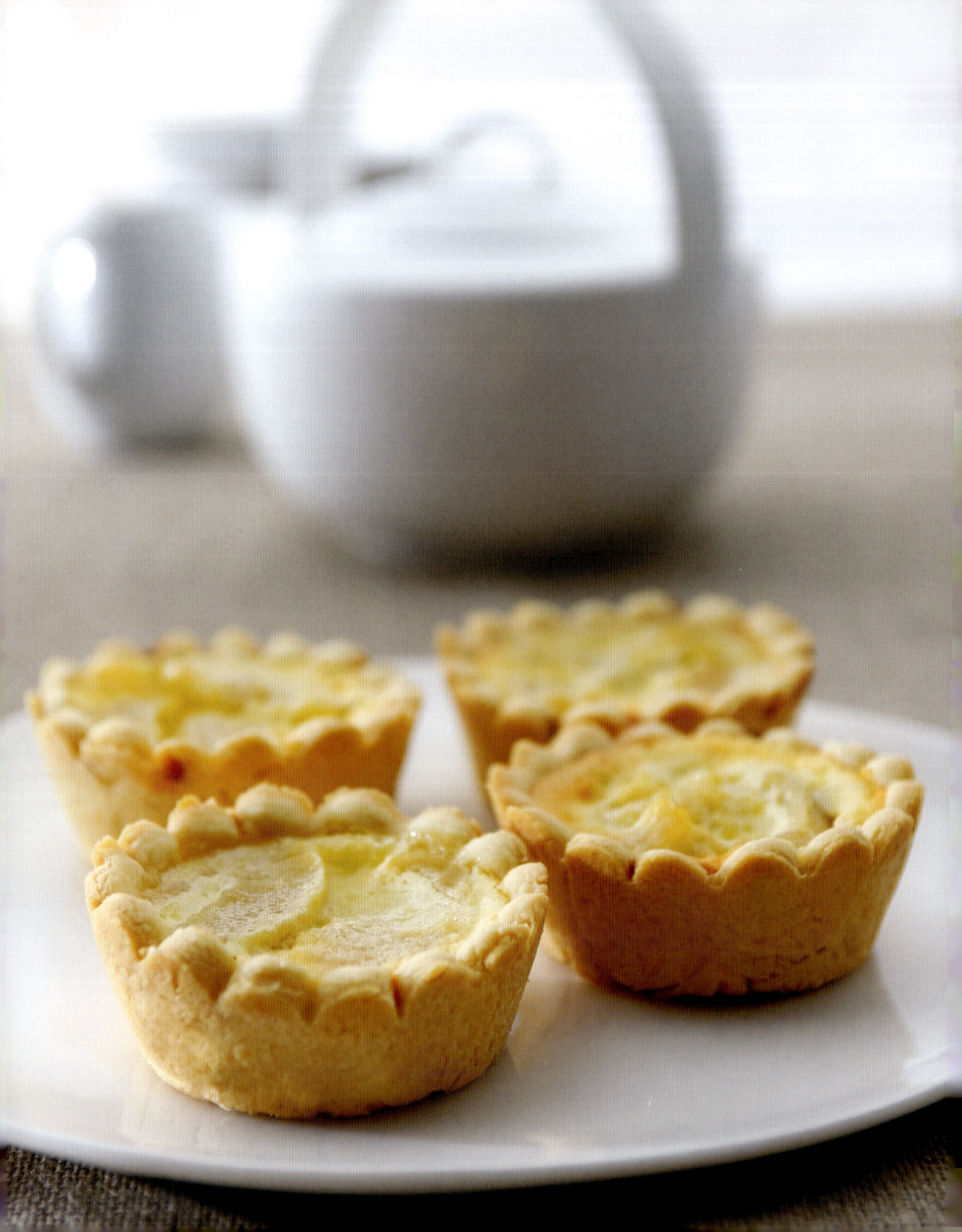

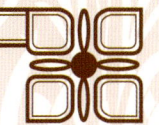

Apple Custard Tarts

INGREDIENTS:

3 cups plain flour

1 teaspoon salt

180 g (6 oz) butter

3 eggs

⅓ cup granulated sugar

1½ cups milk

400 g (14 oz) canned pie apples

Makes 24

METHOD:

1. Preheat oven to 180°C/350°F. Combine flour and teaspoon of salt in mixing bowl. Mix in butter until mixture resembles breadcrumbs. Mix in enough cold water to form a firm dough that sticks together, about 6 tablespoons.
2. Shape dough into a ball. Cut in half. Roll out each half on lightly floured surface until 5 mm (¼ in) thick. Cut 12 circles from each half using fluted biscuit cutter 75 mm (3 in) in diameter. Fit pastry circles into greased muffin cups, pressing sides so they reach rims.
3. Beat eggs with whisk or electric mixer. Stir in sugar and remaining ½ teaspoon salt. Gradually blend in milk.
4. Spoon one tablespoon crushed apples into each pastry case and then spoon custard mixture over apples until each pastry case is full.
5. Bake until knife inserted in centre of custards comes out clean, about 30 minutes. Remove tarts from muffin cups. Cool on wire racks.

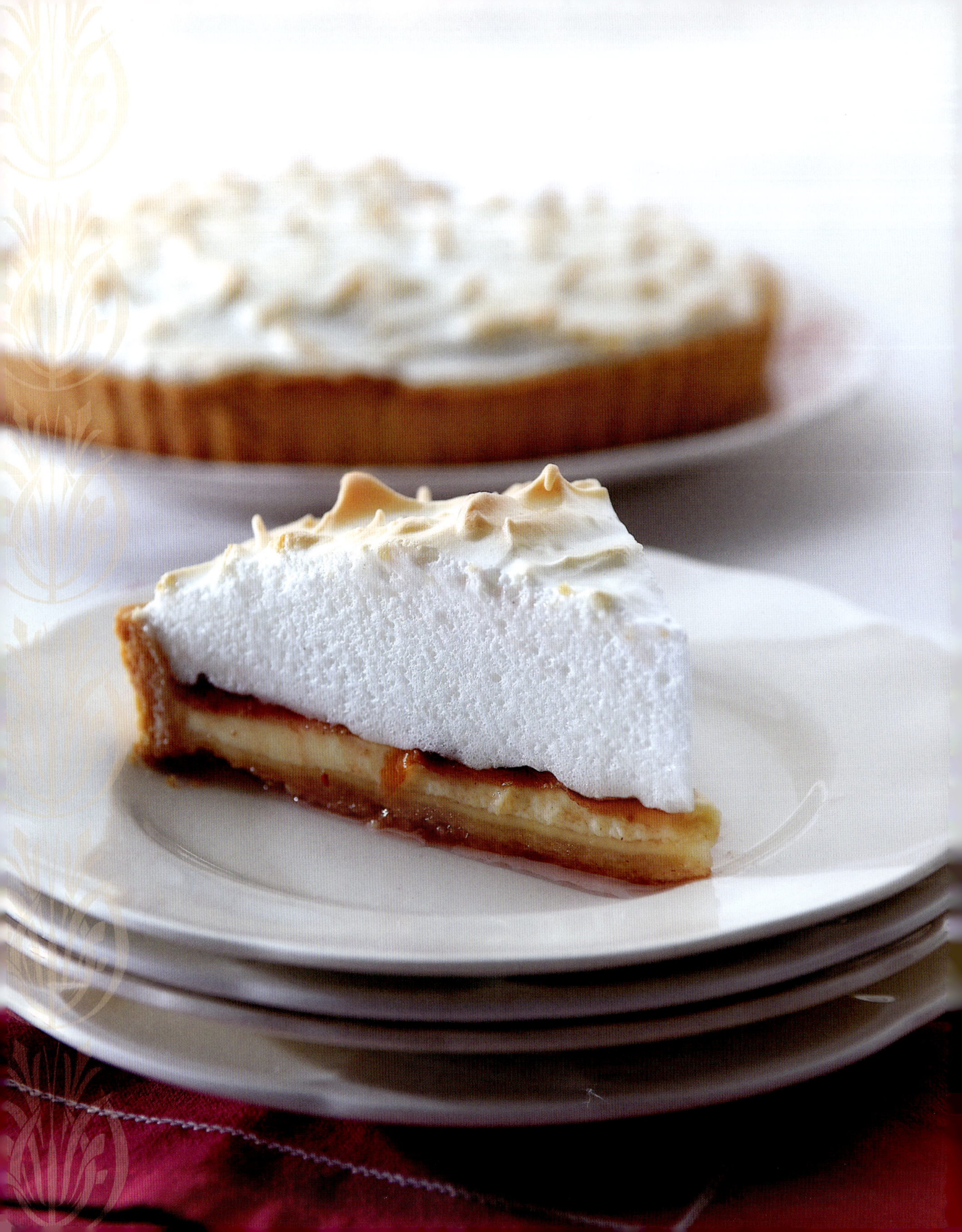

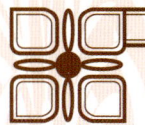

Princess Custard Tart

INGREDIENTS:

175 g (6 oz) plain flour
1 teaspoon baking powder
90 g (3 oz) butter
pinch of salt
30 g (1oz) sugar
¼ cup raspberry jam

CUSTARD

2 teaspoons sugar
1 teaspoon plain flour
2 egg yolks
1 cup milk

MERINGUE

3 egg whites
6 tablespoons sugar

Serves 8

METHOD:

1. Preheat oven to 200°C/400°F. Sift flour and baking powder into butter, salt and sugar and mix with 2 tablespoons cold water to make a firm dough. Roll out pastry to about 6 mm and line the base and sides of a greased 20 cm (8in) springform tin with the pastry.
2. Make custard by mixing sugar, flour, egg yolks and milk together. Fill the pastry case with the custard mixture.
3. Bake for 25 minutes. While baking, make meringue by beating egg whites with 4 tablespoons sugar.
4. Allow tart to cool then spread thinly with raspberry jam and pile meringue on top. Reduce heat to 120°C/250°F and bake until brown.

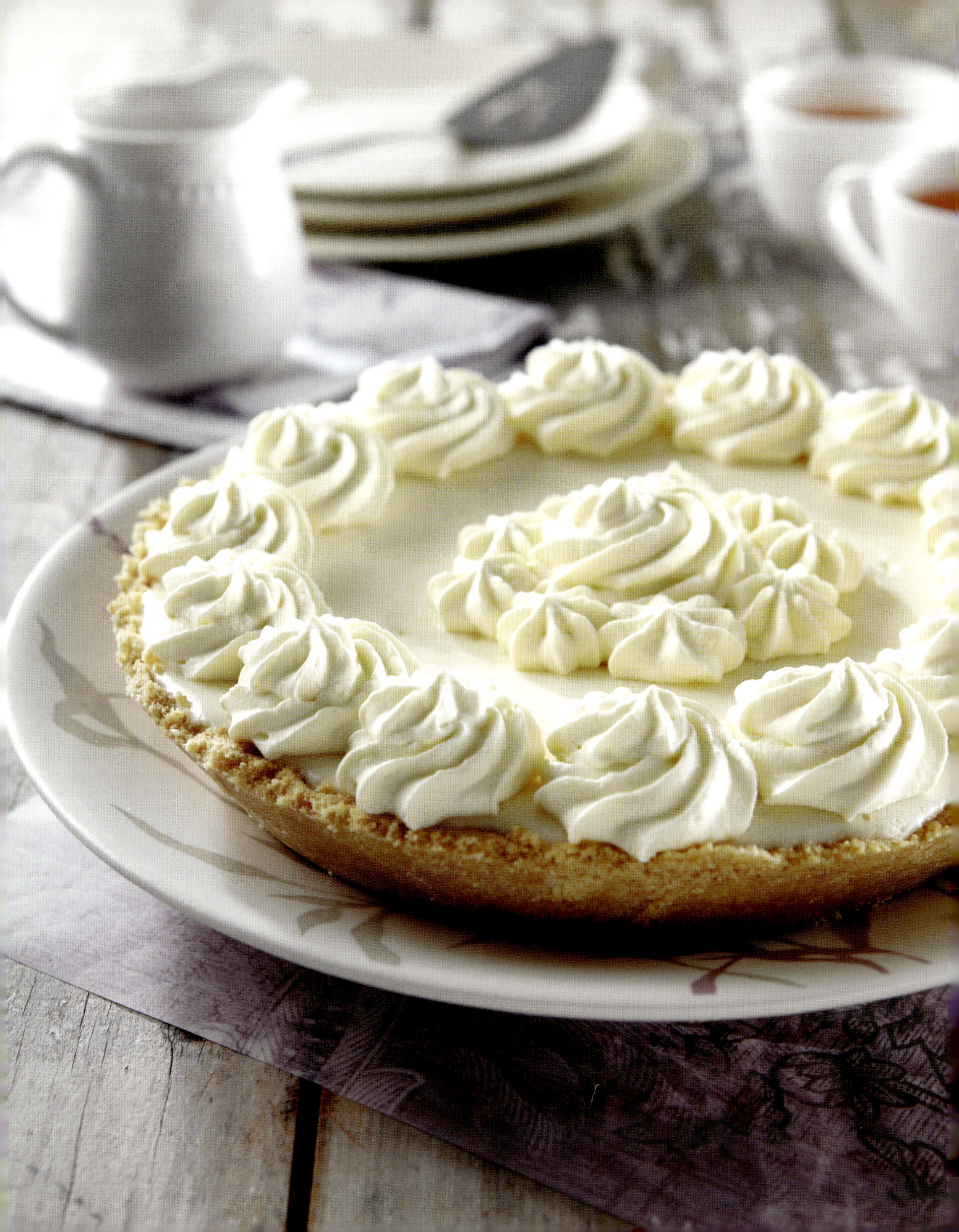

Pineapple Chiffon Flan

INGREDIENTS:

10cm (28 in)
1 sheet or 3 teaspoons gelatin
2 medium sized eggs
425 g (15 oz) can crushed pineapple
½ cup sugar
½ cup cream

Serves 6

METHOD:

1. Add gelatin to ¼ cup hot water, stir briskly with a fork until dissolved. Separate whites from egg yolks.
2. Add ¼ cup sugar to egg yolks and beat until creamy. Add crushed pineapple and juice. To this add the hot gelatin solution.
3. Whip egg whites with the remaining sugar. Fold this through the pineapple mixture. Pour into the prepared crumb case. Refrigerate until set.
4. Whip the cream and pipe onto the set chiffon.

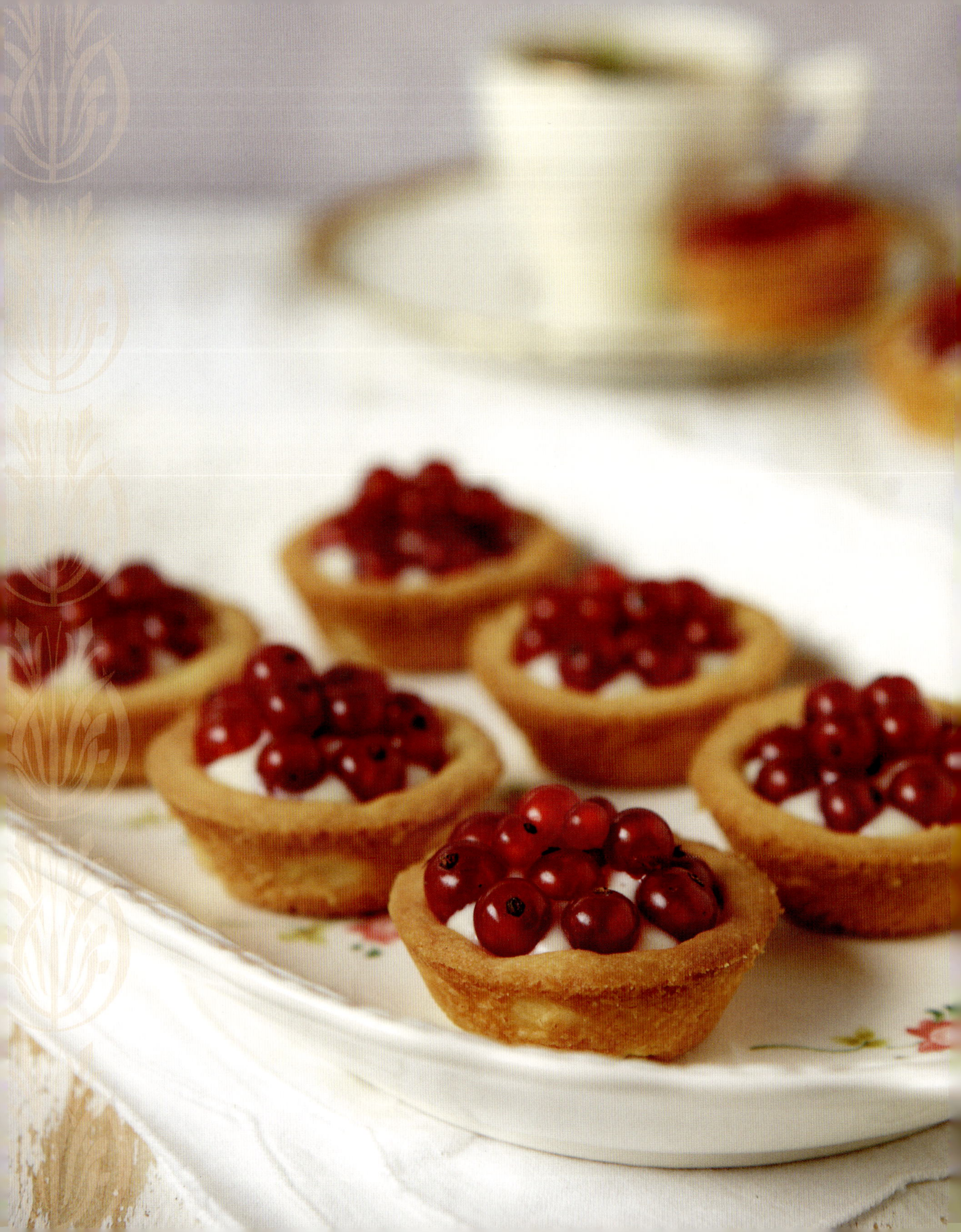

Shortbread Tarts with Cream Cheese

INGREDIENTS:

180g (6½ oz) butter

½ cup icing sugar

1 teaspoon vanilla extract

1½ cups plain flour

2 tablespoons cornflour

⅛ teaspoon salt

CREAM CHEESE FILLING

250g (8oz) cream cheese, softened

200g (7 oz) sweetened condensed milk

⅓ cup freshly squeezed lemon juice

zest of 1 lemon

1 teaspoon vanilla extract

250 g (8 oz) fresh berries or fruit of choice

Makes about 36

METHOD:

1. Preheat oven to 180°C/350°F.
2. Prepare a 36-cup mini muffin tin by buttering lightly.
3. Cream the butter and sugar well. Then add the vanilla, sifted flours and salt and mix until incorporated. Do not overmix. Divide the dough into 36 even pieces and place one ball of dough in the centre of each muffin tin. Press the dough up the sides of the individual muffin tin with your fingers so there is an indentation in the centre.
4. Once filled, place the pan, with the unbaked shells, in the freezer for about 10 minutes so the shortbread can become firm. (This will help to prevent the shortbread from puffing up during baking.)
5. Bake for approximately 18–20 minutes or until lightly browned. About halfway through the baking time, lightly prick the bottom of each shortbread with a fork. Check again after another 5 minutes and prick again if needed. Once they are fully baked, remove from oven and place on a wire rack to cool. When completely cooled, remove the tarts from the tin.
6. To make the cream cheese filling, beat the cream cheese until fluffy. Add the condensed milk, lemon juice, zest, and vanilla and process until smooth. Do not over-process or the filling will be too runny. Transfer the filling to a bowl, cover, and refrigerate until serving time.
7. When ready to serve, fill the tart shells with the cream cheese filling and top with fresh berries or fruit of choice.

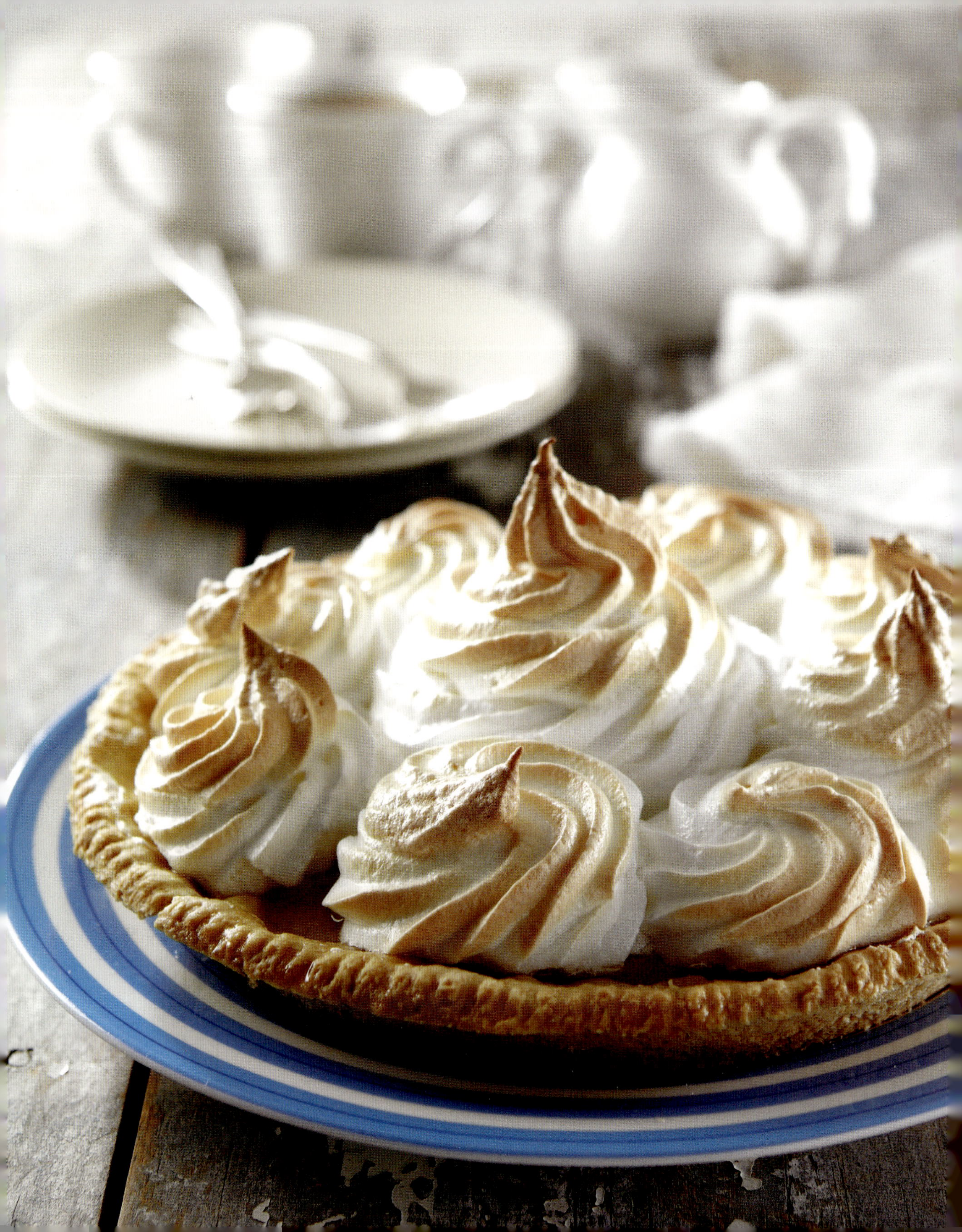

Lemon Meringue Tart

INGREDIENTS:

BISCUIT PASTRY
150 g (5 oz) butter
⅓ cup caster sugar
½ teaspoon vanilla extract
1 small egg
2 cups plain flour
½ teaspoon baking powder
pinch salt

LEMON MERINGUE
4 tablespoons cornflour
¾ cup sugar
juice of 1/2 lemon
2 egg yolks
2 tablespoons butter, softened
grated zest of 1 lemon
3 egg whites
⅓ cup sugar

Serves 6–8

METHOD:

1. Preheat oven to 200°C/400°F. To make the biscuit pastry, sift together flour and baking powder. Cream the butter and sugar with the vanilla until light and fluffy, add the egg. Fold the flour mixture into the creamed butter mixture.

2. Knead lightly until smooth, cover and refrigerate for about 30 minutes before using. Line a buttered 23 cm (9 in) pie plate with the biscuit pastry, decorate the edge and prick the bottom with a fork. Line pastry with baking paper and half-fill with rice and bake. Remove paper and rice and turn out case to cool. Reduce oven temperature to 180°C/360°F.

3. To make the lemon meringue, blend the cornflour and sugar with 1 cup of water, lemon juice and egg yolks. Stir over low heat until the mixture boils and thickens. Beat in the butter and grated lemon zest. Allow to cool and pour into the pastry case.

4. Beat egg whites until stiff, gradually add the sugar and continue beating until thick and glossy. Pipe over the top of lemon filling and bake in the centre of the oven until the meringue is firm and lightly browned.

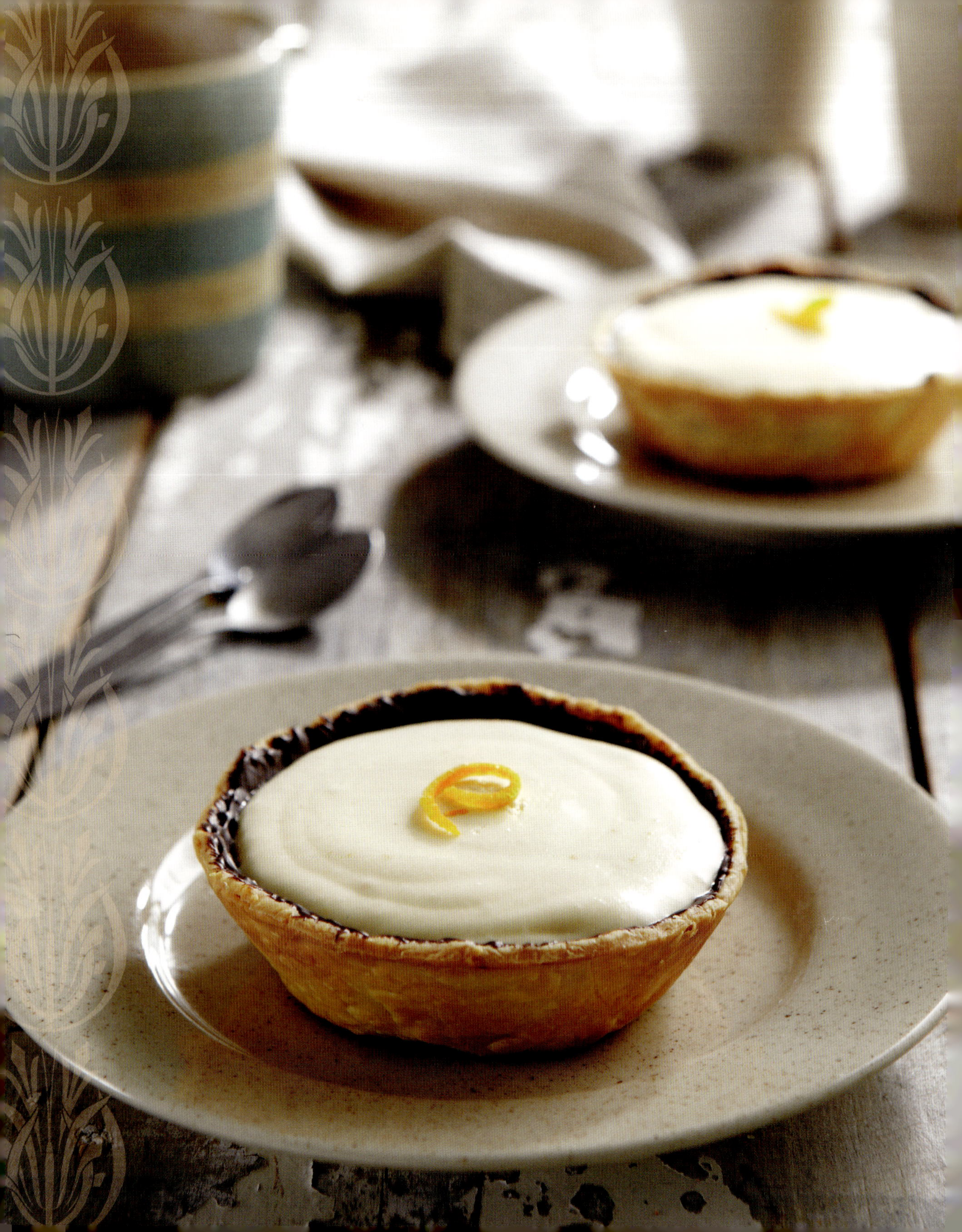

Orange Chocolate Tarts

INGREDIENTS:

370 g (13 oz) prepared shortcrust pastry
125 g (4 oz) dark chocolate, melted

ORANGE FILLING

3 egg yolks
2 tablespoons sugar
1¼ cups milk, scalded
zest of 1/2 orange, finely grated
2 tablespoons Grand Marnier (orange liqueur)
1½ teaspoons gelatine, dissolved in 4 teaspoons hot water, cooled
¼ cup double cream, whipped

Serves 6

METHOD:

1. Preheat oven to 200°C/400°F. Roll pastry out and line six 10cm (4 in) flan tins. Line pastry cases with baking paper and half-fill with uncooked rice. Bake for 8 minutes, then remove rice and paper and bake for 10 minutes longer or until pastry is golden. Set aside to cool completely. Brush cooled pastry cases with melted chocolate and set aside until chocolate sets.

2. To make filling, place egg yolks and sugar in a heatproof bowl over a saucepan of simmering water, beating until a ribbon trail forms when beater is lifted from mixture. Remove bowl from heat and gradually whisk in milk. Transfer mixture to a heavy-based saucepan and cook over a low heat, stirring in a figure eight pattern, until mixture thickens and coats the back of a wooden spoon. Do not allow the mixture to boil. Remove from heat, place in a pan of ice and stir until cool.

3. Stir in orange zest, Grand Marnier and gelatine mixture. Fold in cream, then spoon filling into pastry cases. Refrigerate until set.

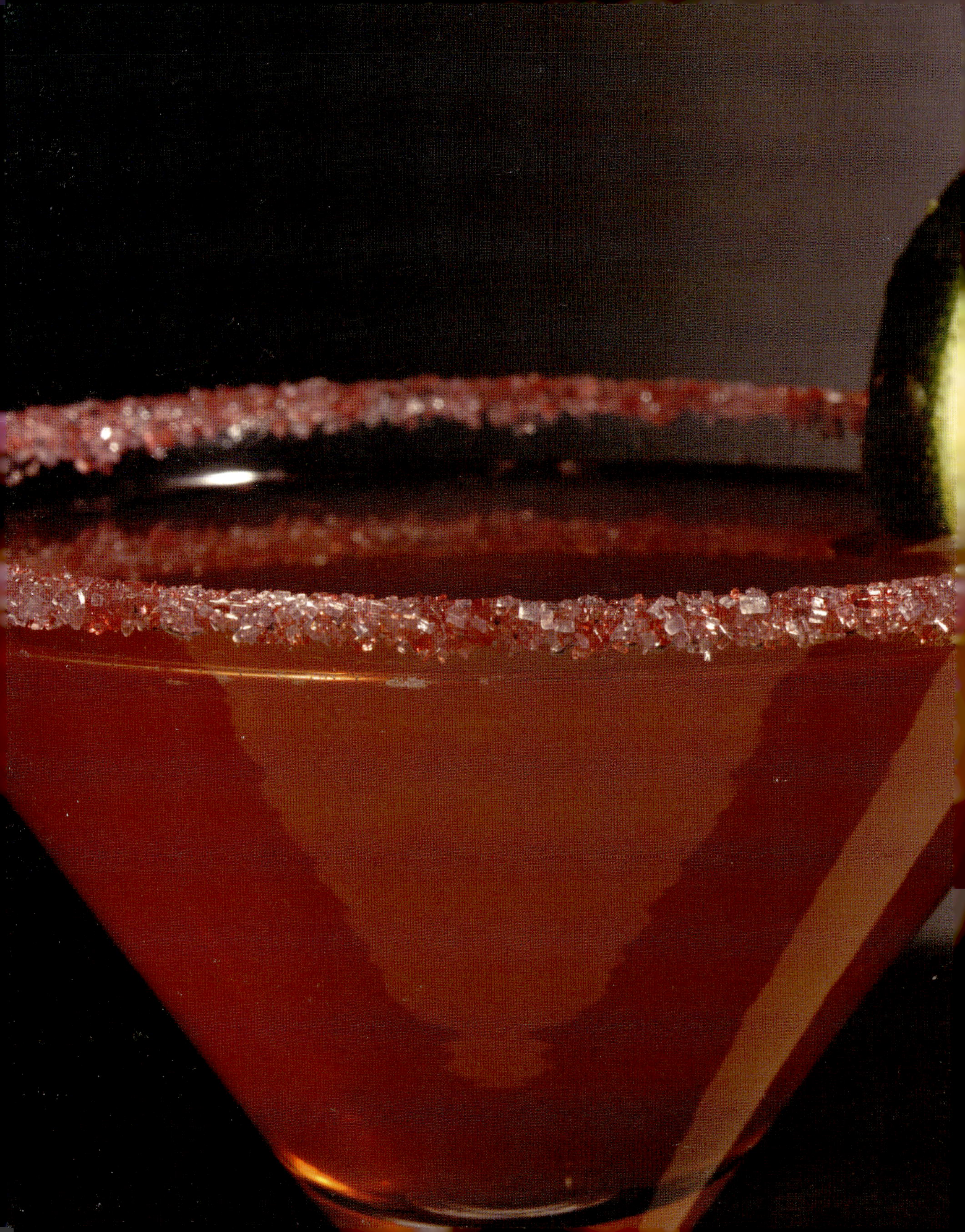

COCKTAILS

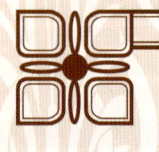

James Bond Martini

INGREDIENTS:

45 ml (1½ fl oz) gin
1½ tsp vodka
1½ tsp dry vermouth
lemon twist, to garnish

GLASS
90 ml (3 fl oz) martini glass

Serves 1

METHOD:

1. Combine the liquid ingredients with cracked ice in a cocktail shaker and shake well. Strain into a chilled glass and garnish with the lemon twist.

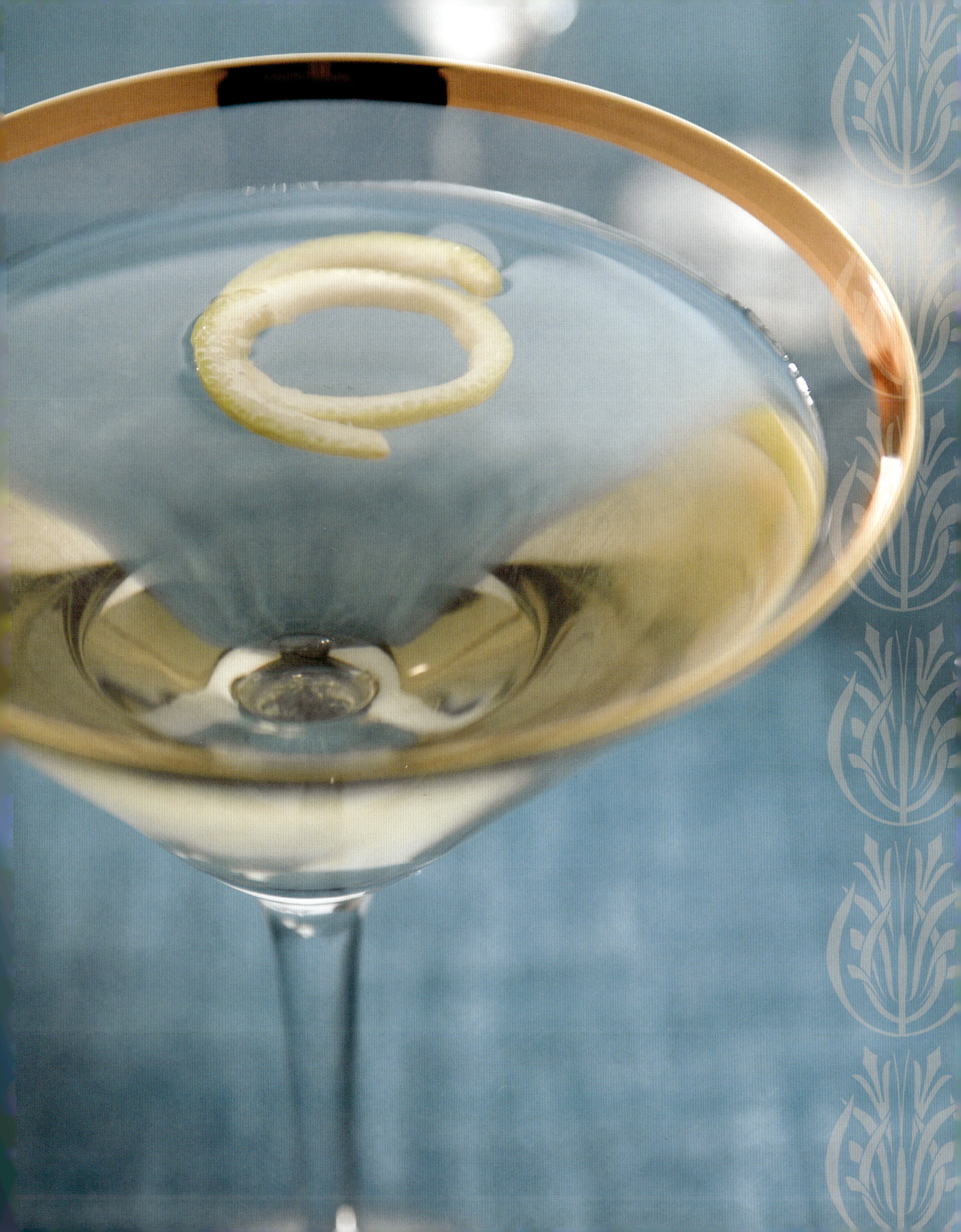

Frozen Lavender Margaritas

INGREDIENTS:

20 ml (1 tbsp) sugar
1 tsp (5 ml) fresh lavender
wedge of lime
250 ml (8 fl oz) tequila
120 ml (4 fl oz) blue curaçao
250 ml (8 fl oz) coconut milk
90 ml (3 fl oz) lime juice
450 g (1 lb) frozen raspberries
450 g (1 lb) frozen blueberries
lavender sprigs, rinsed, to
　garnish

GLASS
350 ml (12 fl oz) margarita
　glass

Serves 8–10

METHOD:

1. Mash the sugar and lavender in a saucer to release the flavour. Rub the glass rims with lime, then frost with the lavender sugar. In a blender, combine the liquids. Gradually add the fruit. Top up with ice. Blend until smooth and slushy. Pour into glasses. Garnish with lavender sprigs.

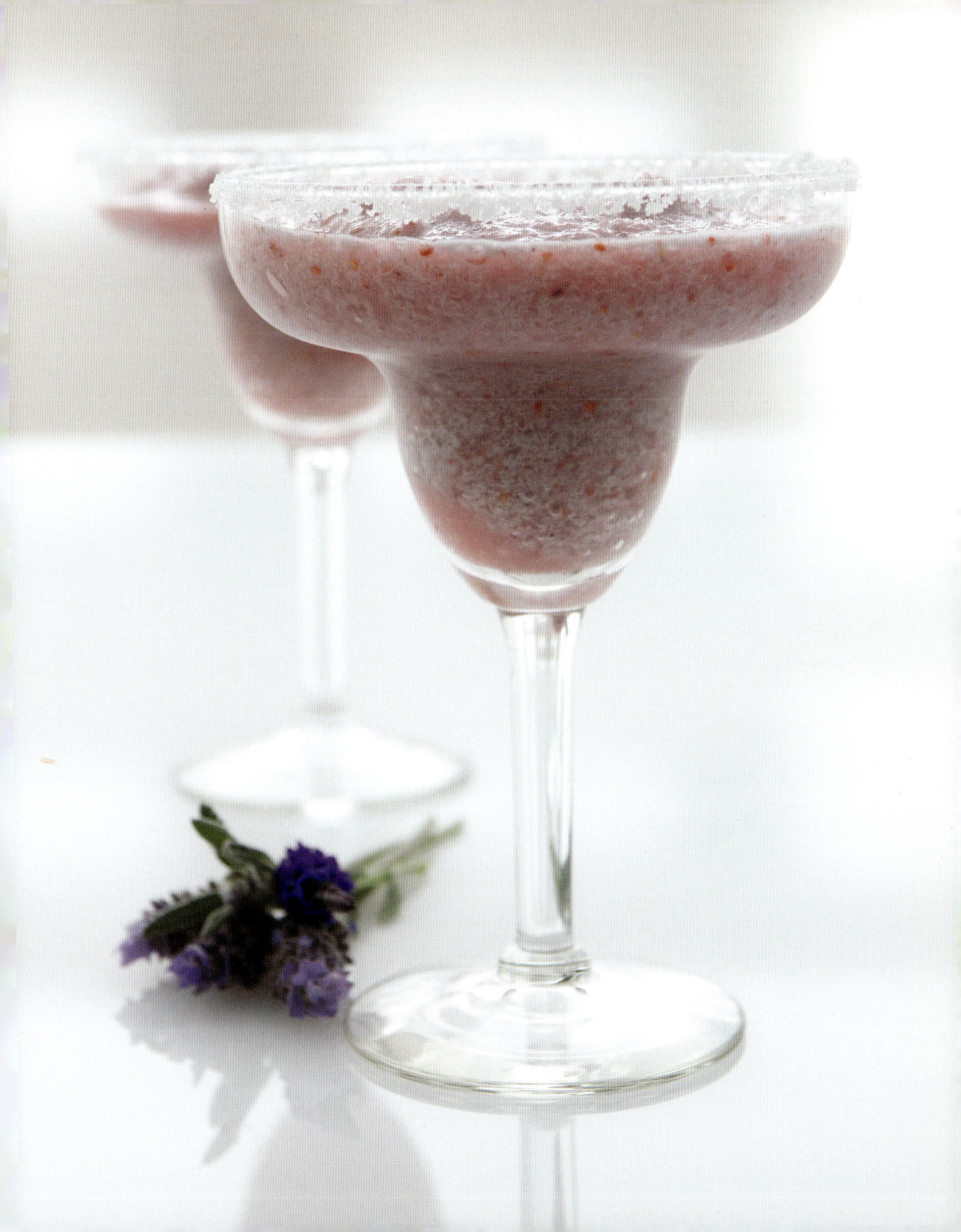

Chocolate Martini

INGREDIENTS:
45 ml (1½ fl oz) gin
1½ tsp (7.5 ml) Mozart chocolate liqueur
chocolate flakes, to garnish

GLASS
90 ml (3 fl oz) martini glass

Serves 1

METHOD:
1 Combine the vodka and liqueur in a mixing glass with ice and stir. Strain into a chilled glass and garnish with chocolate flakes.

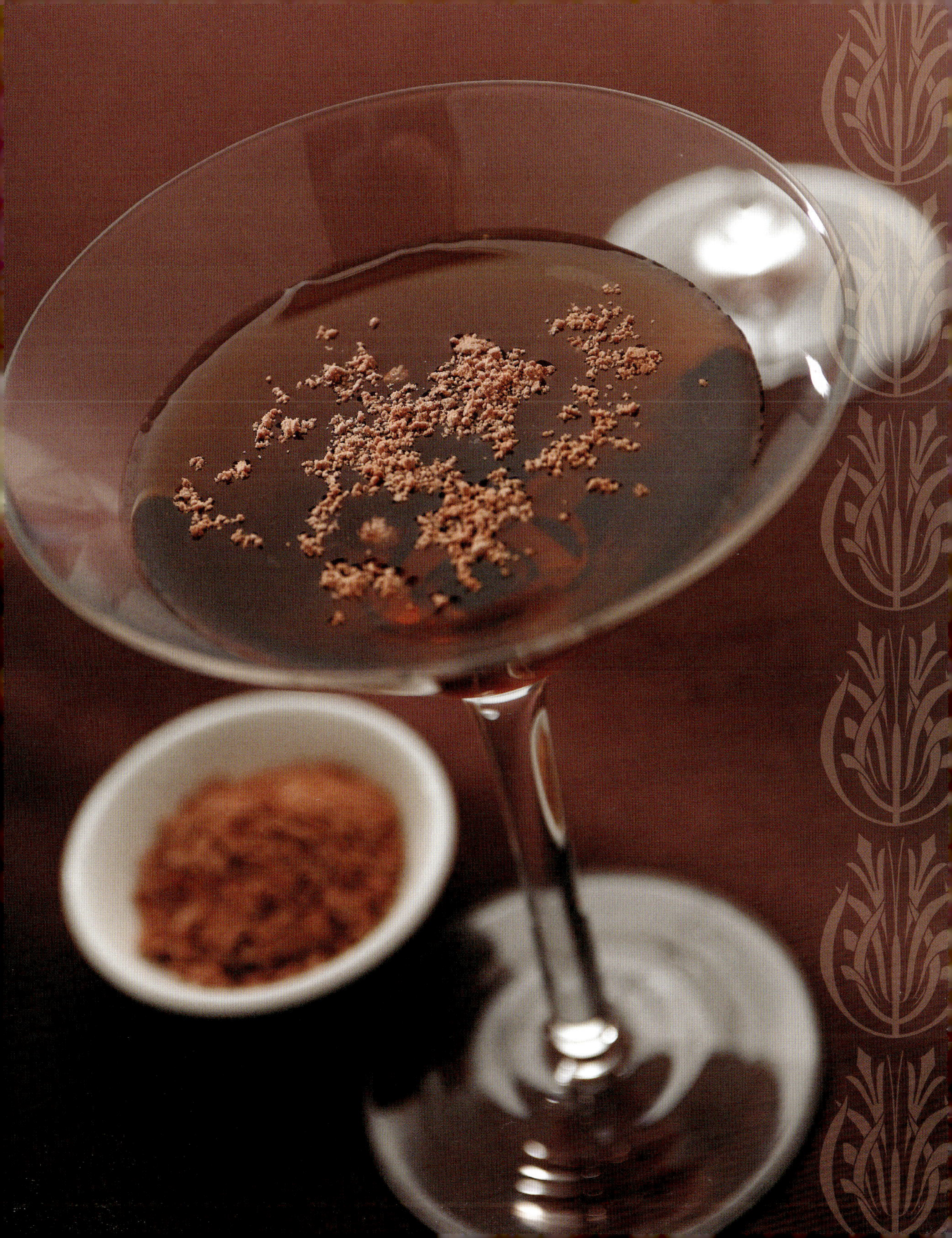

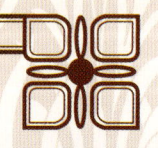

Kir Royal

Kir Imperial is made with grenadine, and crème de cassis and Champagne.

INGREDIENTS:

15 ml (½ fl oz) crème de cassis

Champagne

GLASS
145 ml (5 fl oz) Champagne flute

Serves 1

METHOD:

1 Pour crème de cassis into glass, then top up with chilled Champagne. Serve straight up.

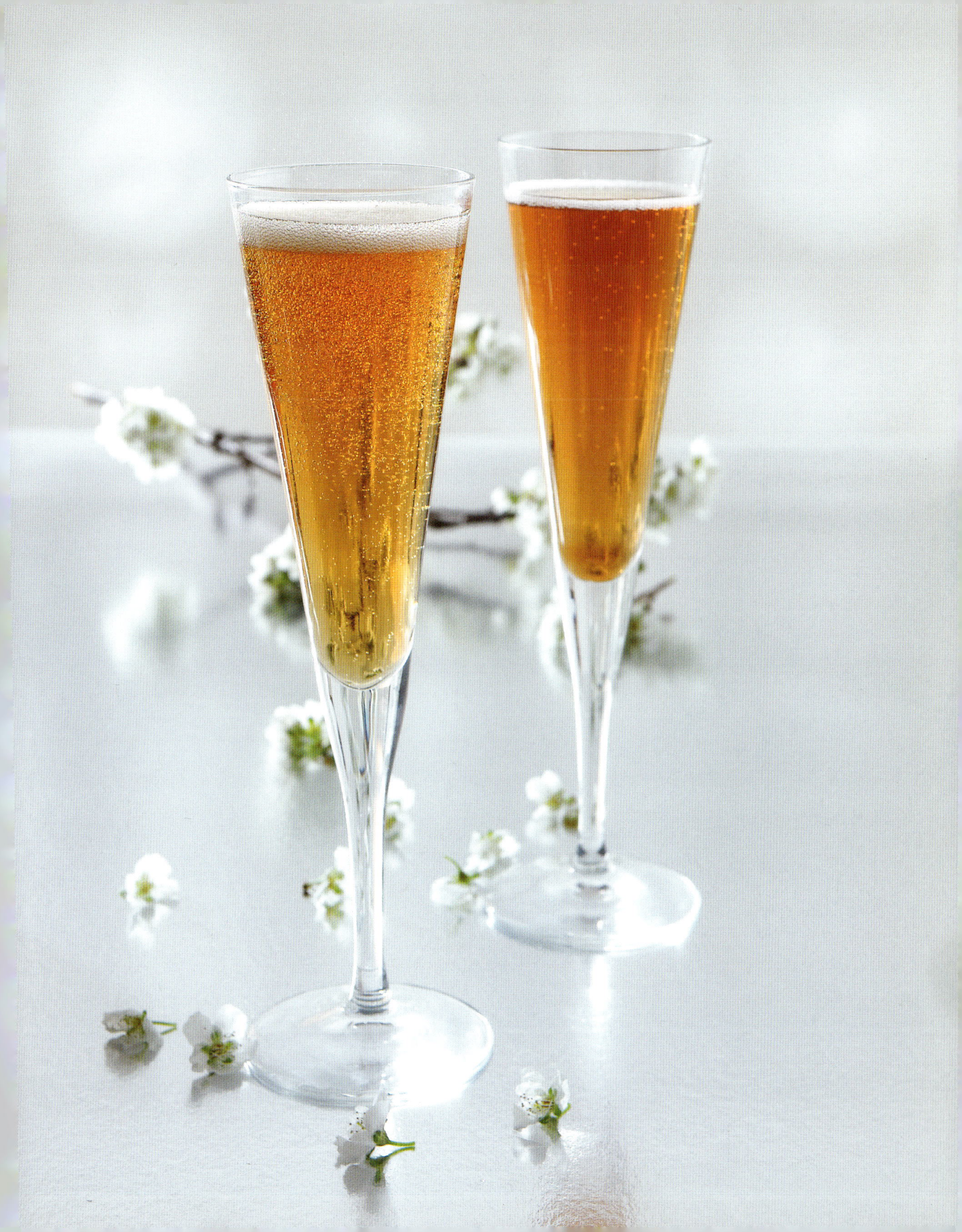

Jumping Margarita

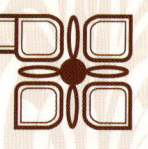

INGREDIENTS

slice of lime, plus extra to garnish
salt
15 ml (½ fl oz) lime juice
90 ml (3 fl oz) lemonade
45 ml (1½ fl oz) tequila
30 ml (1 fl oz) triple sec
45 ml (1½ fl oz) sweet-and-sour mix

SWEET-AND-SOUR MIX
1 egg white
1 cup sugar
2 cups water
2 cups fresh lemon juice

GLASS
200 ml (7 fl oz) cocktail glass

Serves 1

METHOD:

1. Rub the glass rim with the lime slice and frost with salt. Mix the liquid ingredients in a shaker filled with ice; shake well. Strain into a glass. Garnish with lime slice

METHOD FOR SWEET-AND-SOUR MIX:

1. Whisk one egg white until frothy in a medium bowl.
2. Mix in the sugar, then the water and lemon juice. Beat until all the sugar is dissolved.

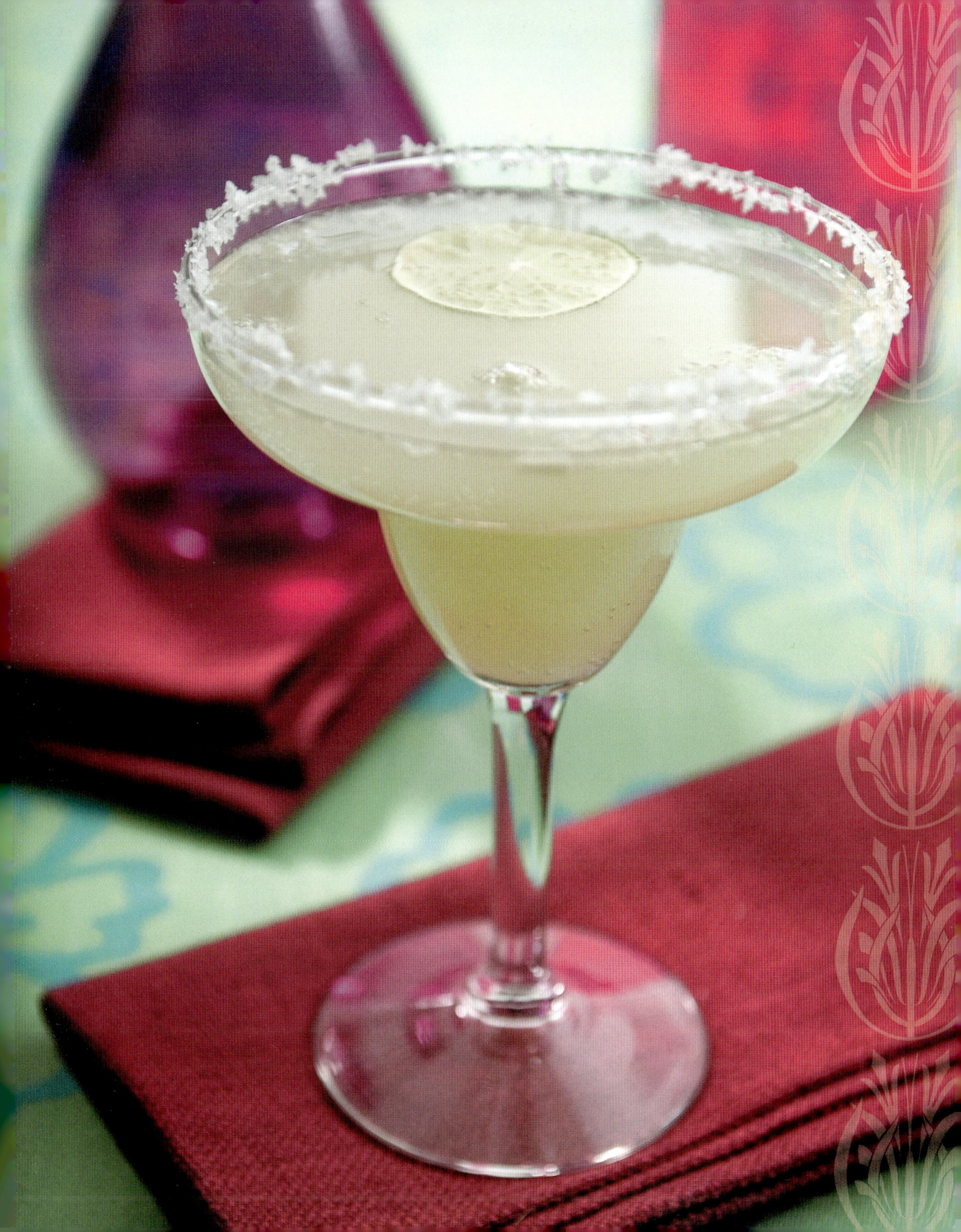

Astoria

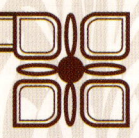

INGREDIENTS:

45 ml (1½ fl oz) gin
30 ml (1 fl oz) dry vermouth
dash of orange bitters
1 olive, to garnish

GLASS
170 ml (6 fl oz) old-fashioned glass

Serves 1

METHOD:

1. Combine all the ingredients except for the olive in a mixing glass with ice and stir well. Strain into the serving glass, then drop the olive into the liquid.

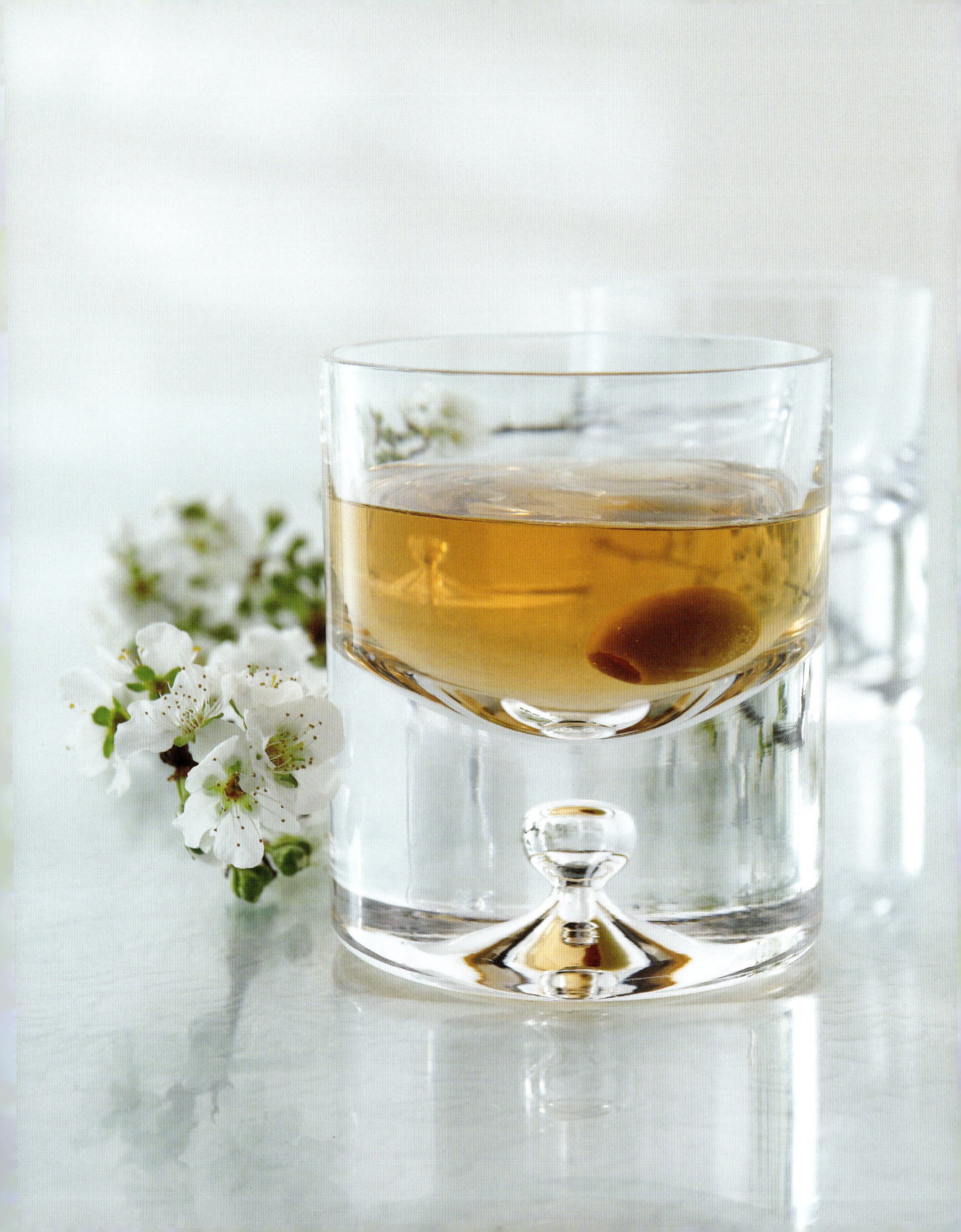

Index

Affogato Agave 28
Almond Biscuits 208
Almond Crisps 200
Almond & Walnut Petits Fours 206
Apple Chiffon Tart 215
Apple Custard Tarts 229
Apple Jam Tarts 221
Apple Tea Cakes 74
Astoria 252

Bergamot Earl Grey Spicy Tea 13
Berry Crumble Muffins 70
Berry Tarts 217
Black Forest Cupcakes 109
Blondies 122
Bourbon Biscuits 192
Brandy Apricot Slice 140
Brownies 136
Butterfly Cupcakes 113

Café Agave 34
Café Oscar 40
Caramel Squares 130
Caribbean Coffee 38
Carrot & Almond Squares 138
Carrot & Sesame Muffins 72

Chai Cupcakes 93
Cheese Scones 64
Cherry Almond Cake 155
Chewy Coffee Cookies 202
Chicken & Walnut Sandwich 49
Choc Fruity Mini Cupcakes 83
Choc-Mint Brownies 124
Chocolate Coffee Tuiles 196
Chocolate Hazelnut Torte 151
Chocolate Martini 246
Chocolate Nougat 144
Chocolate Pear Delights 219
Chocolate Pecan Fingers 146
Chocolate Pecan Torte 155
Chocolate Rum Pudding 78
Chocolate Rum Slice 128
Chocolate Viennese Shortbreads 204
Choc Strawberry Mini Cupcakes 97
Classic Chamomile Tea 23
Coffee & Ginger Almond Crisps 200
Coffee & Walnut Surprises 60
Coffee Break 36
Coffee Kisses 184
Coffee Pecan Biscuits 188
Crab, Chives & Celery Sandwich 51

Custard Tarts 227

Dainty Seafood Circles 47
Dark Choc Truffle Cupcakes 87
Date & Walnut Slice 134
Date Scones 66
Decorated Cupcakes 117
Double Fudge Raspberry Yoghurt Slice 126
Dutch Spice Cake 165

Frozen Lavender Margaritas 244
Fruit, Nut & Chocolate Nougat 144
Frozen Lavender Margaritas 244

Ginger & Nutmeg Tea 15
Guava Strawberry Cheesecake 179

Hazelnut Shortbreads 186

Iced Coffee 30
Irish Coffee 32

James Bond Martini 242
Jaffa Pecan Muffins 76
Jasmine Tea 17

Jumping Margarita 250

Kir Royal 248

Lemon & Blueberry Shortcake Slice 132
Lemon & Raspberry Tart 225
Lemon Meringue Tart 237

Macadamia Coconut Squares 120
Madeleines 210
Madeira Cake 157
Marzipan Triangles 142
Mini Passionfruit Cheesecake 181
Mini Strawberry Princess Custard Tart 231
Mocha Mousse Roll 171
Monte Carlo Biscuits 194

One-step Patty Cakes 99
Orange & Lime Cheesecake 163
Orange Blossom Cupcakes 91
Orange Chocolate Tarts 239
Orange Poppy Cupcakes 95
Peanut Butter Mini Cupcakes 101
Pecan Chocolate Drizzles 198

Pecan Praline Cupcakes 115
Petits Fours 167
Pineapple Chiffon Flan 233
Pistachio Mini Cupcakes 105
Portuguese Custard Tarts 223
Powder Puffs 153

Raspberry Cupcakes 85
Raspberry Chocolate Truffle Cakes 159
Raspberry Muffins 68
Rooibos Tea 19
Rose Hip Tea 21
Royale Coffee 42
Rum & Raisin Mini Cupcakes 107

Shortbread Tarts with Cream Cheese 235
Smoked Salmon & Cucumber 55
Smoked Trout with Lime 53
Smoked Turkey Open Sandwich 57
Sticky Date Cupcakes 103
Strawberry Cake 173
Strawberry Hazelnut Torte 161
Strawberry Meringue Cake 177

Traditional Scones 62
Truffle Cookies 190

Vanilla Rose Petal Cupcakes 101
Vienna Coffee 26

Washington Surprise 169
White Chocolate Cupcakes 89

Published in 2014 by
New Holland Publishers
London • Sydney • Cape Town • Auckland

The Chandlery Unit 114 50 Westminster Bridge Road London SE1 7QY UK
1/66 Gibbes Street Chatswood NSW 2067 Australia
Wembley Square First Floor Solan Road Gardens Cape Town 8001 South Africa
218 Lake Road Northcote Auckland New Zealand

Copyright © 2014 New Holland Publishers
Copyright © 2014 in text: New Holland Publishers and Margaret Roberts (recipes on pages 15 and 19)
Copyright © 2014 in images: New Holland Publishers and Emma Gough (photos on pages 14 and 18)
Istock images: pages 1, 2-3, 6, 9, 10-11, 20, 44-45, 80-81, 118-119, 182-183, 240-241 and 256
Shutterstock images: pages 4-5, 12 and 16

www.newhollandpublishers.com

All rights reserved. No part of this publication may be reproduced, stored in a retrieval system or transmitted, in any form or by any means, electronic, mechanical, photocopying, recording or otherwise, without the prior written permission of the publishers and copyright holders.

A catalogue record of this book is available at the British Library and the National Library of Australia.

ISBN: 9781742575346

Managing Director: Fiona Schultz
Publisher: Fiona Schultz
Designer: Lorena Susak
Project Editor: Emily Carryer
Production Director: Olga Dementiev
Printer: Toppan Leefung Printing Ltd

10 9 8 7 6 5 4 3 2 1

Follow New Holland Publishers on
Facebook: www.facebook.com/NewHollandPublishers